THE LABOR GUIDE TO RETIREMENT PLANS

The Labor Guide to Retirement Plans

James W. Russell

MONTHLY REVIEW PRESS
New York

Copyright © 2021 by James W. Russell
All Rights Reserved

Library of Congress Cataloging-in-Publication Data
available from the publisher

ISBN 978-1-58367-934-0 cloth
ISBN 978-1-58367-933-3 paper
ISBN 978-1-58367-935-7 eBook (trade)
ISBN 978-1-58367-936-4 eBook (institutional)

Typeset in Minion Pro and Brown

MONTHLY REVIEW PRESS, NEW YORK
monthlyreview.org

5 4 3 2 1

Contents

Acknowledgments

B
ooks may be written in isolation, but what goes into them comes out of interactions with the written or spoken words of many people. For understanding Social Security, I learned a great deal from Nancy J. Altman's books, articles, emails, and conversations. She is the co-founder and president of the essential advocacy organization Social Security Works. For struggles over pension plans, Karen Ferguson and Karen Friedman are the experts. Their Pension Rights Center should be the first stop for anyone engaged in a struggle to defend a pension plan from management attempts to eliminate it or cut it back. The National Academy of Social Insurance is an invaluable source of objective information about retirement plans. Chief executive officer William J. Arnone helped me with referrals and his own vast knowledge. I have also learned from the excellent reports of the National Institute on Retirement Security. Manuel Riesco of Chile's Centro de Estudios Nacionales de Desarrollo Alternativo shared his research on the spectacular failure of that country's privatized 401(k)-like system, a cautionary tale for those who think privatization of Social Security in the United States would be a good idea. The same can be said for Elaine Fultz's valuable articles about reversals of social security privatizations in Central and Eastern Europe. A number

of people generously agreed to my interview requests or otherwise answered questions: Jim Kaplan, Marilyn Katz, Adam Krauthamer, Fredrick Kunkle, Steve Lester, Joy Lindsey, Robert J.S. Ross, Kathy Ruffing, Jerry Schlichter, and Kelly Stillwell.

Labor journalist and former organizer Steve Early led me to Monthly Review Press, and I'm glad he did. Going back to the 1960s, I have admired its books and magazine, *Monthly Review*. Much of my early understanding of political economy came from MR Press's books and articles. A lot of that, indeed, led to my current understanding of the political economic importance of retirement plans. Michael D. Yates was an ideal editor and person to work with, as were other members of the MR Press team: Martin Paddio, Rebecca Manski, and Erin Clermont. Holly Watson has used her expert skill to spread word of the existence of this book to those for whom I hope it will be useful.

Introduction

Since the late 1970s, there has been a class war over control of trillions of dollars dedicated to retirement plans of all types. On one side stand Wall Street titans and other members of the financial services industry. They seek to control these funds to profit from them directly. On the other side stand working people, the nominal owners of these funds, who are counting on them being available and sufficient to finance their retirement years.

Social Security is the biggest prize in the retirement plan class war. It's no great mystery why Wall Street–related financial interests and their ideological supporters in political parties and think tanks want to privatize Social Security and are waging a long-term class war to do so. In the most recent year, Social Security collected in revenue just short of one trillion dollars and held in reserve an additional 2.9 trillion, for a total of 3.9 trillion dollars.[1] That's 3.9 trillion dollars out of reach of Wall Street profiteers. At the same time, Social Security is the biggest retirement asset held by most working Americans. Losing it to the financial elite would put a severe dent in their retirement standards of living. Wall Street profit taking would lower the benefits they now receive.

If the battle over Social Security is ongoing and yet to be decided, the Wall Street financial elite can already count a significant victory. Since the early 1980s, it has engineered the transformation of most employer-provided retirement plans from traditional pensions to more profitable 401(k)-like savings and stock market investment schemes. In so doing, it has seized control of a large portion of the collective retirement savings of working Americans. According to Ted Benna, a benefits consultant who was one of the original architects of the transformation, the 401(k) "turned the mutual fund industry from a few cottage-sized businesses into financial giants."[2] This development is one of the major causes of what economists refer to as the financialization of the economy.

The most visible battle of the class war over retirement plans has been the attack on the remaining sector of the workforce that still has traditional pensions: public sector workers. Ideological allies of the financial elite have done an excellent job convincing much of the public that these pension plans are a costly burden on taxpayers, overly generous, threaten to bankrupt governments, and reduce funds for needed public services such as education. Republican and a not insignificant number of Democratic politicians continually introduce bills to replace the pensions with 401(k)s. Yet pension plans cost governments less than 401(k)s for the same benefit amount. Most public pension plans are in sound financial shape despite media focus on the few that are not. The campaign against public pensions, using the scary-sounding term *unfunded liabilities*, spotlights the weakest plans as if they were typical, despite the fact that those plans are weak because of past underfunding. Underlying the campaign is the promotion of pension envy, aimed at most private-sector workers, who are now looking forward to an insecure retirement with insufficient 401(k) savings. The message: it is unfair for public workers to have secure retirements when we don't. Instead of arguing that all those who work for wages deserve secure retirements, workers are urged to form a circular firing squad and end all secure pensions.

The termination of collective pension funds would not only end the most favorable form of retirement plans for working people, it would also end a type of power that they have in the class war:

their collective capital. Pension funds such as the California Public Employees Retirement System (Calpers) hold billions of dollars of investment capital. How they decide to invest what can be called labor's capital has a huge impact on corporations. They can use that capital to influence corporate practices that concern labor. They can withdraw investments from companies with unfair labor practices, as has been done.[3]

I come from a family of labor activists. My wife was a union organizer. My daughter is one. I have been an active union member for most of my life. When I was approaching retirement, I discovered that my 401(k)-like plan would come up very much short in terms of providing the income my family and I needed to maintain our standard of living. Like any conscious union member, I suspected that if I had that problem, then very likely so did a lot of my co-workers. I, though, had an advantage over them. I had studied retirement plans as a part of my work position as a researcher and knew that the fault of our plan coming up short lay not so much in anything we had done or not done but in the type of plan itself. I knew that some co-workers had a different type of plan and that they would be fine in retirement. They were paying less than half what we were in contributions, yet would receive over twice the retirement income. If we could only get into their plan, a real pension plan, we too would be fine.

It was a solution that was both deceptively simple and very difficult to accomplish. Yes, changing plans would deliver much higher retirement income. But to change plans required the agreement of our employer, in this case the state of Connecticut since we were state workers. I first worked out a way that would actually save the ever cash-strapped state money if it allowed us to change plans. I went to state officials with the issue. There was some sympathy for our plight but a unanimous consensus that it was quite impossible, probably even illegal, to allow us to change retirement plans. We were irrevocably bound to the plan we were in. I went to union leaders with the issue. They sympathized too but thought it a lost cause. Putting effort

into trying to obtain it would be a waste of time and resources. I went
to labor lawyers to see if we could sue our way to relief. No, was the
common answer. The lawyers, however, did note that there was nothing illegal about what I was proposing. While the state was under no
obligation to grant the request, there was nothing that legally prohibited it from doing so. It was a matter of somehow getting our employer
to agree to allow us to change plans.

I already knew that they wouldn't accept the proposal to change
retirement plans just because it was a good idea. There's a built-in
lethargy to large bureaucracies. Once they have a system in place that
seems to work, there is a reluctance to change it. I couldn't just ask
them to make a change. I had to find some way to *make* them change
plans.

I had run up against the classic reason workers join together into
unions in the first place. You're not likely to have much success individually confronting an employer. You're much more likely to have
success if all of the workers approach the employer as a collective
force. Or, as the old labor song goes:

> *Many stones can form an arch*
> *Singly none singly none.*[4]

If I wanted that collective force to back up what I knew, based
on my job as a researcher into retirement plans, to be a good idea, I
would have to organize it with others who were in agreement.

I set out to do that. The idea caught on quickly among co-workers deeply worried about going off their own fiscal cliffs when they
retired. Most doubted we could prevail but were willing to listen and
go along just in case. Surprisingly, once we organized, progress came
quickly. The unions responded by filing a supporting grievance, the
remedy of which would be to allow employees to change retirement
plans voluntarily. That led, through twists and turns, to a successful
outcome that allowed state employees to change into the much better
state employee pension plan. The underlying lesson: nothing happened until we got organized.

I wrote about that struggle in *Social Insecurity: 401(k)s and the Retirement Crisis.*[5]

What struck me was how little many union officers, as well as members, knew about retirement plans, despite their importance. Granted, this was the case where I was. There are other union situations where officers and members are keenly aware of the issues involved with their plans. You can see that in the resistance that is often provoked when employers try to cut back or eliminate pension plans. Nevertheless, I suspect that there is much more lack of awareness by employees of the stakes involved in their retirement plans.

When I look at my history, I have to admit that I fell into the lack of awareness category for the major part of my working life, especially when I was young. Like death, retirement is a subject that most young people would prefer not to contemplate. In their eyes, retirement is an unpleasant subject, a step before death, the ultimate unpleasant inevitability. Thinking about retirement when young is thinking about the depressing reality that one day you will no longer be young.

When you are young, life's highway ahead looks very long, stretching into infinity. When you are old, the traveled road looks much shorter. I am now in my seventies and can remember events of my teen years like they happened yesterday. When I was a teenager, I often thought about the millennial year of 2000 as being in the very distant future. It seemed unimaginable to me that I would be fifty-six at the time since I was born in 1944, making me a war baby, just before the famous boomers. I could not imagine reaching that millennial year. Time crept slowly. But 2000 has come and gone and the years since seem to whip by.

When you are young, time is longer in your perception. If you are twenty years old, ten years make up half of the only reality you have directly experienced. When you are seventy, it makes up only one-seventh of your life. The longer you live, the shorter the perceived reality of each year.

At age twenty, retirement at age sixty-five is forty-five years into the distant future. Forty-five years is a long time. It is an even longer time if you are young. But the chronological years do inevitably go by; they seem to go by slowly at first but then they are gone in a rush. At five years before retirement, you realize that it is coming up fast, very fast. You cannot avoid thinking about it now. Worse, if you have not participated in a good retirement plan, there will be little that you can do to make up for lost time.

This is all an argument for learning about retirement plans as early as possible. It's a hard sell because retirement for many is an exceptionally dull subject. It's for older people. You are young or at least not old. It's a reminder that one day you will be a lot closer to death, which is a real bummer, an unpleasant subject. There are a thousand reasons not to think about it. It's easy to put off, like writing a will.

Retirement is the last act before the end of the show, death. And you're still in the first acts. Like in theater, you're dealing with earlier elements of the drama of your life—leaving the home you grew up in, finding a mate or not, having children or not, getting a job. The list goes on and retirement planning is not on it.

I believe that humans are a problem-solving species. Solving small and large problems consumes our lives. What will we wear today? What and how will we eat? How will we get to work? Issues to be solved always fill workdays. Having problems is a normal part of life. It's only when we are dead that we do not have problems.

Some problems have immediacy; they stare us in the face and must be dealt with now. Your child has cut herself badly while playing. Other problems don't or at least don't seem to require immediate action. Retirement planning is like that the younger you are. We can store the problem in a remote region of the brain for later attention.

But the problem of putting it off, kicking the can down the road, is that some things are a lot easier and less painful to do earlier than later. If your retirement security depends on how much you've saved, the more you put away beforehand, the less you will have to set aside later. While that may seem obvious, there is a part that is not so obvious. Retirement savings have two parts: how much of it grows as a result of new contributions and how much of it grows as a result of investment gains. At a certain point, the latter becomes more substantial than the former. Savers don't just have to put in contributions, they also have to leave in the money there for a long time to render maximum returns and assure retirement security. It is challenging to make up for lost ground later in life. There are inherent problems with this approach that I will discuss. But if you're stuck with it, you should be aware of the need to start contributing early and not put it off.

At the same time, no one should have to spend their early decades obsessing about their retirement years. Other problems require attention. Nevertheless, retirement can't be ignored entirely. At least a few decisions must be made, and the more knowledgeably those decisions are made, the better. That's why this book is here.

People reading this so far who have 401(k)s may believe either (a) I was completely wrong, and their experiences are or will be different, or (b) they are doomed, and the situation is hopeless. It is not my purpose to promote either conclusion. I don't agree with (a) or I wouldn't be a critic of 401(k)s. But at the same time, I am not a futilist, the (b) option.

Most people in the United States now, if they have an employer-provided retirement plan, are in a 401(k)-type plan. Their deficiencies require a national reckoning. To have that reckoning, one that leads to reforms to rectify them, will require an understanding by their participants of what is wrong with them. Union and rank-and-file activists will need to understand the nature of the beast and what they are up against.

Retirement plans are complicated. That is one of the main reasons many participants prefer to avoid thinking about them, hoping for the best. They all have different features, even within the broad types of traditional pensions and individual retirement savings and investment plans like 401(k)s. They are complicated because finance in and of itself is complicated. They are complicated because they require information that is not always readily available, such as how long one is likely to live in the retirement years. But just because something can be complicated or opaque does not mean it cannot be understood.

In the course of my professional work and labor activism, I have counseled hundreds of people about their retirement plans, and I have spoken to many more about labor struggles regarding them. A common observation is that they don't know as much about those plans as they should. A union leader in charge of negotiating a retirement benefit told me with a sigh that he was an English major in college, hardly preparation for what he had to deal with now. All the retirement experts, he complained, seem to be on the other side. He very much wanted to do the right thing for his members, and he understood the severe consequences if management cut retirement benefits. He wished he knew more to defend member interests adequately.

In our Connecticut struggle, the state employee unions formed a coalition to bargain retirement and other benefits. Representing the coalition in negotiations was an exceptionally skilled lawyer who was a genuine expert on retirement plans. We were lucky to have him. But that expertise did not spread through the ranks of the labor officials. When members had questions, even basic ones, the officials were ill-equipped to answer them. At one point, I commented to a pension attorney that I didn't think there were more than twenty-five people in the state who understood how the state employee pension plan worked. He agreed and then added that there were a lot more people who thought they did, especially politicians who were proposing reforms to it. Conversations I had with several journalists who had been writing about it confirmed this lack of general understanding. In one case, I spent an hour in a coffee shop explaining to a journalist how the pension plan worked. She was very appreciative, and her reporting on it became much better.

It's easy to see how union officials and reporters would not necessarily know much about retirement plans. They have many other concerns. Union officials confront a wide variety of problems. Reporters go from story to story. When a retirement plan problem or issue presents itself, they have to deal with it even if they do not have the full understanding to do so. Members of retirement plans, of course, should also know much more than they likely do. When I was counseling employees about their plan options, I discovered just how little most people knew. Those baffled by their retirement plans included heads of economics departments and other economists whom the *New York Times* quoted as experts knowing something.

It's also true that retirement plans can be very complicated. But here it's necessary to distinguish between fundamental plan principles and the often opaque features that managers have added. Underneath a maze of specifics, such as different rates of benefit accrual, will be a straightforward structure. There are other types of complications that require the expertise of lawyers and actuaries to decipher. But most of what needs to be understood does not require technical, legal, or mathematical specialization. It is accessible to plan members, labor organizers and officials, and others who are called upon from time to time to assess retirement plans.

With respect to knowledge of the basics of retirement plans and those areas that require specialized expertise, I aim at the former in this book. Its goal is to provide the basics of what labor people should know, including employees and their union representatives, if they have them. This is somewhat like health advice books. There is a distinction between what everyone should know to take care of essential health needs and when to call the doctor. Here, it is the distinction between what you should know and when you need to call a technical, legal, or other type of expert.

Knowing the nuts and bolts of retirement plans will allow employees to critically assess changes to plans that employers advocate or make. Employers always present these changes as being in employees' interests, but unless you are naive enough to believe that employers without exception have the best interests of their employees in mind rather than their own, it is best to be equipped to assess them critically.

This book is not a neutral account. It will evaluate types of plans and features in terms of which are better and which are worse for working people. Also, I will, out of necessity, address national issues, since, ultimately, retirement is a national issue. From a labor perspective, there are national as well as workplace reforms needed to resolve the country's chronic retirement problems.

The purpose of this book is broadly educational. For readers, to help them navigate through the complicated and often impenetrable world of retirement plans so that they will be in a position to defend themselves and their interests. For employees, it will be strategic information for charting their strategies. For union organizers, it will be information and understandings that they can use to navigate the retirement benefit provision of contracts. It will also be information that they can pass on to members in terms of labor education and as responses to their questions and concerns.

In this book I will share what I have learned from years of study and retirement activism. I will present the material in as understandable a manner as possible. In many cases, it took me a great deal of time to understand an issue because no one else had explained it well, perhaps because they did not themselves understand it. Writing can be annoying when you suspect the writer is trying to hide a lack of understanding by not clearly explaining a critical concept or idea. I hope not to be guilty of that type of incomplete or lazy writing in the pages to come. I have made sure that I understand what I am writing about, so that I can explain it well.

--- 1 ---

The Retirement System

Retirement is a personal and family concern for individuals. It is a social and political concern for societies. To the extent that individuals worry about it, which tends to be as they get older and begin to think about what comes after their work careers, they want and hope they will have enough income to go on living as they are accustomed to living. No one wants to suddenly have to live on a lot less when they retire. A few will have more income in retirement than during their working years, but the vast majority of retirees will have less. A little less will not have much impact on their standards of living, but at some point, even a small decline in income will be felt. First, there is an inability to afford conveniences and wants that undergird the quality of life. Eating out becomes less affordable. And if the decline is steep enough, it begins to eat into necessities. There's less money to spend on weekly grocery shopping. If there are still home mortgages, paying them becomes more of a strain.

Retirement in the past was a family as well as a personal concern. Younger family members often had to support older retired ones without income. The multigenerational farm family was the classic, with elderly grandparents living in the house. As the proportion of the workforce engaged in farming declined and small towns and cities correspondingly grew, parts of the farming culture carried over. Elderly retired family members continued to live in attics, but now the houses were in the small towns and cities.

That was the situation through the beginning of the past century in the United States. Farmers, factory workers, and middle-class merchants and professionals either worked until they died or assumed they would live with their adult children if they lived long enough to stop working. It was a situation that grew increasingly untenable off the farm. Not every older person had adult children. And not every adult child was in a position to provide for elderly parents in small-town and urban conditions. An essential part of what farm families did was to produce food and other necessities for home consumption, including for non-producing elderly members. Those living away from farms had to obtain enough cash to buy those necessities. That, in turn, assumed that the factory workers and others had sufficient income to buy enough for the elderly household members as well as for themselves and their children. The economics of the factory and urban economy were stacked against adult children being able to support retired parents financially.

Retirement provision thus became a social and political issue. Families were unable to continue shouldering the responsibility for the complete financial support of elderly members. What was needed were ways that workers could continue receiving income after retirement. That would enable them to continue supporting themselves if they did not have adult children who were willing and able to provide that support. It would relieve financial pressure on families already burdened with other expenses.

What emerged in fits and starts were government, employer, and personal retirement plans. Taken together, these form a retirement system, though it is far from a unified one. Individual families may still be providing support for elderly members but far less than in the past. They have moved from a primary to supplementary role.

If the retirement system arose to meet the need to support the retired financially, it could be analyzed in terms of its forms of support and judged in terms of how well those forms of support provide adequate support.

Sources of Retirement Income

The American retirement system has three parts: Social Security, employer-sponsored retirement plans, and individual savings. That is the so-called three-legged stool of retirement, so called because it was never a good analogy. For a three-legged stool to be stable, the legs must be of equal length. Very few people have equal amounts of retirement income from Social Security, work plans, and their savings. Many, perhaps a majority, do not have income from all three. Many have income from only one, most likely Social Security. Virtually everyone who has income from two or three of the sources has unequal income from each.

We can dispense with the analogy, but not with the reality that the system does indeed have three sources or tiers of retirement income, if not for everyone within it. As a system, it is more like a pyramid. Social Security is at the base, accounting for the most income; workplace plans are in the middle, making up the next most significant income; and then individual savings and assets, accounting for the least income, are at the pinnacle.

Table 1.1 (page 22) gives a more exact notion. Social Security accounts for 57.1 percent of the income for the entire 65 and older population, employer retirement plans for 15.8 percent, and savings and assets 6.4 percent. Note that 17.1 percent comes from the earnings of people still working. That percentage drops off after the age of 65. For the 80 and older population, it is only 3.7 percent.

The pyramid analogy is a good starting point for looking at the system as a whole, but it does not necessarily apply to all experiences within it. Sources of individual retirement income may not look like a pyramid at all, and if they do, they may not look like the overall national proportions in Table 1.1. For about a quarter of the senior population, over 90 percent of income comes from Social Security.[1] They have little or no income from employer-sponsored plans or

TABLE 1.1: Sources of Income

Sources of Income	Aged 65 or older (%)	Aged 80 or older (%)
RETIREMENT INCOME		
Social Security	57.1	71.1
Employer Plans	15.8	14.5
Savings and Assets	6.4	7.7
OTHER INCOME		
Earnings	17.1	3.7
Other	3.9	3.0
TOTAL	100.0	100.0

Source: Social Security Administration, Income of the Population 55 or Older, 2014, Table 8.A1.

individual savings. Many retirees have income from Social Security and employer plans but none from individual savings. A minority receive more income from workplace plans than Social Security. Those are the people most likely to have financially comfortable retirements. There is also a tiny subset of people for whom individual savings provide the greatest amount of income. This may have been the result of selling a business upon retirement or unusually successful real estate or stock investments.

It is hardly a unified system since individual results vary so much. That's one of the reasons why it's necessary to treat statistical averages with caution. The average person has a certain amount of Social Security income. But there is a huge spread around that average. Some have a lot more and some a lot less. Close to half the workforce at any one time have employer-sponsored plans. But that doesn't necessarily mean that half of retirees receive significant income from those plans. Some do, but many are not in those plans long enough to attain significant benefits. And, as we will see, two people can be in different plans for the same length of time and make equal contributions but receive dramatically different retirement incomes depending on the natures of the plans.

Another way to look at the sources of income is that one, Social

Security, is relatively fixed. It covers 94 percent of formal economy jobs. People can take for granted that they are accruing retirement credits in Social Security as they move from job to job. The second tier of employer-sponsored plans is much more problematic. Half of jobs, as mentioned, don't have retirement plans, and there is an enormous variation in the plans of those that come with retirement benefits. Employers can't get away with not offering, decreasing, or eliminating Social Security benefits. They, by law, must make those contributions. But they can do all of the above with their own or lack of retirement benefits. Though Social Security is a reliable source of future retirement income for the vast majority of workers, what they will encounter in terms of employer-sponsored benefits is iffy. The plans of those that have them vary significantly between excellent and paltry. Some will keep jobs they hate because of excellent retirement benefits. Others will keep jobs they love despite the gnawing under-standing that they won't have much to show for all of the time and effort they put into the job year after year in terms of later retirement income. Knowing that they can't expect much from their employer, some will want to build alternative personal retirement plans through investments or side businesses. However, very few are successful at this type of entrepreneurial self-help. For most people, solutions lie in building up the first two tiers: Social Security and employer-spon-sored plans.

Types of Employer-Sponsored Plans

There are two fundamental types of employer-sponsored retirement plans: pensions and individual savings accounts, of which 401(k)s are the most well known. In the first, employers, with or without employee contributions, make contributions into collective funds from which they pay pensions to individual retirees. In the second, employers and employees make contributions to personal savings and investment accounts. The accumulated balances of those accounts are then used by their holders to finance their retirement years.

A traditional pension plan set lifetime retirement incomes according to how long employees had worked for the employer sponsoring the plan and what their final salaries were. These are *final-salary pension plans*. More recently, employers have developed a second type of pension plan, the *cash balance plan*. With it, employers and employees continue to make contributions to a collective trust fund. But unlike final-salary plans, the employees individually accrue cash credits in those accounts according to the contributions and credited interest payments. The size of the cash balance then determines the size of the pension upon retirement.

Retirement savings plans, in addition to 401(k)s, include 403(b)s and 457s. The numbers refer to provisions in the Internal Revenue Service code that govern their use. Individual Retirement Accounts (IRAs) are also a type of retirement savings plan, though not sponsored by employers.

Retirement plan experts express the difference between pension and retirement savings plans as a difference between defined benefit and defined contribution plans. In the first, there are specified guaranteed benefits that accrue each year. In the second, all that is specified is that employers or employees will make specific contribution to individual savings accounts each pay period. There is no specification or guarantee of the retirement benefit, that is, income. Social Security, while not an employer-sponsored plan, is structured as a defined-benefit pension plan since its benefits are specified and guaranteed according to average career incomes.

The basic idea of a pension system is that contributions by employers, with or without those of current workers, go into a collective fund out of which lifetime payments—pensions—are paid to retirees (pensioners).

*Pension Plan: Contributions → Collective Fund →
Individual Pensions*

Social Security is a national public pension system. Private and public sector employers maintain separate supplementary pension systems. 401(k)s and other retirement savings plans are *not* pension systems, despite many people confusing the two. What differentiates them is that 401(k)-like contributions go into individual accounts rather than collective funds to provide the bases for withdrawals during retirement. In both pension plans and 401(k)s, the contributions are saved and usually invested. The difference is that the first goes into a collective account and the second into an individual one.

401(k): Contributions → Individual Savings Accounts →
Individual Withdrawals

The misidentification of 401(k)s as pensions glosses over the vast differences between the two. An actual pension plan pools contributions and is structured so that it will produce a life-income in retirement, that is, regular pension checks until death. Personal retirement savings accounts like 401(k)s don't necessarily lead to life incomes in retirement. In this book, pension plans will always mean the collective funds that produce life incomes in retirement.

The difference between having a pension plan and having a 401(k)-retirement savings account would look like this: Jack has a pension plan. Each pay period, his employer contributes 8 percent of his salary to a trust fund. Pension checks drawn from the trust fund are paid to retired members of the company. What is left over in the trust fund is invested in a second stream of revenue for the trust fund. Contributions are the first stream; investment returns the second. Jack doesn't pay much attention to this. Like his Social Security, he takes it for granted that he will receive a pension when he retires.

Jack's cousin Jill is in a 401(k) plan instead. Each pay period 5 percent of her pay is deducted and sent to Prudential, which administers her plan. Her employer matches her contribution by sending an additional 5 percent of her salary to Prudential to be credited to her account. Jill decides how to invest this money in the stock market. The administrators of her retirement plan have given her a set of options from which to choose. She doesn't know much about investing and takes the advice of a co-worker who says her brother-in-law is a financial advisor. Every three months, she receives a quarterly statement from Prudential that tells her how much her balance has increased, or decreased if the market is not doing well. The statement also contains pages of other information that she does not understand and ignores. She's not sure how but assumes that all will work out in the end, and she will have enough to retire.

It's not always an either-or situation. A relatively large number of employers with pension plans also sponsor supplementary retirement savings plans. These workers can look forward to something like the three-legged stool of Social Security, a pension, and savings. Most workers, though, will have the two-wheel bicycle of Social Security and a 401(k)-like retirement savings account. (Being a cyclist, I might add that there are many unorthodox bicycles with one wheel larger than the other like these hypothetical retirement bicycles.)

The Central Goal of Retirement Plans

The goal of retirement plans is to provide enough income in retirement so that individuals and families can maintain their pre-retirement standards of living. Keeping them out of poverty is, of course, important, but that can only be a minimum goal. No middle-class person would look forward to living just above the poverty line in retirement. At the other extreme, the purpose of retirement plans is not to make people rich in retirement, nice as the fantasy may be. It is instead to make it possible for individuals to make the economic transition from work to retirement in a way that they can keep living in their usual manner. They should have a steady income that is sufficient to cover their expenses. Given that we live in a society with a highly unequal distribution of income, it follows that retirement incomes reflect that inequality. The amount, though not the proportion, of income needed to maintain a middle-class standard of living will be higher than that required to maintain a lower-class one.

The *replacement rate* is the technical term for the proportion of working income replaced by retirement income. It is a measure that we will return to often as we evaluate different types of retirement plans and modifications to them, including management-promoted cutbacks. The higher the replacement rate, the more retirees maintain their pre-retirement standards of living. There is no general agreement among retirement experts as to how much replacement rate is needed to maintain pre-retirement standards of living. There is, though, a general rule of thumb that retirees need at least 70 percent of final pre-retirement wages from all sources together, including Social Security.

Why not 100 percent? Good question. A central assumption supporting the lower 70 percent replacement rate is that retirees are past having the expenses of child-raising. They are supporting just themselves and perhaps a spouse as opposed to families that include children. As a generalization, that is true. But in many individual circumstances, it is not, as when retirees must continue supporting adult children who are unable to work. In that case, the drop to 70 percent of pre-retirement income would lower the standard of living of the family as a whole. It's also true that as people age, their medical expenses increase. It is thus difficult to quantify what the replacement rate needs to be in each circumstance. All that is certain is that it differs. Nevertheless, we will accept the 70 percent replacement rate as a rule of thumb in these pages to evaluate how well different types of retirement plans achieve at least this.

It's important to understand that, in most cases, what is needed is at least 70 percent of *final* or highest income to maintain standards of living. People have different incomes during their working lives. In general, as a result of seniority and promotions, people have their highest incomes right before they retire. But there are exceptions. People laid off in their fifties may not be able to find an equally paying position and have to settle for lower incomes during their final working years. We have to distinguish between the general principle of replacement of final incomes and individual circumstances in which the replacement of average career earnings may be higher. Whichever is higher would be what any retiree would want.

The difference between replacement of final and replacement of average income is evident in how Social Security presents its replacement rates. That average replacement rate is 41 percent of pre-retirement income. This does not mean that all Social Security participants will receive 41 percent of their pre-retirement income. That is what average earners who have always been average earners will receive—41 percent of both their career average and earnings adjusted for inflation since their career averages equal their final incomes. But virtually no one fits this profile. If a person started with a minimum-wage job and then slowly advanced to an average wage just before retirement, her actual replacement of final income in retirement would be 31 percent.

We will return to this rather complicated issue. For now, suffice it to say that Social Security replacement rates may not be as high as one might assume. This means that obtaining the goal of a 70 percent replacement rate will require more income from employer-sponsored plans and savings. As we will see, that will be at a time when employer-sponsored plans are delivering less replacement income. Those are the trends that are contributing to the retirement income crisis.

The Best Retirement Plans

Social Security is a sound basis for the retirement system. It could be better if it delivered more income, as do comparable European national pension plans. Increasing Social Security retirement incomes is undoubtedly a worthy goal for labor advocacy policy. We can and will later make an argument that Social Security should take up more of the retirement needs of the country and employer-sponsored plans less.

The reality now, however, is that in the absence of Social Security expansion, workers are dependent on employer-sponsored plans to make up the gap between their Social Security income and the 70 percent replacement income needed. If we know the different major types of employer-sponsored retirement plans, a logical question for any employee is, which is the best in terms of delivering the highest income replacement rate? The question is not as difficult to answer as it may seem. It is true that retirement plans, even within the same types, differ significantly according to their features. That makes it possible, depending on the variable elements, for any of the three major types—final salary pension, cash balance pension, or 401(k)—to be the best, as when comparing the plans of three different workers. And that's probably the way most people encounter plans when they go from job to job. They're all different, making it difficult to know which is better or best. Plans with varying rates of contribution will have different outcomes. There are many 401(k) plans to which employers contribute nothing and leave it up to employees to determine how much to contribute. Pension plans also have different contribution rates and benefit formulas.

To make worthwhile comparisons, we have to compare oranges to oranges. We have to compare plans that have the same contribution rates and look at their outcomes for the same periods. We can compare three hypothetical plans—final salary, cash balance, and 401(k)—that have the same contribution rates, say 8 percent of wages, for 25-year employees who retire at age 65. When we do that, the differences in terms of replacement rates are apparent. Final salary pensions deliver the highest replacement rates for reasons that will be discussed in the coming chapters. 401(k)-like plans provide the lowest replacement rates, also for reasons to be explained. Cash balance plans are somewhere in the middle as are a newer scheme, "adjustable," sometimes called variable, pension plans (see chapter 8).

A quick explanation of the terms used in Table 1.2 (page 30) is in order. By collective fund, we mean a plan whose assets are held in a trust fund from which retirement benefits are paid.

By investment risks, we mean that the chances that plan assets and future benefits will decline because of stock market downturns. With all types of pension plans, if the market goes down, management cannot reduce already accrued benefits. By accrual, we mean a benefit that once obtained cannot be lost regardless of investment losses. With cash balance and adjustable pension plans, market declines can only affect the rates at which future benefits are accrued. Once the earned benefit is in the bank, so to speak, it cannot be reduced. With final-salary pension plans, market downturns have no impact on future as well as accrued benefits, as all market risk is the responsibility of

Table 1.2: Major Types of Employer-Sponsored Retirement Plans

	RETIREMENT SAVINGS PLANS	PENSION PLANS	
Types	401(k), 403(b), 457, IRA, ESOP	Cash Balance Plan, Adjustable/Variable Pension Plan	Final Salary
Account	Personal Account	Collective trust fund	Collective trust fund
Investment Risk	Borne by employees	Shared by employer and employees	Borne by employer
Accrued Benefits Each Year that Cannot Be Reduced	No	Yes	Yes
Lifetime Income Upon Retirement	No	Yes	Yes
Portable	Yes	Varies	Mostly No
Retirement Income Amount	Low	Higher	Highest

Note: Amount of retirement income comparison assumes equal contributions and years of participation.

management. With 401(k)s, employees bear all market risks with no accrual rights. If the market drops, so too will the accumulated balance. In the 2008 Great Recession, 401(k) participants lost 30 to 40 percent of their accumulations, which significantly harmed those close to retirement.

By life pension or annuity, we mean a regular, often monthly, payment made from collective plan funds for the remaining life of the retiree. By law, all pension plans must have default pension or annuity options. 401(k)-type plans rarely have embedded annuity options.

Portability means that job changers can transfer accumulated benefits from old to new job retirement plans. 401(k) and cash balance plans are portable, whereas adjustable and final-salary pension plans generally are not. Multi-employer pension plans, such as in the trucking and construction industries, are exceptions, assuming that old and new employers both participate in the same plan. With 401(k)-type and cash balance plans, job changers can combine account balances from old and new job plans. Final-salary pension plan accrued benefits stay with the original plan. That can present a disadvantage if the salary of the old job is much lower than that of the job from which the worker retires.

A close reading of Table 1.2 indicates that there is no perfect plan design that covers all career possibilities. A final salary pension plan is the gold standard for long-term employees who will retire from that position. It will deliver the most retirement income with the most security. And there are many long-term police officers, government employees, teachers, health workers, and firefighters, among others, who are well served by traditional final salary pension plans. But there are also a lot of people in the labor force who change jobs and geographical locations fairly frequently for whom lower portable benefits are the only current option. *Current* is the crucial qualifier here because, with appropriate national reforms, job changers would not have to sacrifice retirement income for portability.

The meaning of retirement income amount is self-evident. The conclusions of low, higher, and highest come from modeling, using assumptions of equal contributions and years of work in each of the plan types.

PART I

SOCIAL SECURITY
AND
MEDICARE

2

Social Security: The National Pension Plan

Social Security, our national pension plan, covers more people, collects more contributions, and delivers more benefits than employer-provided programs or individual savings. It is also the federal government's most popular program. The National Academy for Social Insurance found that 68 percent of adults had a favorable view of Social Security. It is popular with virtually all demographics: young and old, high- and low-income classes, all racial and ethnic groups, Republicans as well as Democrats.[1] It is only unpopular among certain conservative elites who have outsize influence in creating the false perception that the program is going broke and that the country needs to replace it with a Wall Street-benefiting program of personal savings and investment accounts.

A top reason why people like Social Security is that they don't have to think about it. They don't have to write a check and send contributions anywhere. That is all done automatically. They don't have to think about or worry about investing it. What Social Security does with its trust fund happens behind the scenes. When they retire, they receive retirement incomes that last the rest of their lives. They can't outlive them, as they can with personal retirement savings accounts such as 401(k)s.

That is what is immediately attractive. There is a lot more with which most people are less familiar. Social Security also insures against disability. If participants become unable to work due to injury or long-term sickness, they are eligible to receive income to partially replace their lost employment income. If participants die during working years, their surviving dependent children and spouses are eligible to receive support. If dependent children of participating workers are injured or born with or develop illnesses that prevent them from working as adults, they are eligible to receive incomes and medical insurance. That program spares parents of some of the financial hardships that accompany supporting disabled adult children.

Conservative Origins

In 1880, conservative German Chancellor Otto von Bismarck faced a political problem. The socialist Social Democratic Party was gaining strength. Many of its members adhered to the radical anti-capitalist ideas of Karl Marx and Friedrich Engels. The Social Democrats appealed to German workers who were suffering from deep economic insecurities bred by the tumultuous early history of industrialization through which the country was going: long working hours, unsafe working conditions, low pay. It was a system in which workers bore all of the risks. If they got sick, disabled, or became too old to work and earn income, they were on their own. Bismarck feared that the insecurities bred alienation from the German government and potential votes for the Social Democrats.

By addressing worker insecurities, Bismarck thought he could forestall a revolution. He would give workers an incentive to keep the current government. If there were a retirement plan along with other changes to address medical and disability issues, there would be something, in the eyes of workers, worth preserving in the existing economic and political system.

At first, socialist parties and many labor unions opposed reforms such as those initiated by Bismarck. They thought the changes would prolong the existence of capitalism, which needed to collapse so that a much better system, socialism, could take its place. It is difficult to overemphasize the point that early socialist and labor movements operated on the assumption that capitalism was about to collapse and therefore resisted reforms that could temper its worst features. In the decades that followed, much history happened, including two world wars and the spread of communist governments in countries that contained one-third of the world's population. Despite the spread of communism, the staying power of capitalism became clear to socialist parties and labor unions in the capitalist countries. Their beliefs that capitalism was on its last legs and that reforms such as retirement security would just serve to delay the desirable inevitable withered. They then began to embrace, fight for, and defend those reforms.

Bismarck, of course, did not see things as the early socialists did. He moved to address old-age insecurity and other issues as a tactical maneuver to check the rise of his political rivals. He was not assuming or wishing for the demise of capitalism.

Social Insurance

What made the most sense to Bismarck and his advisors was to create social insurance funds to address each of the problems of healthcare, disability, and old age. The German retirement system thus based itself from the beginning on state-sponsored social insurance rather than private insurance or individual savings and investment. Social insurance operates like any other insurance to protect people against risk. One buys car insurance to protect against the risk of having an accident; one buys health insurance to protect against the extraordinary financial expenses of accidents and sicknesses; one buys fire insurance to protect against the risk of losing a home due to fire. And one contributes to social insurance to protect against the risk of not having income once retired.

Bismarck was clear that these should be social rather than private insurance. They should not be profit-making businesses in which owners siphon off profits from pooled contributions. In his view, entities sponsored by the German government would collect, hold, and distribute the contributions.

All insurance plans, whether social or private, collect contributions from participants into a pool, out of which they pay benefits. Automobile owners pay premiums each month that the insurance company amasses into a fund. If the owner has an accident, the company will then pay the damage costs from the fund. The probability of any individual having an accident is quite small. But the loss from an accident can be catastrophic, tens of thousands of dollars or more. It is thus in the interest of the prudent driver to part with a small amount of money each month. The driver is not hoping to collect from the insurance company eventually. No one greets an automobile accident as a fortunate event so that they can collect on their insurance policy. Instead, they part with their money in order to have peace of mind, knowing that in the unfortunate event that they suffer a costly accident, it will not be financially ruinous.

Every insurance fund has to balance income from participants' contributions and other possible revenue sources with what it pays out. For that, they employ actuaries whose job it is to calculate both sides of the equation and adjust accordingly to keep the fund in balance. Any actuary or accountant, for that matter, can tell you that it is a simple proposition to keep an insurance fund solvent: make sure that income matches or exceeds expenses. If it looks like costs are beginning to exceed income, then either the company must increase revenue from participant contributions or other sources or it must decrease benefits paid out or some combination of the two.

Every insurance fund operates on the principle of sharing of risk. The assumption is that the insured condition or event will only occur to a minority of participants at any given time. The majority—those who do not suffer the event—transfer to the minority who suffer the event as much of their accumulated contributions as are needed to cover the costs of the event. There must always be a sufficient number of people in an insurance plan who do not need its benefits at any given time to cover the costs of those who do.

Occasionally, prominent people can run roughshod over this basic principle. In a case of political rhetoric going out of control, former Republican Speaker of the House of Representatives Paul Ryan once stated opposition to the mandatory participation requirement of the Obama Administration's Affordable Care Act, that is, the requirement that all people carry health insurance. Speaker Ryan countered that it was wrong that "the people who are healthy pay for the people who are sick. It's not working, and that's why [Obamacare] is in a death spiral."[2] That sounded superficially reasonable, and no doubt accomplished his purpose of whipping up opposition to Obamacare. But no insurance plan would be able to function if people only paid contributions when they were collecting benefits.

How did the insurance principle work with the problems confronting Chancellor Bismarck? To protect themselves against the risks of health problems, workers and their employers would pay into a government-administered insurance fund to cover medical expenses. It was somewhat different for disability insurance. In that case, what was insured was not set expenses such as doctor and hospital bills. Instead, it was income that would be lost due to an accident or illness, causing a worker to be unable to continue earning income from working. But the principle was the same: the able-bodied majority would subsidize the disabled minority. It would not be out of charitable concern. It would be out of self-interest, since today's able-bodied persons could very well be disabled tomorrow or at some other point in the future.

Retirement was still another issue. Accidents, sicknesses, and disability are all unusual conditions that befall people. Retirement is a usual condition which all workers who survive that long will experience. In this case, the notion of "risk" has a different meaning. The risk involved is that the worker will be without income. In the weird language of insurance, there is longevity risk that you will live to the time of retirement. Of course, living that long is a good thing. The risk involved is that you will not have the income to support yourself because you no longer have income from work. The insurance principle can be applied here as well. Every worker—with or without employer contributions—pays into a fund while they are working and do not need money from the fund. Thus when they are no longer working and need the income, they will have it.

In the purest form of retirement social insurance, benefits are only paid to retirees and stop when they die. If they die before becoming eligible for benefits, their estates receive nothing. Their contributions remain within the system to support others who make it to retirement age. That transfer of funds allows the benefits to be higher than they otherwise would be. The short-lived thus subsidize the long-lived. For some, this seems unfair. If death keeps them from receiving retirement benefits, at least their contributions should go to their estates to be inherited by other family members. But closer examination indicates that it is entirely consistent with the logic of social insurance.

Social insurance retirement plans have a single purpose: retirement security for those who are too old to work. Using the plans to build up private wealth would be at the expense of that primary purpose. Also, while an inheritance would be welcome as an income windfall for those receiving it, it is irrational for retirement security. It would be providing income to usually younger members of families who are still earning income from working and not needing retirement income.

Bismarck's government enacted its social insurance retirement plan in 1889. It has continued, with modifications and reforms, down to the present. It even functioned in and survived the Nazi period.[3] Eighteen European countries plus the Union of Soviet Socialist Republics and Chile followed suit by the early 1930s with social insurance retirement plans of their own. Six other countries had limited programs. Following are countries that adopted retirement social insurance plans before 1935:[4]

- Germany (1889)
- France (1910)
- Luxembourg (1911)
- Romania (1912)
- Netherlands (1913)

- Sweden (1913)
- Italy (1919)
- Portugal (1919)
- Spain (1919)
- Greece (1922)
- Serbo-Croat-Slovene Kingdom (1922)
- Union of Soviet Socialist Republics (1922)
- Belgium (1924)
- Bulgaria (1924)
- Chile (1924)
- Czechoslovakia (1924)
- Austria (1925)
- Great Britain (1925)
- Hungary (1928)
- Poland (1933)

Origins in the United States

As other countries were developing national social insurance retirement and other plans, activists and organizations sought parallel action at the state and national level in the United States. Organizations included the National Consumers League, founded in 1899, and the American Association for Labor Legislation, founded in 1906. The AALL sought, among other goals, to develop European-style social insurance protections for American workers. Much of the early origins of what would become the social insurance intellectual infrastructure for Social Security would advance through advocates for labor legislation such as Richard Ely, Henry Farnam, and Frances Perkins. Perkins would later become the Secretary of Labor under Franklin D. Roosevelt and a principal proponent of Social Security. Of particular note was a circle at the University of Wisconsin that included the economist John R. Commons and his students Arthur Altmeyer and Edwin Witte. Altmeyer and Witte would later become key designers of Social Security in the Roosevelt administration.[5]

The 1929 stock market crash and ensuing Great Depression threw the country into economic, social, and political crises. Existing labor legislation and programs were insufficient to handle the ensuing massive unemployment and poverty. The Great Depression also brought into relief the problems of lack of support for old-age citizens.

On September 30, 1933, an unemployed medical doctor, Francis E. Townsend, sent a letter to the *Long Beach Press-Telegram*. In it, he advocated that the government provide each person 60 or older with a $200 monthly pension—roughly equivalent to $3,871 today. The requirements were being retired and not a criminal, and that the money be spent entirely within thirty days. The last condition, according to Townsend, would help to pull the economy out of the Depression.[6]

It is doubtful that Townsend had much awareness of the social insurance plans already in existence in Europe and other countries, much less the work of social insurance proponents in the United States. He had concocted his scheme entirely out of whole cloth from his own experience and what made sense to him. His scheme proved wildly popular. By the end of 1934, there were 1,000 Townsend Clubs with at least 125,000 members in the United States.[7]

The Townsend Plan, while lending urgency to the need to develop a national retirement plan, did not form a basis for what would become Social Security. The Roosevelt administration never seriously considered it as a model for legislation. There was, by that time, a much sounder basis in the already existing European social insurance plans that had expert advocates in the United States.

The social insurance approach also appealed to Roosevelt, who saw it as an attractive alternative to welfare. It would be an earned benefit based on contributions and work history rather than a government handout. It would be a way for ordinary non-poor working people to efficiently and effectively provide for their retirement years. They would earn that support as opposed to having to beg for it as charity. Roosevelt also saw the social insurance approach as having a built-in self-protection against the whims of politicians. If workers paid for it, they would see it as theirs and fiercely resist any political attempts to take it away. In 1941, Roosevelt was asked whether it had been a mistake to add the Social Security payroll tax during the Great Depression. He responded:

> I guess you're right on the economics. They are politics all the way through. We put those payroll contributions there so as to give the contributors a legal, moral, and political right to collect their pensions and their unemployment benefits. With those taxes in there, no damn politician can ever scrap my social security program. Those taxes aren't a matter of economics, they're straight politics.

Roosevelt's words were prophetic. Future public mobilizations would block all attempts to eliminate or cut back the program. It is common to call Social Security the third rail of American politics. Politicians touch it, as with the electrified third rails of train systems, and they will be shocked. In the same interview, Roosevelt also indicated that payroll contributions had the psychological effect of nullifying any notion that Social Security was like welfare relief.[8]

The Original Program

Congress passed the Social Security Act by votes of 372 to 33 in the House and 77 to 6 in the Senate, which Roosevelt then signed into law on August 14, 1935. The program had just one type of benefit: pensions for insured retired workers over 65. It would begin to collect 1 percent of salary from employers and employees each in 1937. Like any social insurance program, these would go into a collective fund out of which pensions were to be paid, beginning in 1940.

Social Security issued its first monthly pension check to 65-year-old Ida May Fuller, a former schoolteacher and legal secretary, on January 31, 1940. It was for $22.54 (equivalent to $405 today). It replaced 30 percent of her final salary. That was far lower than the $200 that Townsend and his followers had demanded. It was nevertheless welcome income and a great deal for her. With three years of contributions before retirement, she had put a total of $24.75 into the program. She lived to be 100 and collected a total of $22,888.92.[9]

Legislation in 1939 established the formula for calculating Ida May Fuller's benefit. That formula would remain in effect during the 1940s: 40 percent of the first $50 average monthly income + 10 percent of the next $200 monthly income + 1 percent for each year of coverage.[10] That worked out in her case, based on an average monthly income of $68.75, to $20 + $1.87 + 0.67 = $22.54.

The benefit formula has changed over the years. Eligibility now requires at least forty quarters (three-month periods) or ten years of covered employment if born in 1929 or later. Ms. Fuller had slightly less than three years but was born before 1929. From a strictly actuarial point of view, Ms. Fuller was a bit of a free rider. She received benefits for which she did not fully pay. There were good reasons not to have the vesting requirement for the earliest beneficiaries. The country was still in the Great Depression and needed to get income to retirees to stimulate the economy. If people close to retirement knew that they were making contributions for naught, they would not have supported the program.

Expansion

In the years since 1935, Social Security expanded by covering more categories of workers and adding new types of benefits. When Social Security began, it covered under 60 percent of the labor force. Major excluded groups were agricultural workers (many of whom were Blacks and other minorities), domestics (primarily Black), and self-employed workers. Congress extended coverage to these groups in 1950. Today, the program covers approximately 94 percent of the labor force.[11]

Over the first decade and a half of its existence, Congress added survivor, dependent, and disability benefits. In addition to retirement pensions, insured workers—that is, anyone who paid Social Security taxes—also would be eligible for a disability pension for themselves and survivor and dependent benefits for eligible family members. Details of the benefits would change in subsequent years but not their purposes—to reduce social insecurities—and structuring.

Survivor Benefits (1939): If an insured worker with dependent children dies prematurely before retirement age, Social Security will pay monthly benefits to a surviving spouse who is caring for the children, as well as for each of the children. The benefits will last until the children reach age 18, or 19 if still in secondary school. The higher the average wage of the insured workers, the higher the benefit checks for their survivors. At the same time, the benefits for widowed mothers and fathers will be proportionately reduced if there is income from other sources. The Social Security income for children of deceased workers will remain the same regardless of income increases of parents.

The addition of survivor benefits for minor children of covered workers addressed one of the great anxieties of parents: how will their children be supported if they die? For insured workers who die or become disabled but who have children, Social Security currently provides up to $500,000 in insurance coverage until age 18 or 19. For many young parents, it is their most valuable asset, even if they are not aware of that fact. Some 1.9 million children of deceased workers receive an average monthly payment of $902 for their upkeep from Social Security.[12]

Dependent Benefits (1939): These benefits cover primarily dependent spouses of retired insured workers. The spouses upon reaching retirement age themselves become eligible to receive their own pensions, which can be up to 50 percent of those of their insured spouses. Should the insured retired worker die, the dependent spouse will receive 100 percent of the insured spouse's pension. If there are still dependent minor children when insured workers retire, their families will be eligible for additional benefits to support their care. As with survivor benefits, the higher the average wage of insured retired workers, the higher the benefit checks that their dependent spouses and minor children will receive.

Disability Benefits (1950): Should participants become unable to work because of accidents or chronic illnesses, they are eligible for disability pensions. The pensions, with amounts based on their earnings records while still able to work, last until they reach full retirement age. The Social Security Administration then transfers them to the Old Age Insurance program, where they continue to receive the same indexed benefits for the rest of their lives.

Initially, Social Security assumed a family where the male was the breadwinner and the wife a stay-at-home homemaker and mother. It also assumed a couple that stayed married. During the decades after the 1930s, though, more women entered the labor force, and divorce became more prevalent. Social Security adapted to these changes by adjusting its benefits to take them into account. The addition of eligibility for divorced spouses in 1950 for dependent benefits partially resolved the unfairness of situations in which women took care of children and households so that husbands could advance in careers, only to divorce them in later years.

Cost of Living Adjustments (1950): During the 1940s, the Consumer Price Index rose by 72 percent, while Social Security benefit amounts remained the same.[13] In essence, the value of pension checks decreased by 72 percent. Congress addressed the problem in 1950 by approving a significant 77 percent cost-of-living raise. It would be the first of several Cost-of-Living Adjustment (COLA) increases during the next two decades until 1972 when an automatic annual COLA was approved that would begin in 1975 and continues today.

It is difficult to overestimate the value of a COLA to any retirement income. As costs of living increase due to inflation, flat retirement incomes, which many private pensioners have, lose value. Consider someone who retired in 1999 at age 65 with a flat pension of $1,000 a month. In 2019, at age 65, because of inflation as measured by the Consumer Price Index, the $1,000 in 2019 dollars would only be worth $652 in 1999 dollars. And 1999 to 2019 was a period of relatively low inflation. The loss in real income has been much higher in more inflationary periods, with there being no guarantee that such periods won't return. Like taxes and death, inflation, high or low, is an inevitability and risk to pensioners with flat incomes.

Social Security's automatic annual COLA avoids much of the inflation problem, but it may not prevent all of it. There are debates about whether it is enough given increased, especially medical, expenses that many retired people face.

Medicare (1965): The Johnson administration in 1965 created Medicare, part of its War on Poverty, to provide health insurance to the over-65 population. The Social Security Administration initially administered Medicare directly and today interconnects its retirement and disability benefits with it. Because health insurance is an especially crucial necessity for the retired population, I will devote chapter 7 to the subject.

Supplemental Security Income (1972): In 1972, Congress created Supplemental Security Income (SSI) to provide minimum income to impoverished people who are 65 or older, blind, or disabled. Social Security administers but does not fund SSI. Technically, SSI is not social insurance since general tax revenue funds it as a means-tested welfare program targeted at the poor.

Contraction of Benefits

When Congress approved automatic COLAs in 1972, it also approved a last one-time COLA of a huge 20 percent, which aided President Nixon's reelection that November. The COLA bonanza, along with a faulty reconfiguration of the benefit formula, would contribute to a growing funding crisis that was clear by 1973, when the economy dove into recession. The 1973 Social Security trustees' report projected the first deficit in the program's thirty-eight-year history. In their 1975 report, they projected that the trust fund would be depleted by 1979.[14] In 1977, Congress passed legislation to address the growing financial crisis. The bill included two benefit cutbacks:

Benefit Formula Change (1977): In the first cutback, Congress reconfigured the benefit formula to correct the problems of the 1972 reconfiguration. This reconfiguration produced a small decrease in benefits over what the 1972 method had allowed.

Government Pension Offset (1977): The second cutback was the introduction of the Government Pension Offset, which went into effect in 1982. The GPO reduces dependent benefits by two-thirds if spouses of retired workers have government pensions and did not contribute to Social Security. For example, a retirement-age married or divorced spouse of a retired insured worker with a Social Security pension of $1,600 usually would be eligible for a dependent pension of $800. But if she had a $900 pension from a government job for which she did not pay Social Security taxes, the dependent pension would be reduced by $600 (two-thirds of $900) to $200. The rationale for the reduction is that the framers of the dependent benefit in 1939 mainly intended to cover widows who otherwise did not have incomes. Many consider that condition to be obsolete today with the prevalence of two-wage-earner families and call for the repeal of the GPO. A further argument for its repeal is that the insured workers paid for the coverage.

The 1977 amendments were not sufficient to fully stabilize Social Security's financing in the face of double-digit inflation beginning in 1978 and a new recession starting in 1980. In 1980, the Social Security trustees reported again that the program was in financial trouble. This was also the election year in which Ronald Reagan defeated Jimmy Carter to usher in a significant conservative revolution that included political forces opposed to Social Security.

The Reagan administration, after some political missteps (discussed in chapter 5), created a bipartisan commission, headed by Alan Greenspan, to examine the financing of Social Security and make recommendations. The commission's recommendations were quickly debated in Congress, passed overwhelmingly, and signed into law by President Reagan in 1983. The reforms included measures to increase program revenues by phasing in increases in the contribution rate from 5.08 to 6.2 percent of labor income. It reached the 6.2 percent rate in 1990, where it has remained, resulting in the most prolonged period of no contribution rate increase in Social Security history. The reforms also included three measures to reduce benefits:

Raise Retirement Age (1983): The first measure raised the full retirement age gradually from 65 to 67, the first such rise in Social Security history. That would reduce the total amount of lifetime benefits that a retiree could receive. Under the old rules, a 65-year-old retiree who lived to age 80 could receive a monthly check of, say, $1,500 for fifteen years for a total amount of $270,000, not considering COLA increases. Under the new rules, he or she would receive the same monthly check of $1,500 but for only thirteen years and a total amount of $234,000, 13.3 percent less.

Taxation of Benefits (1983): The second cutback mandated taxation of benefits for the first time, though at lower rates than general taxes. Revenue from the taxes recycle back into the program rather than going into general federal revenues.

Windfall Elimination Provision (1983): The WEP reduced the retirement benefit for participants who have both covered years of contributions to Social Security and uncovered years during which they participated in a retirement plan. The current Social Security benefit formula averages the 35 years of highest earnings. It then applies an adjustment that favors low earners, as the architects of Social Security intended, so that the program's retirement incomes would reduce elderly poverty. Before 1983, middle- and higher-income earners had zeros for their non-contributory years. As a result, their career averages sank to the range of low earners, making them eligible for the poverty reduction benefit adjustment—an unmerited windfall. The Greenspan Commission sought to correct that problem as a way to reduce overall Social Security expenditures. At the same time, it provoked considerable opposition, with an ongoing campaign by many to repeal the WEP.

The WEP issue arose in part out of miscommunications by Social Security with its annual statements that it used to send out in print form. Social Security included an estimate of pension amounts at full and early retirement ages for which it did not consider possible WEP reductions. Those subject to them did not find out about the cuts until they retired. The bigger problem is the continued existence of uncovered employment. This lack of coverage is a problem for many public school teachers. For them, it seems, and is, unfair that other public employees may be receiving both Social Security and employer-provided pensions, whereas they are only receiving the latter. The extra WEP ding is a final straw.

Strengths and Limits

It is difficult to overstate the importance of Social Security for tens of millions of retirees and their dependents who rely on its monthly pension checks. Were Social Security not to exist, 39.2 percent of that elderly population would be living below the poverty line. Instead, a very significantly reduced 9.2 percent live below it.[15] For just over half the retiree population, Social Security checks constitute the majority of their income. For about one in four, it provides 90 percent or more. It gives even higher proportions for Blacks and Latinos—a reflection of their lower incomes for which the progressive Social Security benefit formula produces higher replacement incomes.[16]

No other retirement program comes remotely close to covering as much of the working population and the work it does. Employer-sponsored plans include just over 50 percent, much less than the 94 percent that Social Security covers. Social Security covers workers who employers don't want to cover and who financial services industry companies consider unprofitable to have to deal with because their incomes are too low and erratic. Part-time and temporary workers, a growing portion of the labor force, are much more likely to be covered by Social Security than employer-sponsored programs. That includes the part-time and adjunct faculty who now do over half the teaching at many universities. Even if they only teach one course for a few hundred dollars' salary, Social Security covers, with few exceptions, this work.

Employer payment of their share of Social Security taxes, whether they like it or not, is mandatory and firmly entrenched. For employees, no matter how low the income, it is a good investment. If thought of as matching, employers must match 6.2 percent of employee contributions, which is a significantly higher rate than for most 401(k) plans in the corporate world. Because of Social Security's progressive benefit formula, the lower the income, the better the deal for employees.

For employers, sponsorship of their own retirement plan is entirely voluntary. As a result, as workers go from job to job, they may or may not be covered by employer-sponsored plans and receive retirement credits. Unlike many employer plans, there is no waiting period for Social Security coverage to kick in. Employers cannot pay Social Security tax contributions on some but not other categories of workers. If their full-time employees are covered, their part-time and temporary ones must be as well.

Social Security is the model portable retirement plan. The Social Security number goes with workers from job to job, with their contributions going into a unitary system that keeps lifetime track of them for them. It is not a fragmented system like employer plans scattered among many different financial services industry companies. Even contract workers, such as Uber drivers, are covered so that they build up Social Security credit. Granted, they have to pay both the employer and employee contributions, because they are still considered self-employed. But it is still worth doing, despite the unfairness of having to pay the employer parts.

There are other features of Social Security, such as disability and survivor coverage, that are very important but not the focus of our concern with retirement benefits. But it is worth mentioning that payment of Social Security tax contributions gets people more than retirement coverage, though that is the major part. For this reason, it is not an oranges-to-oranges comparison to argue that one could receive more from investing the 6.2 percent of salary contribution in the stock market, which in most cases is not true anyway.

Social Security is very efficient. It expends over 99 percent of its revenues on benefits. It spends less than one-half of 1 percent on the costs of administrating the program, which includes field offices throughout the country.[17] Private retirement plans minimally expend 20 percent of participant contributions on overhead expenses, including high top management salaries, profits, commissions, and advertising budgets. According to a Congressional Budget Office study, individuals who purchase annuities from private life insurance, which are similar to Social Security retirement life incomes, receive back in payouts 15 and 20 percent less than what they would if there were no administrative costs.[18] That compares to the less than one-half of 1 percent lost to Social Security administrative costs.

The companies that manage private retirement plans, because they are competing against each other, spend heavily on advertising. Those costs come out of the potential retirement incomes of plan partici-pants. Social Security does not have those costs. Its advertising budget is minimal. This explains why most people cannot remember seeing a Social Security advertisement. Financial service company advertise-ments, however, are all over television and in many magazines. In addition to high advertising expenses, CEOs and other top financial services company managers command yearly compensation packages in the tens of millions of dollars, which, like advertising costs, their companies glean from the contributions and investment gains of plan members. The highest salary for a Social Security official in 2018 was $189,600.[19]

But despite all these positive virtues, Social Security, as it currently functions, does not deliver enough retirement income. This is not an argument for going to a different system, despite there being financial interests that would like to divert the money to Wall Street with false claims that retirees would be better off. It is instead an argument for putting more resources into Social Security so that its benefits can be adequate for the needs of the retiree population. There are many financially sustainable ways to do that, which I will discuss in the next and final chapters. Social Security, in other words, already provides a sound basis for achieving benefit adequacy. All that is needed is to put more resources into it. That would be a better-paying investment than putting them into retirement savings accounts. In the long run, it could also form an alternative way for employers to provide retirement benefits. Instead of directing their contributions to private financial service companies to administer and invest, they could send them to Social Security in return for higher employee pensions. Instead of sending 6.2 percent of salary to Social Security, they could send, say, 12 percent, and stop contributions to private plans. To sweeten it further, employees could choose between having their retirement benefit sent to Social Security or sent to a private plan. That would constitute a public option in the employer retirement plan market.

---- 3 ----

What to Expect at Retirement

Social Security keeps detailed records of quarterly and yearly earnings for all participants. The participant can apply for early retirement benefits at age 62 and full retirement benefits currently at age 66, an age that is gradually rising. They can also defer receiving benefits until age 70. Taking early retirement results in reduced monthly payments; taking deferred retirement gives increased amounts. Social Security, like all life annuity providers, is calculating your total payments based on average longevities. If you retire early, you will receive more monthly payments than retiring at age 66. Each monthly check, though, must be less to make the lifetime payment the same as if you had retired at age 66. Vice versa for deferred retirement. Each monthly payment can be more because there will be fewer of them.

To determine the initial monthly pension amount for a retiree at full retirement age, Social Security applies a formula to the thirty-five years of highest earnings. It does not include any earnings that may be over maximums, known as "caps," for any of the years since payroll taxes were not paid on these. Social Security (1) takes each year's earnings under the cap for that year and multiplies them by an index factor to control for inflation. It (2) adds up those indexed earnings and divides that sum by 420 (the number of months in 35 years). The result is the average indexed monthly earning. It (3) then divides the average indexed earning into three parts. It multiples the first $960 in 2020 by .90. Then it multiplies the amount between $960 and $5,785 by .32. It multiplies any remaining amount by .15. Adding the products of these multiplications together produces the monthly benefit amount. It is a bit tricky: the .90, .32, and .15 are always constant, but what they multiply—referred to as "bend points"—change each year. The bend points, like the index factors, can be found online. Further, the bend points to be used are those in existence at age 62, even if the retirement age is later. Because the multipliers of the bend points decrease as income increases, Social Security distributes benefit amounts progressively. The lower the income, the higher the replacement rate. This is intentional to reduce elderly poverty.

Three things stand out about the formula. It bases itself on average rather than final earnings, to be discussed presently. It applies indexing to control for the effects of inflation. And, it results in a progressive distribution of benefits while it collects contributions on the basis of flat payroll taxes.

If the goal of retirement policy is to ensure enough replacement income to maintain pre-retirement standards of living, with 70 percent being the most common rule of thumb, then we can start by examining how far Social Security takes us toward that goal.

It is common to state that the designers of Social Security never meant to provide all that income. It was supposed to supply just part of it, with employer-sponsored retirement plans and individual savings making up the balance. That three-legged stool assumption may not necessarily be correct. In any event, we need to evaluate how well current Social Security is functioning.

According to Social Security studies (see Table 3.1, page 56), for average earners, the program replaces about 41 percent of their pre-retirement income. Because Social Security distributes its benefits progressively, high-income retirees have less of a percentage of income replaced (though receiving more dollars), and low-income retirees have a higher percentage replacement. At one extreme, Social

TABLE 3.1: Social Security Average Career Incomes, Benefits, and Replacement Rates at Full Retirement Age, 2020

Income Class	Average Career Income (2019 dollars)	Initial Yearly Benefit**	Percent of Career Average Earnings
Very Low	$12,949	$9,843	76.0
Low	$23,308	$12,884	55.3
Middle	$51,795	$21,248	41.0
High	$82,872	$28,147	34.0
Maximum	$127,061	$34,343	27.1

Source: Michael Clingman, Kyle Burkhalter, and Chris Chaplain, "Replacement Rates for Hypothetical Retired Workers," Social Security Administration Actuarial Noted 2019.9 (April 2019), Table C.
** Reaches full retirement age in 2019.

Security identifies the "very low" income retirees. They do not work a full year since their total yearly incomes are less than that of full-time minimum wage workers. At the other extreme are maximum-income workers. They have always paid contributions on the Social Security maximum income for thirty-five years.

But there is more here than meets the eye. The Social Security study is not referring to final earnings but *average career* earnings, and there can be a vast difference between the two depending upon different career patterns. The replacement rates cited in the study for very low, low, medium, high, and maximum income workers assume that they have always earned the average income for their class. Virtually no one has. They've received more or less, and they've received different amounts at different times. The earning of different wages at different times may make their career averages higher or lower than their final incomes. Social Security research has concluded that average and final salary replacement rates are close because of the use of index factors in the benefit formula.[1] This closeness may be empirically true in terms of averages, but only because many people's incomes decline in their final work years. For those who receive significant raises in those years, it is not true. Individual earnings patterns, it turns out, can be all over the place.

How wide can they range? To answer that question, we can design an extreme set of career-pattern scenarios. Workers would receive full-time minimum wages for thirty-four years. Then for the thirty-fifth, their final year, somehow, they would receive a salary that brought them up to one or another of the low, medium, high, or maximum incomes listed in Table 3.1. This career pattern, of course, is very unlikely, if not impossible. But it is useful for establishing the range for full-time workers with thirty-five years of contributions before retiring at full retirement age (66 in 2019). The results (Table 3.2, below) show that actual replacement rates could be considerably lower than average ones. In the case of middle-income workers, that is, average income workers, the spread is between a replacement rate of 20.3 and 41 percent.

Now, the lower ends of those ranges are very unlikely extremes—minimum-wage income for thirty-four years and then enormous jumps for the final year before retirement. What would be a more likely career wage pattern? There are many. But it would be impossible to account for all of them without producing a thick volume of spreadsheets. Instead, let's hypothesize a situation in which a worker begins at age 18 with a minimum-wage job and then works full-time until retirement at age 66. These would be workers who steadily worked their way up to one or another of the low, medium, high, or maximum salaries for the final year. Table 3.3 (page 58) presents those scenarios. As we can see, there are still considerably lower replacement incomes for each of the low, medium, high, and maximum levels than those of average workers. The average-income worker at

TABLE 3.2: Social Security Incomes, Range of Benefits, and Range of Final Salary Replacement Rates at Full Retirement Age, 2020

Income Class	Final Income	Initial Yearly Benefit (range)	Percent of Final Earnings (range)
Very Low	$12,949	$9,843	76.0
Low	$23,308	$10,236 – $12,884	43.9 – 55.3
Middle	$51,795	$10,524 – $21,248	20.3 – 41.0
High	$82,872	$10,932 – $28,147	13.2 – 34.0
Maximum	$127,061	$12,576 – $34,383	9.9 – 27.1

TABLE 3.3: Steady Climber's Social Security Incomes, Benefits, and Final Salary Replacement Rates

Income Class	Final Salary	Initial Yearly Benefit	Percent of Final Earnings	Percent Wage Increase per Year
Very Low	$12,949	$9,864	76.2	2.8
Low	$23,308	$12,000	51.5	4.2
Middle	$51,795	$16,034	31.0	5.9
High	$82,872	$20,328	24.5	6.9
Maximum	$127,061	$25,032	19.7	8.0

Note: "Steady Climber" assumes work career begins at age 18 with a minimum-wage job and then receives steady wage increases until retirement.

the medium level drops from a 41 to 31 percent replacement income, nearly a quarter less. The maximum-income worker from 27.1 to 19.7 percent.

Anyone who starts a career with low earnings that then rise due to promotions or attaining better-paying jobs faces this problem. Indeed, it was mine, and the primary reason why I became sensitive to it. My actual Social Security benefit was 43 percent less than the average for the income class to which I belonged. What I had been counting on turned out to be considerably less. This discrepancy, I suspect, is the same for many others who have assumed that their benefits would closely approximate the Social Security averages.

In sum, what to expect from Social Security at retirement depends overall on the top thirty-five years of earnings and how they occurred. To put that into perspective, most retirement advisors recommend that overall retirement income from all sources, including Social Security, be at least 70 percent of the final salary. Social Security's advertised average replacement rate is 41 percent, leaving 29 percent to come from other sources, mainly employer-sponsored retirement plans. But many people do not receive the average 41 percent of their final incomes. The first reason is that Social Security calculates the 41 percent on average career rather than final salaries. Those most likely to receive the average are middle-income workers who have always been middle-income workers or who had higher incomes earlier in their careers and then lower incomes in their final years. For those who earned their highest salaries during their last years, their replacement rates will be lower than their income class averages.

For individuals trying to make sense of this for estimating their retirement incomes, Social Security provides an estimate of retirement income that can be accessed through the www.ssa.gov website. The closer you are to retirement, the more accurate the forecast. If individuals can estimate their final wages or salaries, they can see what proportion of those incomes Social Security's estimate of their retirement incomes replaces.

No one should take at face value that Social Security replaces, on average, 41 percent of income. Workers may be in for a rude awakening if it returns a lot less of their final salaries. The problem is not that Social Security is a defective retirement system. It is instead that the country must expand it if we want it to be capable of replacing more income.

4

Not a Ponzi Scheme

n one respect, the financing of Social Security is straightforward. It has three parts: (1) revenues collected that go into a (2) collective trust fund out of which (3) it pays benefits. The plan is in financial balance as long as the trust fund contains enough to pay out owed benefits. If owed benefits exceed what is in the trust fund, the plan can be put back into balance, as any accountant knows, by increasing revenues, decreasing benefit expenses, or some combination of the two. Beyond that pure accounting mathematics, however, are a host of political issues regarding whether to increase revenues to maintain or increase benefit levels or to decrease those benefit levels. It seems that Republicans and Democrats agree on what the elements or variables of that mathematical equation are but disagree on how to manipulate them. Democrats generally, though not always, prefer to maintain or increase benefits, while most Republicans would like to do the opposite. We will return to this topic, but first we need to account for what the sources of Social Security revenue are.

Contributions from employers and employees are the largest sources of Social Security revenue. The program, from its beginning, has been based primarily on those two sources of revenue. It began in January 1937 to collect 1 percent of employee pay with employers making an equal match of 1 percent. Over the years, the size of the payroll deduction has risen to 6.2 percent each. This is the FICA (Federal Insurance Contributions Act) deduction on payroll stubs.

Employer and employee payroll taxes account for 86 percent of Social Security's income. FICA payroll taxes are dedicated taxes. They solely fund the Social Security program. The federal government cannot use them for other expenses or to balance its general budget. At the same time, Social Security gets no support from general federal tax revenues. General taxes and Social Security payroll taxes fund separate budgets. Other Social Security systems, such as that of Germany, have additional contributions from general tax revenues. There are thus alternate sources of income to fund social insurance systems beyond employer and employee contributions. Any future expansion of Social Security could tap those sources.

The combined 12.4 percent of payroll collected by Social Security is low in comparison to European social insurance systems. According to the Organization for Economic Cooperation and Development (Table 4.1, page 62), the majority of Western European countries invest higher percentages of their GDP (Gross Domestic Product) in public pension systems than the United States. Five countries—Ireland, Netherlands, Norway, Switzerland, the United Kingdom—compensate for their relatively low expenditures by spending more on mandatory employer-provided retirement plans or other social benefits, expending overall more than the United States on retirement plans or additional benefits for retired people.[1] In the Netherlands, nearly all workers have substantial employer-provided pensions, unlike in the United States. In the United Kingdom, the National Health Service provides more free healthcare for retired people than does Medicare in the United States.

What Social Security collects is recycled into benefit payments. That which exceeds what it has to pay out goes into its long-term trust fund. That money, in turn, is invested in interest-paying Treasury bonds. These are most likely the most secure investment in the world, though their interest payments are low. There is, in essence, a trade-off between modest interest payments and high security. The interest

TABLE 4.1: Public Expenditures on Old Age and Survivors' Benefits 2015

Country	Percent of GDP
Austria	13.3
Belgium	10.7
Denmark	8.1
Finland	11.4
France	13.9
Germany	10.1
Greece	16.9
Ireland	3.6
Italy	16.2
Luxembourg	8.4
Netherlands	5.4
Norway	6.6
Portugal	13.3
Spain	11.0
Sweden	7.2
Switzerland	6.5
United Kingdom	6.2
European average	9.9
United States	7.1

Source: OECD, *Pensions at a Glance 2019* (Paris: OECD Publishing, 2019), Table 8.3.

obtained from Treasury bonds makes up the second stream of Social Security revenue.

Opponents of Social Security have spread the myth that the surplus doesn't exist. In one version, widely circulated on the internet and Facebook, in particular, Congress has stolen the surplus to fund other programs. Congress indeed uses the excess to fund other government expenses. But Social Security *loans* those funds. Those loans in the form of Treasury bonds must be paid back with interest. The second version, spread by former President George W. Bush when he was trying to generate public support for legislation to partially privatize Social Security, alleged that the Treasury bonds owned by Social Security were "worthless I.O.U.s." Any economist viewing that allegation cringed at the thought of a president implying that the U.S. government would default on the payment of Treasury bills. Such an action would crash a good part of the world economy. Treasury bonds are backed by "the full faith and credit of the U.S. government." This means that the government must use all of its means, including raising taxes, to repay the principal plus interest of a bond when it is due. Since the dollar is the world's dominant reserve currency, there is virtually no risk of the U.S. government defaulting on its debts, and it has never done so. The reserve portion of the Social Security Trust Fund is thus parked in what is the most secure place in the world, hardly in "worthless I.O.U.s," as alleged by former president George W. Bush.

In 1985, as mentioned earlier, the Internal Revenue Service began to tax Social Security income, though at a lesser rate than general taxes. Those tax revenues go back into the Social Security trust fund. They are, in short, dedicated to supporting the program. The federal government cannot divert the tax revenues to other government expenses. They make up the third and final source of Social Security revenue.

Honest Misunderstandings and Dishonest Manufactured Myths

It should be clear by now that social insurance plans, such as Social Security, are not like individual bank checking, savings, or investment accounts. Many people mistakenly believe that they are. It is thus worth highlighting the differences. In a demand checking or savings account, depositors have a right to withdraw as much of their deposited money as they want at any time. This is not true of Social Security

TABLE 4.2: Social Security Income and Expenditures (in Billions), 2019

	OASI	DI	Total
INCOME	$917.9	$143.9	$1,061.8
Payroll Taxes	$805.1	$139.4	$944.5
Interest	$77.9	$2.9	$80.8
Taxation and Benefits	$34.9	$1.6	$36.5
EXPENDITURES	$911.4	$147.9	$1,059.3
Benefits	$902.8	$145.1	$1,047.9
Administrative Cost	$3.7	$2.7	$6.4
EXCESS INCOME OVER EXPENSES	$6.5	−$4.0	$2.5
TOTAL TRUST FUND RESERVES	$2,804.3	$93.1	$2,897.4

Source: 2020 OASIDI Trustees Report, Office of the Chief Actuary, Social Security Administration, Washington, DC, 2020, Table II.B1.
Note: OASI is the Old Age and Survivors Insurance Fund, DI is the Disability Insurance Fund.

contributions. Social Security can distribute deposits to participants only under set conditions, such as when they retire or become disabled. With a bank account, you cannot withdraw more than what you have deposited plus any accumulated interest. Amounts of deposits plus interest set the absolute limits for what account holders can withdraw. There are situations where Social Security participants can receive more than they contributed, such as if they live to 106, since the program delivers guaranteed payments for life, long or short as that may be. The corollary is that there are also situations in which individuals receive less than they contributed, such as if they die shortly after retirement, or nothing at all if they die before retirement.

With a bank account, the size of deposits plus interest credited to them determines what account holders can withdraw. With social insurance plans, the size of the overall contributions plus other sources of revenue also determines how much participants can receive as benefits. But the individual's contributions do not determine all that he or she can receive as benefits. There is not a one-to-one relationship as there is with bank accounts. Those who have higher contributions owing to higher earnings are eligible for higher retirement incomes. But the total amount received is also based on the longevity of the beneficiary. Regardless of how much pensioners contributed during working years, those who live to 90—assuming equal initial monthly benefit checks—will collect much more during their lifetimes than those who live to 75.

Beyond honest misunderstandings are myths that the enemies of Social Security intentionally create and spread in the court of public opinion. The favorable view of Social Security that is held by most of the public is a stumbling block for those seeking its total or partial elimination. For that reason, they engage in campaigns to either tar the program in unfavorable terms or undermine confidence in its basic viability and solvency.

Social Security is not welfare. Its enemies put that label on it to confuse people. They want people to think of Social Security income as something shameful to accept. The right-wing campaigns against welfare and Social Security have operated in tandem since the late

1970s, with the former approaching absolute demonization. In the United States, many people take the term "welfare" to mean programs that benefit the poor. In a more generous and caring society, that would be as it should be, with the more fortunate extending a hand to the less fortunate. But there has long been an (originally) Calvinist hostility toward the poor in this country, viewing them as undeserving parasites living off and taking advantage of hard-working, overtaxed citizens. To identify Social Security this way with welfare accomplishes the goal of its enemies to make acceptance of its benefits shameful.

Europeans take the concept of welfare differently. They embrace their welfare states as being beneficial to all citizens. Welfare programs for them comprise all of the publicly sponsored programs that seek to provide income, retirement, health, and other forms of social security that, in turn, make for the well-being of whole societies. A subset of those programs target poverty alleviation, which Europeans do a much better job of accomplishing than Americans. Most Europeans consider their anti-poverty programs as prudent social investments to undergird social peace, which benefits everyone.

The United States, of course, has public programs that benefit the non-poor such as student grants and subsidized loans, tax abatements for corporations, and non-taxation of churches. Americans, though, are less likely to perceive these programs as parts of a broader welfare state.[2]

Taking the narrow American meaning of welfare programs as only those exclusively targeted toward the poor, Social Security does not qualify. Social Security has become a critical source of the retirement income of non-poor persons and families. Many more working- and middle-class persons benefit from it than do the strictly poor. Removal of that income would lead to a severe drop in the number of people who could maintain working- and middle-class standards of living in retirement while swelling the ranks of the elderly poor.

Social Security is not an entitlement, at least not in the prevailing current politicized connotation of that term. The concept of an entitlement used to be noncontroversial in American discourse, meaning something like "a right to," as in the right to free public education. But then as conservatives sought to cut social spending, they began using the term as a pejorative, implying that an entitlement was somehow an unearned gift at the expense of taxpayers, like welfare, as opposed to something earned through hard work. "You're not *entitled* to anything in this land of opportunity: you have to *work* for it" became the common intended misunderstanding. No one, however, would disagree that workers are entitled to wages or salaries. Words in discourse can be slippery, their meanings dependent on context and inflection.

Social Security is an entitlement only in the original neutral, not the politically motivated pejorative, meaning. People paid during their working lives for the benefit, which they are entitled to receive in retirement income. It is an earned benefit, which a number of its advocates use to describe it now due to the political corruption of the original meaning of entitlement. It can also be viewed as a deferred wage since original wages would have been higher had they not been subjected to Social Security payroll taxes.

Not a Ponzi Scheme

Social Security is not a Ponzi scheme. Its enemies often levy this charge at the program with a knowing look to indicate that it is a house of cards that will fall of its own so that it won't be there for today's young workers when they retire. Like in a Ponzi scheme, its enemies allege, most will have contributed money that they will never get back.

Charles Ponzi (1882–1949), an Italian immigrant to Boston, is the namesake of the scheme. In January 1920, he set up a company that promised investors 100 percent returns within ninety days. They would be investing in the purchase of foreign stamps that the company would redeem at higher values in the United States. Like all successful confidence men, he had a magnetic personality that inspired trust. As more people invested, he had enough revenue to pay off previous investors, at least for a while. That inspired more people to part with their money, quickly setting off an investment frenzy. It was a get-rich-quick promise that seemed to be trustworthy. But his pay-offs came from the new rapidly increasing investments rather than legitimate profits from the stamp business. Suspicious critics began to ask questions. This inspired early investors to try to pull their money out rather than reinvest it. That, in turn, led to a rapid reversal that plunged the scheme into the red, making it collapse altogether in August 1920, just eight months after it began. His investors lost millions of dollars. Ponzi was arrested, tried, and jailed for fraud. He spent twelve years in jail and then was deported back to Italy in 1934.

Ponzi's immortalized name serves as a metaphor for financial frauds that use later investments rather than legitimate profits to pay early investors and then motivate others to invest.

Once, while in junior high school, I went to the Oklahoma State Fair in Muskogee. My mother had warned me to stick to the rides and stay away from the barkers. That, of course, made me more curi-ous about the barkers. One was drawing a crowd. He had a pile of mystery gift boxes for five dollars each, which was a lot of money for me then. The first person, no doubt a shill, handed over five dollars and received back a box with a portable radio, a much more valuable item then than now. A portable radio was at the top of my adolescent wishlist of must-haves to listen to rock and roll and baseball games. A second and third person received back similarly much more valuable gifts than their five-dollar payments. People were competing now to have the barker accept their five-dollar bills. I debated with myself because five dollars was all I had for the rest of the fair. I don't part with money easily, then or now. But my greed got the better part of me, and I made the payment. By this time, the barker was just taking money and a lot of it. When he had shaken down the crowd for about as much as he thought he could get—I was one of the last ones—he handed out the gift boxes. Mine contained a cheap keychain. My fellow suckers did no better. I had been Ponzied. Lesson learned.

A more recent and much more consequential example was the Bernie Madoff swindle. The bitter joke was that Madoff was the only one jailed because he was the only one who robbed rich people.

Several Republican politicians, including former Wyoming Senator Alan Simpson, former Texas Governor Rick Perry, and former President Donald Trump, have branded Social Security a Ponzi scheme, a charge that has spread widely among opponents of the program. Like a Ponzi scheme, they claim, Social Security only works if more and more people pay into it to pay off the benefits of earlier contributors. But that can't happen now, they claim, with the aging of the population and an increasing ratio of beneficiaries to contributors.

While seeming like an apt comparison, it is an entirely false one. Social Security is not a Ponzi scheme, first and foremost, because it does not depend on increasing numbers of contributors to pay off earlier entrants. Instead, the Social Security Administration carefully estimates with actuarial methods its future required expenditures on pensions and other benefits. Ponzi schemers never do that. They're only interested in pocketing inflows of cash without worrying about having to make good on future promised payments. When Social Security contributions and benefits are out of balance, Social Security puts them back in balance through congressional legislation by increasing contribution rates, decreasing benefits, or some combination of the two.

Second, Social Security's finances are completely transparent, unlike those of Ponzi, who relied on deception as did the Oklahoma barker. Each year the trustees release a report on the program's finances that is readily available for public viewing online.

Third, unlike Social Security, which is backed by the U.S. government, Ponzi schemes are criminal enterprises that are accountable to no one other than their partners in crime. When Ponzi's scheme collapsed, its victims had no recourse to get their lost money back. When Social Security ran into financial problems in the 1970s, there were plenty of remedies to make sure that participants would keep receiving their earned and promised benefits.

Finally, a Ponzi scheme is usually short-lived due to its fundamental financial instability. Ponzi's scheme lasted just eight months before collapsing. Social Security has more than eight decades of existence, during which it has never failed to make a benefit payment.

The original German model from 1889 has lasted well over a century. Social insurance funds can last forever with appropriate management. No amount of managerial skill on Ponzi's part would have been able to overcome the fundamental flaws of his scheme.

Another charge against Social Security is that it is a primary driver of the national deficit and debt. The clear implication is that cutting Social Security benefits is required to reduce both. It is a key part of the presumed necessity of entitlement reform.

Social Security has nothing to do with either the deficit or debt. Deficits occur when Congress and the administration spend more in a given year than is collected from taxes and other sources of revenue. The government must borrow the difference. All of the accumulated liabilities of the federal government make up the national debt. Deficit spending adds to the national debt. How much either one does or doesn't represent a problem for the country need not concern us here.

Social Security finances, however, are separate from those of the rest of the federal government that contribute to its deficits and the national debt. Social Security, as discussed, is a self-financed and self-contained program that has a budget separate from that of the rest of the federal government. There is no commingling of funds. Far from having continual budgetary deficits, with rare exceptions, Social Security's revenues have exceeded its expenditures. Far from having an accumulated debt, the program had an accumulated surplus of $2.9 trillion as of 2019.

None of this is to say that the program does not have financial challenges for the future. But those are easily manageable challenges, assuming the willingness of Congress and the administration. On the other hand, "entitlement reform" that reduced Social Security benefits would not affect the federal deficit or debt.

Nancy Altman, president of the labor-backed advocacy organization Social Security Works, summed up the issue: "Social Security's current projected shortfall, modest in size and still years away, is not a 'crisis,' as too many politicians assert, but a call for simple maintenance. If your car needs an oil change, it's not a crisis. But if you do nothing, and wait until your engine is blown, it can become a crisis."[3]

— 5 —

Privatizers and Means Testers

From its inception in 1935 until the 1970s, Social Security was relatively uncontroversial. American workers quickly warmed to the New Deal program, its benefit checks being a welcome source of needed income. Democrats took credit for initiating the program, and Republicans went along. For sure, it had critics, but their influence was limited. Republican president Dwight D. Eisenhower dismissed the program's opponents as a tiny group of Texas oil millionaires.

From the Great Depression to the end of the 1960s, there was a Keynesian political consensus that government programs, like Social Security, were needed not only by their direct beneficiaries but by the capitalist system itself. They kept income circulating rather than being bottled up at the top. If the lower and working classes had too little income, they would not be able to purchase enough goods and services to keep the economy growing.

A small group of conservative economists, most prominently Milton Friedman at the University of Chicago, never accepted the Keynesian argument. They viewed government regulations and redistribution programs as interfering with the optimal functioning of markets. As early as 1962, Friedman took aim at Social Security.[1] He didn't like it for three reasons. First, it was a mandatory government program that required employers and employees to contribute. Government mandates rankled his libertarian values. It was fine for individuals voluntarily to save money for retirement, but governments should not make them do so. Second, the contributions went through the government rather than the private financial services industry. Rather than serving as a basis for private capital accumulation, they bolstered the economic power of government. Third, Social Security benefits were redistributive. The benefit formula returned relatively more to lower- than upper-income groups in line with the original goal of the program to reduce elderly poverty. Friedman, like other conservatives, was dead-set against governments redistributing income. Market success, not government, should determine the nature of income distribution, including how many ended up impoverished.

Friedman and other economists like him remained voices in the wilderness until the 1970s and the lead-up to Reagan Republicanism, coming to power in 1981. They helped to prepare the policy changes that conservatives would introduce as part of the Reagan agenda, including attempts to transform Social Security with an ultimate goal being its complete privatization. One of the ways that Friedman directly participated in policy development was to have a close association with the libertarian Koch brothers' Cato Institute, which has continued to have a Social Security privatization project down to the present.

Writers have used various labels to describe the ideological opposition to Social Security, including that of Friedman. Among the more prominent labels have been libertarianism, neoliberalism, conservatism, and neoconservatism. The names taken together seem confusing and contradictory. However, each has a coherent logic of its own. It depends on the school of thought that its user is employing. Libertarians believe that government—the state in its classic formulation—is the primary source of oppression. Reducing government oppression would require reducing government power to the necessary absolute minimum. All government programs and control, whether economic or social, should be eliminated or minimized. Governments should not regulate the private economy or individual behavior, so no prohibitions on price fixing or smoking dope. Libertarians are very pro-capitalism, while taking a classic liberal attitude toward maximizing individual liberties.

Commentators have also labeled Friedman and those like him as neoliberals and conservatives. The discourse of liberalism and conservatism cross-cuts that of libertarianism. The classical liberalism of the early nineteenth century, like libertarianism, opposed excessive government economic and political power. At a time when semifeudal institutions were significantly frustrating the development of European capitalism, liberals wanted to liberate the market. The term retains that meaning in parts of Europe today, which is different than its contemporary American use where liberalism means support for government programs and economic regulations. The term "neoliberal," literally *new* liberal, refers to the original meaning of support for free markets.

The term "conservative" has different connotations in the United States and Europe. In the United States, it is economically indistinguishable from libertarian and neoliberal, with its embrace of free-market capitalism with minimal or no government interference. However, on social questions such as abortion and street drugs, conservatives very much believe in government regulation. In European conservatism, there is no embrace of free-market capitalism. There, conservatives have accepted the welfare state in the same way that Republicans in the United States in the 1950s acknowledged Social Security as necessary and useful.

Right-wing think tanks, such as Cato, the American Enterprise Institute, and the Manhattan Institute, have ideological motives for opposing Social Security. Those motives are mostly but not entirely consistent with the economic interests of the financial services industry—the private investment, insurance, and other companies that process and profit from controlling retirement savings. Partial or complete Social Security privatization would bring them a bonanza of new business and profits. But not all of it would be profitable. They would lose money having to administer the accounts of low-income participants. There is a parallel with health insurance companies preferring to insure healthy rather than sick people. Financial services companies prefer to manage accounts of people who have a lot rather than a little to invest.

Reagan and the Greenspan Commission

When the Reagan administration came into office in 1981, Social Security, as we have seen, was facing a real financial shortfall. Conservatives in and out of the administration saw that as an opportunity, a pretext to reduce the program. David Stockman, the director of the Office of Management and Budget, proposed a budget that cut both taxes and spending. He considered Social Security to be part of a unified federal budget despite the separation of its funds from those of the rest of the federal government, something that President Reagan would eventually learn. He could not, for example, transfer funds from the Social Security trust fund to balance the general budget.

Stockman prepared the first direct attack on Social Security by a federal official. His opposition to the program was evident when he referred to it as "closet socialism." He would later write that he had prepared "a frontal assault on the very inner fortress of the American welfare state—the giant Social Security system, on which one-seventh of the nation's populace depended for its well-being."[2] There had been earlier reforms in 1978 under the Carter administration. But their purpose had been to try to bring the accounts into balance without prejudice against the very idea of Social Security.

By spring 1981, Congress passed a budget prepared by Stockman that cut back two Social Security benefits: extending support for surviving children until age 22 if they went to college and a subsidized minimum retirement benefit. Then Stockman aimed at Social Security's early retirement program that allowed participants to take reduced benefits starting at age 62. Social Security's actuaries had calculated the total lifetime benefits that participants would receive if they began to draw them at the full retirement age of 65 and survived an average amount of years. They then added three years—the

additional years of payments if they started at age 62—and calculated the necessary reduction to the monthly checks to keep the total
lifetime amount paid out the same. The result was that the early retirement monthly check was 80 percent of the full retirement age version.

Stockman and his staff proposed reducing the 80 percent check to
55 percent to gain more savings for their concept of the federal budget
that falsely combined Social Security with the government's general
expenditures. The 55 percent figure had nothing to do with Social
Security's technical actuarial needs.

When the proposed early retirement benefits reduction leaked to
the press, it set off a firestorm of public opposition. Phones rang off
the wall in congressional offices from angry constituents. Complained
Representative Carroll A. Campbell, Jr. (R-SC): "I've got thousands
of sixty-year-old textile workers who think it's the end of the world.
What the hell am I supposed to tell them?"[3] The Senate then passed
a non-binding resolution 96–0 that opposed any reform that would
"precipitously and unfairly penalize early retirees."[4]

The administration's anti-Social Security proposals stimulated
a series of labor and community organizations to defend Social
Security, adding organized pressure to the spontaneous public opposition. By the fall of 1981, the administration beat a retreat on further
Social Security cutbacks, including the reduction of early retirement
benefits. The president sought to save face by naming the bipartisan National Committee on Social Security Reform (the Greenspan
Commission) to develop a plan to stabilize Social Security's financing.

The Greenspan Commission would make an honest effort to stabilize Social Security's financing through increasing its revenues by
speeding up payroll tax rate increases to 6.2 percent and beginning
the taxation of benefits, and through moderately reducing benefits by
raising the retirement age and other measures. What it was unable to
anticipate and control were the rates at which income inequality and
financialization, both of which removed income from Social Security
taxation, would increase from the 1990s going forward. But before
examining those dynamics, there is still ground to cover on more
efforts to undermine Social Security.

While the results of the Greenspan Commission and earlier Reagan administration legislation produced reductions in Social Security benefits, they did not challenge Social Security's basic defined-benefit pension approach. That frustrated many of the administration's conservative allies. They wanted, more than a reduction of benefits, the elimination of Social Security as a competitor to the private financial services industry for the nation's retirement plan dollars.

The Chilean Precedent and the World Bank

Social insurance privatizers would be more successful in Chile, which from 1973 to 1990 was governed by a right-wing military dictatorship. Students and followers of Milton Friedman, called "the Chicago boys" in the Latin American press, in 1981 ended the country's social insurance–based social security system for new workers, replacing it with a 401(k)-like system. Whereas in the United States, 401(k)s were beginning to displace employer-provided traditional pensions as adjuncts to Social Security, in Chile, the dictatorship replaced the social security system itself. The privatized Chilean system survived the restoration of democracy in 1991 and became the model for neoliberal public pension reform throughout much of the world with encouragement from the World Bank. The privatizers were particularly successful in Latin America. During the 1990s, they succeeded in privatizing or partially privatizing national public retirement systems to which half the region's workers belonged.

In the United States, right-wing and libertarian foundations in the 1990s continued their long-term goal of privatizing Social Security, including attempts to undermine public confidence that the program was stable enough financially to be in existence for long. The first of the broadsides against Social Security, written in 1982 by Peter J. Ferrara of the Cato Institute, was titled *Social Security: Averting the Crisis.*[5] By 1994, what had been a right-wing fringe campaign mainstreamed when the World Bank issued an influential report with a suspiciously similar title, *Averting the Old Age Crisis.* Averting is a relatively unusual gerund, making its choice for both titles more than coincidental. Confirming the ideological proclivities of the title, Estelle James, the writer of the report, after leaving the World Bank, went to work for the libertarian Koch brothers–funded National Center for Policy Analysis.

Averting the Old Age Crisis is the best single source for knowing what to expect from opponents of Social Security in the now ongoing battle over its future. The World Bank's model national retirement system had three parts or pillars in its terms:[6]

1. Mandatory tax-funded means-tested programs to reduce poverty;
2. Mandatory personal savings accounts based on employee deductions;
3. Voluntary supplementary plans or accounts.

If the U.S. government applied the World Bank model to Social Security, it would shrink the retirement program to a means-tested program for the elderly poor and privatize the rest into 401(k)-like personal accounts. In the years since the Bank published *Averting the Old Age Crisis*, there have been prominent proposals to means-test Social Security benefits and to privatize substantial parts of its program.

Means-testing of benefits sounds deceptively reasonable when the examples used to support the idea are millionaires drawing Social Security checks they don't need. But the proponents' goal is also to take away Social Security checks from the less-than-millionaire non-poor, which means most ordinary people. That would transform Social Security from a social insurance program that benefits most working- and middle-class people into a welfare program that would help only the poor.

As with other poverty-alleviating welfare programs, according to the Bank, general taxes rather than dedicated social insurance contributions should fund national social security programs. That, however, would make the program vulnerable to politically motivated budgetary reductions. One can imagine how tempting it would be for Congress to cut Social Security's funds in years of tight budgets. Its constituency, unlike that of the current Social Security, would represent only a small percentage of voters, and ones often maligned as undeserving of taxpayer support. There is a saying in Washington: "A program for the poor has poor support."

Retirement provision for the non-poor, according to the Bank prescriptions, should be based on individual savings and investment 401(k)-like plans. Since these are privately managed accounts, the government would get out of the business of facilitating retirement support for the non-poor. It would then no longer be liable for making good on benefit promises. This government exit from retirement provision would also free up capital—currently, government-held—for the private market.

Bush and Social Security Partial Privatization

Republicans and Democrats don't exactly take marching orders from the World Bank. Still, its report served to frame policy options for Republicans and corporate-friendly Democrats. Republicans ultimately want to transform Social Security from a social insurance program with a cross-class base to a tax-funded welfare program for only the poor. The boldest expression of this came in 2005 when President George W. Bush attempted to privatize Social Security partially. A significant number of, but not all, Democrats wanted to curtail further growth of Social Security while encouraging individual savings and investment accounts.

Bush announced the partial privatization plan right after being reelected in 2004 as his top second-term domestic policy goal. With his proposal, instead of the combined employer-employee payroll tax of 12.4 percent of employee payroll going to Social Security, up to a third could be diverted to personal savings and investment accounts. It would represent a partial privatization, no doubt, as a first step toward more comprehensive privatization in the future. In the early months of 2005, Bush traveled the country, talking up the plan as a central pillar of "the ownership society." People, not the government, he stated, would own the accumulations from these individual accounts. But the more he talked about the proposal, the more public opinion became opposed to it. In August, he abandoned it to pursue other domestic policy goals.

The Democrats' answer to Bush's carve-out proposal, which would have turned Social Security financing into turmoil, had been announced by former vice president Al Gore in a 2000 presidential debate. They would create "add on" provisions instead. They would facilitate individual savings and investment accounts that would supplement traditional Social Security, whose contribution rates would remain the same.

The Democratic add-on proposal would not undermine Social Security financing, but it would contain it. It would foreclose the possibility of raising future contribution rates to stabilize or expand the program. All future contribution increases, instead, would go into individual savings and investment accounts.

Both the Democratic and Republican proposals were thus consistent with the World Bank prescriptions, the first with partial privatization and the second through making sure that any future increase in mandatory retirement payroll deductions would go toward private plans.

After the Partial Privatization Debacle

There has been no further movement on the attempt to privatize part or all of existing Social Security. The Obama administration, however, named a commission headed by two enemies of Social Security: Republican Alan Simpson and Democrat Erskine Bowles. Simpson had described Social Security, in an email to the executive director of the National Older Women's League, as "like a milk cow with 310 million tits." He later apologized.[7]

The commission's draft final report recommended changing the benefit formula. Benefits would remain the same for the lowest-income group of $9,000 or less. Every income group above $9,000 would have its benefits cut by progressively more substantial amounts.[8]

The effect would be to make Social Security a program that benefited mainly the poor, consistent with the 1994 World Bank report. Nonpoor classes would receive significantly less replacement income than under the current benefit formula. That would force them to rely more on 401(k)s and other retirement savings plans, again consistent with World Bank recommendations. The report also recommended raising the full retirement age to 69. That would, even if the benefit formula were not changed, result in a reduction in total lifetime benefits. The announcement of the proposals sparked widespread opposition from senior, labor, and community groups, similar to the opposition to Bush's 2005 partial privatization effort. The report failed to be supported by enough commission members to become the official report to be voted upon by Congress.

The Obama administration then issued a second threat to Social Security beneficiaries when it proposed lowering long-term benefits by changing the Cost of Living Adjustment (COLA) formula. That, too, drew considerable activist and public opposition and was eventually withdrawn.

Democrats generally have supported add-on plans so that new government-mandated retirement dollars would be circulated through the private financial services industry rather than publicly administered and held as those of Social Security are. During its second term, the Obama administration proceeded in that direction. In his 2014 State of the Union address, President Obama announced that he would direct the Department of the Treasury to create a new retirement savings plan for workers who do not have 401(k)s. Called My Retirement Account, or MyRA, it would allow them to purchase savings bonds with guaranteed rates of interest through automatic payroll deductions. He introduced the program by urging, "Let's do more to help Americans save for retirement." The new plan, however, drew little participation. The Trump administration ended it with scant opposition.

That MyRA plan was followed up by Democrat-supported state plans in California, Oregon, Connecticut, and elsewhere. All of these are essentially add-on individual savings and investment plans. Instead of building upon the sound social-insurance base of Social

TABLE 5.1: Defeated Social Security Privatization and Cut-Back Proposals Since 2005

Initiative		Proposal
2005	George W. Bush partial privatization proposal	Divert XX percent of FICA contribution into private retirement savings accounts
2010	Simpson-Bowles Commission	Lower benefits for all income groups above the lowest; increase full retirement age to 69
2013	Obama COLA Reduction	Change calculation of COLA from CPI to lower chained CPI

Security, they divert future public-sponsored retirement plan dollars into private plans. The plans benefit the financial services industry, while not delivering as much to participants that equal contributions to Social Security would.

Decreasing Tax Support from the Rich

In 1990, the Greenspan Commission's scheduled phased-in Social Security FICA tax rate for covered labor and self-employment income reached a maximum of 6.2 percent, where it has stayed ever since. As expected, the percent of national individual income contributed to Social Security also rose, from 3.5 in 1980 to 4.2 percent. But then by 2000, it dropped back to 3.9 percent, where it has remained. What happened to reduce the percent of national individual income that went to Social Security?

According to Congressional Budget Office figures, market income inequality grew by 7.8 percent in the 1990s.[9] For Social Security revenue to keep up with inequality, it has to raise the cap on covered labor income. Between 1982 and the present, though, raises in the cap have lagged behind increases in income inequality. In 1982, 9 percent of labor and self-employment income was untaxed because it was above the cap. By 2016 it had jumped to 15.4 percent.[10] A second dynamic is that, during the same time, investment income, which Social Security does not tax, has commanded a higher proportion of total national individual income. From 1990 to 2016, it increased from 15.6 to 18.8 percent.[11]

The rich are the clear beneficiaries of not taxing all individual income for Social Security since they are the ones who have uncovered wages and salaries above the cap and significant investment income. Whereas people with up to $200,000 have over three-quarters of their income taxable by Social Security, those with over $10 million have just 0.4 percent taxable (Table 5.2, below).

People with million-dollar or more incomes—the top 0.27 percent of tax filers—take 13 percent of total national individual income. Still, they pay just 5.8 percent of the cost of Social Security. On the other end of the distribution, the bottom 95.4 percent of filers take 66 percent of total national individual income but pay 88.1 percent of the cost of Social Security.[12]

TABLE 5.2: Individual Income Class by Percent Income Taxable by Social Security

Income Class	Percent Income Taxable by Social Security
Under $25,000	87.6
$25,000 under $50,000	85.3
$50,000 under $75,000	79.3
$75,000 under $100,000	77.7
$100,000 under $200,000	77.2
$200,000 under $500,000	41.0
$500,000 under $1 million	18.4
$1 million under $1.5 million	10.0
$1.5 million under $2 million	6.8
$2 million under $5 million	4.0
$5 million under $10 million	1.7
$10 million and more	0.4

Note: Income includes wage, salary, self-employment, and investment income.
Source: Calculated from Internal Revenue Service, *Statistics of Income, Basic Tables—All Returns Filed and Sources of Income, Tax Year 2016*, Table 1.4. https://www.irs.gov/statistics/soi-tax-stats-individual-income-tax-returns-publication-1304-complete-report#_pt1.

TABLE 5.3: Uncovered Income for Social Security Taxation, 2016

		POTENTIAL EXTRA REVENUE IF TAXED	
	Untaxed Amount (millions)	Amount (millions)	Percent Increase
Wages above Cap	$1,164.8	$144.4	17.3
Self-Employment above Cap	235.2	29.2	3.5
Investment	1,947.1	241.4	28.9
TOTAL	3,347.1	415.0	49.6

Note: % Increase is increase over the actual Social Security (OASI + DI) income of $836.2 billion for 2016. Sources: Calculated from Social Security Administration, Annual *Statistical Supplement 2017*, Table 4.B2; and Internal Revenue Service, *Statistics of Income, Basic Tables—All Returns Filed and Sources of Income, Tax Year 2016*, Table 1.4, https://www.irs.gov/statistics/soi-tax-stats-individual-income-tax-returns-publication-1304-complete-report#_pt1.

That the rich don't pay their share of the cost of Social Security is well known. Most attention for the cause of this tax privileging concentrates on the existence of the cap on labor income that is taxed. In 2016, Social Security taxed the first $118,500 of labor and self-employment income. All income above was untaxed. The total labor and self-employment income of 94 percent of Social Security contributors fell below that cap.[13] The remaining 6 percent of contributors had untaxed labor and self-employment income above that cap. Were that untaxed income taxed, it would bring in an additional 173.6 billion dollars, which would have increased Social Security's 2016 revenue by just over a fifth.

It is clear that the cap, which rises every year, has not kept up with the rise of inequality, and, as mentioned above, kept the increase in the contribution rate to 6.2 percent in 1990 from stabilizing Social Security's finances. Stabilization would require either raising the contribution rate or the cap on labor and self-employment income taxed or some combination of the two.

As important as the low cap on labor and self-employment income taxed is, that is less than half the story. The other half is the lack of taxation on investment income—interest, dividends, capital gains, partnerships, rents, and royalties—which are the primary sources of income for the rich. While the elimination of the cap would have produced 20.8 percent extra revenue for Social Security, taxation of investment income would have provided an additional 28.9 percent extra revenue, nearly doubling it. Taxing investment as well as labor and self-employment income above the cap would have produced a whopping 49.6 percent increase, much more than enough to financially stabilize the program for the future and increase benefits (Table 5.3, page 82).

6

Reversing Privatization

The 2005 Bush administration's failed attempt to partially privatize Social Security occurred during a period of substantial privatizations of comparable social insurance retirement systems in other countries. Their experiences offer insight into what could have happened if the Bush plan had succeeded or what could happen if a similar change occurred in the future.

From 1993 to 2008, thirteen Latin American countries followed the Chilean precedent, most with World Bank encouragement, and fully or partially privatized their public retirement systems. By 2000, half the region's citizens lived in countries with those systems. Massive retirement system privatizations also took place in the former communist countries of Eastern and Central Europe and others that had been a part of the old Union of Soviet Socialist Republics. By 2000, the majority of the population of the formerly communist region had fully or partially privatized systems. To a smaller extent, the wave extended to Africa. Nigeria, the continent's most populous country, fully privatized its system in 2004, and Ghana partially privatized its system in 2010. Advisors from Chile were instrumental in guiding the development of many of these new personal account retirement savings and investment systems.

TABLE 6.1: Social Security Systems Privatizations, 1981–2016

Country	Privatization Year	Degree of Privatization
LATIN AMERICA		
Chile	1981	Full
Peru	1993	
Argentina	1994	Partial
Colombia	1994	
Uruguay	1996	Partial
Bolivia	1997	Full
Mexico	1997	Full
Venezuela	1997	
El Salvador	1998	Full
Nicaragua	2000	Full
Costa Rica	2001	Partial
Ecuador	2001	
Dominican Republic	2003	Full
Panama	2008	
FORMER COMMUNIST		
Hungary	1998	Partial
Kazakhstan	1998	Full
Croatia	1999	Partial
Poland	1999	Partial
Latvia	2001	Partial
Bulgaria	2002	Partial
Estonia	2002	Partial
Russian Federation	2002	Partial
Lithuania	2004	Partial
Romania	2004	Partial
Slovakia	2005	Partial
Macedonia	2006	Partial
Czech Republic	2013	
Armenia	2014	
AFRICA		
Nigeria	2004	Full
Ghana	2010	Partial

Source: Isabel Ortiz, Fabio Dura-Valverde, Stefan Urban, and Veronika Wodsak, *Reversing Pension Privatizations* (Geneva: International Labour Organization, 2018), 3–4, 8.

Fully privatized meant that the country ended its public social insurance system, at least for new employees. In some cases, such as Chile, existing participants in the government-sponsored social insurance system were given the choice of remaining in it or transferring to the new private savings accounts system. Partial privatization meant that the country diverted some of the contributions of individuals from the existing public social insurance system to newly created private savings accounts. It was the latter partial privatization that President George W. Bush attempted for Social Security in 2005.

The Latin American transformation that was the most significant and most closely followed the Chilean precedent took place in Mexico. In December 1995, the year of a serious peso crisis, the Mexican Chamber of

Deputies and Senate, over massive public protest and with the active encouragement of the World Bank, passed the privatization measure.[1] What made the unpopular move possible was that the dominant political party, the Partido de la Revolución Institucional (PRI), under President Ernesto Zedillo, still had semi-authoritarian control with disciplined majorities in the Chamber of Deputies and Senate. The legislation established companies to administer the accounts—Administradoras de Fondos para el Retiro (AFORES).

The purported purpose of the privatization was to increase the country's savings rate and thereby decrease its reliance on foreign capital for development.[2] This was putting highly regressive legislation in its most publicly palatable form. It would be hard to argue against allowing the country to find a way to finance its development and be less vulnerable to external control. But beneath the manipulated appearance was a deeper purpose. What the privatization did was to transform collective workers' retirement savings into a new source of capital accumulation for investment in the Mexican and other stock markets that private capital could control. Meanwhile, workers assumed all of the risks of the investments and lost the guarantees of retirement income that they had with traditional pensions. The risks included those of any market investment due to unfavorable market conditions. Also, private managers of the retirement accounts were able to charge considerable administrative fees.

In Mexico, where there has been a historical culture of public and private corruption and lax controls over consumer fraud, the social security privatization provided a new way for the powerful to take advantage of the weak. Instead of corrupt officials pilfering public accounts, in the new neoliberalized Mexico, corporate managers, many of them former public officials, now had access to largely unprotected workers' private accounts to use to their advantage.

The Chilean Model Fails

Through the 1990s, there was little realization, even among left-wing Chileans, that their privatized social security system would produce far lower benefits than the public one. One prescient exception was a 1995 graduate thesis by economist Doris Elter that doubted on theoretical grounds the claim that the privatized system would deliver adequate retirement benefits.[3] In 2001, researchers at the Centro de Estudios Nacionales de Desarrollo Alternativo (CENDA) in Santiago de Chile, led by Manuel Riesco, confirmed the theoretical analysis with an extensive empirical study of accounts in the privatized system.[4] CENDA then engaged in a public campaign to educate Chileans about the severe inadequacies of the system and urge a reform that would allow participants to switch back to the older public system. The inadequacy of the privatized system became the major issue of the 2005 election, with all sides agreeing that it was in crisis. At the same time, President Bush was touting the Chilean model as he was urging partial privatization of Social Security.

While CENDA and other left organizations urged that people be allowed to transfer out of the privatized system, that reform was not adopted. Instead, there was a much milder reform that preserved the privatized system but increased its minimum retirement benefit with an infusion of public money. In other words, the Chilean government began to subsidize the privatized system to lessen its production of elderly poverty. The reform was consistent with the evolving World Bank policy to accept a role for governments in limited retirement provision. Public plans, in the Bank's view, should be able to provide just enough retirement income to keep the elderly out of poverty. But all income above the poverty line should come from private investments.

Lower Benefits and Higher Costs

In a major 2018 study, the International Labour Organization of the United Nations (ILO) reviewed the outcomes of the privatizations in thirty countries. It found that benefits deteriorated. In Chile, the model for pension privatization, the median replacement rate was just 15 percent,[5] far below the ILO absolute standard of 40 percent and 45 percent for workers with thirty years of contributions. This can be compared to

TABLE 6.2: Lowered Benefits in Privatized Systems: Wage Replacement Rate

	Previous Public System	Privatized System
Chile	-	15%
Bolivia	-	20%
Hungary (partial privatization)	-	9% to 12.5% lower
Poland	67%	40%
Kazakhstan	60%	29.27%

Source: Ortiz et al., *Reversing Pension Privatizations* (Geneva: International Labour Organization),15.

the 41 percent median replacement rate for U.S. Social Security, which is also below the higher ILO standard. In terms of Chilean pesos converted to U.S. dollars, the median monthly payment in 2018 was $200, which is below the country's poverty line of $231.[6]

Rising public protests against the lower benefits of the privatized Chilean system forced the government to adopt a new tax-supported minimum income in 2008. Since then, Chilean governments have responded to waves of public protest by raising the minimum benefit while retaining the overall system of private accounts.

For the other countries that provided sufficient information, the ILO found lowered benefits also for Bolivia, Hungary, Poland, and Kazakhstan (Table 6.3, page 89).

Privatization is exceptionally costly, and the high costs result in lowered benefits. The first expense are transition costs. When a system privatizes, reduced contributions go into the replaced system, which owes benefits to its participants. Other parts of the government budget have to provide those funding shortfalls. That would have been a severe problem if President Bush's proposed partial privatization of Social Security had succeeded. With that proposal, nearly one-third of payroll contributions would have been diverted to private accounts and would be thereby unavailable to pay regular Social Security benefits. What could have been a problem in the United States had the proposal succeeded was an actual problem for the thirty countries that followed through with some form of privatization.

TABLE 6.3: Administrative Costs Before and After Privatizations

	Before Privatization (in billions)	After Privatization (in billions)	Increased Costs (%)
Argentina	$6.6 (1990)	$50.8 (2002)	670
Bolivia	8.6 (1992)	18.1 (2002)	110
Hungary	2.0 (1998)	14.5 (2007)	625
Colombia	2.6 (1993)	25.9 (2002)	896
Chile	8.0 (1980)	19.5 (2002)	144
El Salvador	7.8 (1996)	21.3 (2002)	173
Peru	NA	30.5 (2002)	N.A.
Mexico	NA	40.3 (2002)	N.A.
Uruguay	6.5 (1990)	18.2 (2002)	180

Source: Ortiz et al., *Reversing Pension Privatizations*, Table 3, 23.

In a study of nine Central and Eastern European formerly communist countries with private accounts, senior ILO researchers Elaine Fultz and Kenichi Hirose found that, in reaction to the 2008 economic crisis, most of the countries reduced the diversion of contributions from the public system to the private accounts with reforms being ongoing.[7]

Administrative costs of privatized savings systems are much higher than those of public social insurance ones. For that, the ILO study was able to identify nine international examples. For those countries, administrative costs jumped between 110 and 896 percent after privatization (see Table 6.3). The highest expenses were in Argentina and Mexico. In Argentina, administrative fees consumed half of all new contributions. Put differently, the financial companies that administered the private accounts extracted half their value. According to a study cited by the ILO, financial companies took out from the accounts "administration charges, investment management fees, custodian fees, guarantee fees, audit fees, marketing fees and legal fees, among others."[8]

The World Bank had promoted pension privatization as a way to increase economic growth, remove strains on public financing, and benefit retirees. By 2008, it was becoming increasingly clear that none of this was happening. The privatization experiment, first imposed by a military dictatorship in Chile in 1981, had been a failure. The sole beneficiary was the financial services industry, which was able to profit handsomely from the new privatized accounts. The World Bank quietly dropped its international privatization advocacy.[9]

Reversing Privatization

Proponents of privatization of retirement accounts refer to the period between 1981 and 2000, when retirement privatization swept through Latin America and the former communist countries, as the "second generation" of retirement reforms. The first generation was the prior period when countries developed national social insurance pension plans. Unforeseen by them is that there has been a third generation of pension reforms in which eighteen of the thirty countries that privatized their systems have fully or partially reversed those privatizations. Those that fully re-nationalized stopped contributions to private accounts and swept all of their accumulations back into the public social insurance systems. Those that partially re-nationalized reduced the amounts going into individual accounts.

Argentina achieved fame in the 1990s as the Latin American country that most toed the line of neoliberal reforms. Then-president Carlos Menem, a member of the Peronist Justicialista Party, enthusiastically embraced and promoted neoliberal reforms that included privatizing state enterprises and adopting the U.S. dollar as the currency. In what one newspaper called "the mother of all privatizations," Argentina substantially privatized its public retirement system in 1993 with World Bank encouragement.[10]

As with the Chilean Administradoras de Fondos de Pensiones and Mexican AFOREs, different, supposedly competing, private financial services corporations—Administradoras de Fondos de Jubilaciones y Pensiones (AFJPs)—administered the private plans. The new AFJPs aggressively promoted their plans, implying that workers would do much better under them than in the traditional public pension plan. Their advertising campaigns convinced upward of 82 percent of existing and new workers to choose the private plans.[11]

The AFJP industry took off in the middle 1990s as the Argentine economy was going through a growth spurt owing to privatizations of state-owned businesses that were attracting domestic and international investments. But, as in Chile, you can only sell the farm once. By 2001, the privatization growth spurt had spent itself, and the economy spectacularly crashed, taking down with it accumulated personal savings in the AFJPs. The crash produced a social explosion and multiple political crises. Over three weeks in late 2001 and early 2002, Argentina had three different presidents. The country began to stabilize with the election of Néstor Kirchner, a center-left Peronist, in 2003. The next election, in 2007, was won overwhelmingly by Cristina Fernández de Kirchner, the wife of Néstor Kirchner.

Though the Kirchners were from the same political party as Carlos Menem, who was responsible for the privatization binge, they saw the need to use public investments, regulations, and programs to contain and reverse the crisis. They modified or completely reversed many of the Menem administration's neoliberal reforms. It is in this context that they began to have serious reservations about what had been wrought by the 1993 pension privatization.

There were two sides of the damage: what it was doing to retiree income and what it was doing to government financial capability. In terms of the former, as with all cases where defined contribution plans replace defined benefit ones, participants eventually realize that they will get much less income under the new than under the old system. As the realization grew, trade unions began to take up the issue. "For me, the AFJP is one of the greatest swindles ever perpetrated on the Argentinean people," stated Hugo Moyano, Secretary-General of the General Confederation of Labor, known as the CGT by its Spanish acronym, the largest labor union in the country.[12]

The other issue was the potential damage that the system was doing to the country. Both domestic and foreign AFJP administrators were increasingly investing the funds abroad. Instead of the funds spurring growth and development of the national economy, the funds were taken out of the country. The rationale was that the AFJPs were in search of higher rates of return that would benefit retirees directly. But

TABLE 6.4: Social Security Systems: Reversals of Privatizations, 2000–2013

	Privatization	Reversal of Privatization	Degree of Reversal
Latin America			
Argentina	1994	2008	full
Bolivia	1997	2009	full
Venezuela	1997	2000	full
Nicaragua	2000	2005	full
Ecuador	2001	2002	full
Eastern and Central Europe, former USSR			
Hungary	1998	2010	full
Kazakhstan	1998	2013	partial
Croatia	1999	2011	partial
Poland	1999	2011	full
Latvia	2001	2009	partial
Bulgaria	2002	2007	partial
Estonia	2002	2009	partial
Russian Federation	2002	2012	full
Lithuania	2004	2009	partial
Romania	2004	2017	partial
Slovakia	2005	2008	partial
Macedonia	2006	2011	partial
Czech Republic	2013	2016	full

Note: Countries that have not reversed privatizations as of 2019: Chile, Peru, Colombia, Uruguay, Mexico, El Salvador, Costa Rica, Dominican Republic, Panama, Armenia, Nigeria, Ghana.

at the same time, any domestic investment would help the national economy and, therefore, retirees indirectly. The system also produced the strange situation in which money from the retirement funds that the government earlier controlled to loan or invest for national purposes was now in the hands of the AFJPs to *lend* to the government, shifting the government from being a creditor to a debtor.

On February 13, 2007, the Argentinean Senate voted unanimously for a reform that would allow participants in the AFJP a 180-day window of opportunity once every five years to switch to the public plan. By the end of the first window of opportunity, 1.2 million workers, 20 percent of the total, switched. Those who changed were disproportionately women and over 40 years of age.

In 2008, after the window of opportunity closed, the recession hit full force, and those still in the AFJPs saw their accounts begin to sink dramatically. Then, in October, the government intervened decisively. It introduced a measure to pass the remainder of the AFJPs to the public system. The bill passed in the Congress overwhelmingly, and Argentina became the first country to completely reverse a social security privatization by essentially re-nationalizing the system. The government justified its action as aimed at protecting AFJP participants whose accounts were dramatically shrinking and freeing the funds for more socially productive purposes, including countering the impacts of the economic recession. AFJP participants who switched over would receive the same guaranteed pensions as those who had been in the public system their entire work lives. What they lost by joining the AFJP system was restored.

In December 2010, Bolivia followed the Argentinean example and became the second country to re-nationalize its privatized retirement system. Bolivia had established a defined benefit pension system in 1959. In the 1990s, in line with World Bank and International Monetary Fund orthodoxy, the country instituted widespread neoliberal reforms, including privatization of its retirement system in 1997. As the shortcomings of similar privatized systems were manifesting in the bordering countries of Chile and Argentina, criticisms arose in Bolivia. The coming to power of the left-wing Evo Morales presidency in 2005 created an opportunity to examine the system critically. In August 2008, the Centro Obrero Boliviano, the country's largest trade union federation, called a general strike that included the demand to re-nationalize the retirement system to return to a defined benefit plan. A year and a half later the Congress passed, and Evo Morales signed, the bill.

7

Medicare

Two great bangs were responsible for the formation of the American welfare state. The first was the original 1935 Social Security legislation. The second was the 1965 legislation that created Medicare government health insurance for citizens 65 and older and Medicaid government health insurance for the poor.

As in 1880s Germany under Bismarck, where medical and old-age social insurance began within a few years of each other, the original proponents of Social Security assumed that the program would add a healthcare component for all covered workers, retirees, and their dependents. This proved not possible in the 1940s. By the 1950s, it was an ever more remote possibility as the private health insurance industry grew more profitable and powerful. Providing medical insurance for the retired population then became a fallback goal that finally succeeded under the Johnson administration. A number of the people who had worked on the original 1935 Social Security legislation, including Robert M. Ball and Wilbur J. Cohen, were instrumental in designing the 1965 Medicare legislation.[1] The name Medicare originated from the name of the Canadian system, which was established in 1962, three years earlier, as single-payer coverage for all ages.[2] The progressive Medicare for All campaign is consistent with the original goals for Social Security expansion.

H.R. 6675, the originating Act signed into law by President Johnson, shows the interrelationship between Social Security and Medicare in its long, convoluted description: "An Act to provide a hospital insurance program for the aged under the Social Security Act with a supplementary medical benefits program and an expanded program of medical assistance, to increase benefits under the Old-Age, Survivors, and Disability Insurance System, to improve the Federal-State public assistance programs, and for other purposes." The Social Security Administration carried out its implementation and administration until 1977 when the Health Care Financing Administration—renamed the Centers for Medicare and Medicaid Services (CMA) in 2001—was established. Currently, Social Security continues to enroll people in Medicare, while CMA administers the program.

Access to healthcare is a vital part of any person's well-being. It is especially crucial for the retired. Sicknesses become more frequent, serious, and expensive after retirement. The per capita cost of healthcare for those 19 to 64 is $7,153. For those 65 and older it is $19,098.[3] With most people getting health insurance as an employee benefit, before Medicare, the retired were left in the lurch at precisely the time when they needed it more.

A special sixty-fifth birthday gift for many today is Medicare coverage kicking in. For those approaching retirement between the ages of 45 and 64, a full 9.3 percent have no health insurance. That percentage drops to 1.3 percent for those 65 and older.[4] The United States has come closest to universal coverage for the Medicare-age population at 98.7 percent. No other age group comes close to that percentage. Without Medicare, over 90 percent of the sixty-five and older population would be without health insurance.

The availability of Medicare insurance has saved an enormous number of lives. Compared to the United Kingdom and Germany, the United States has overall many more preventable deaths per capita; that is, deaths due to the lack of timely and effective medical treatment. However, for its over-65 population, which has access to Medicare insurance, the statistics for preventable death rates are nearly identical.[5]

Medicare Parts

Medicare has four parts. Part A covers inpatient hospital, skilled nursing, and hospice stays. It also covers some home healthcare. Part B covers doctor and outpatient bills, medical supplies, and preventive services. Part C, Medicare Advantage, was added in 1997 as a privatized alternative to traditional Medicare. Part D, added in 2006, covers prescription drugs.

Traditional Medicare covers about two-thirds of enrollees. The rest have Medicare Advantage plans. The latter privatized plans likely will grow in the coming years. They are privatized in the sense that Medicare contracts with private insurance companies to administer benefits. Put differently, Medicare finances Medicare Advantage plans while private insurance companies administer and profit from them.

With traditional Medicare, Medicare directly pays service providers. With Medicare Advantage, it pays set per person fees to private insurance companies, which in turn pay providers. All Medicare Advantage plans must cover what traditional Medicare covers. They can include additional services, such as dental and vision, for extra fees. All Medicare Advantage members pay the fixed Medicare part B monthly fees plus any additional premiums charged by their plan for its extra costs and services.

Medicare, like Social Security, is social insurance. Employers and employees contribute 1.45 percent of salary to a fund. Unlike Social Security, the amount of benefits does not depend on the amount of contributions. Once members reach the minimum of forty quarters' contributions, they are entitled to all Parts A, B, and D benefits.

Financing

Medicare has two trust funds: Hospital Insurance, which covers Part A, and Supplementary Medical Insurance, which covers Parts B and D. The Hospital Insurance Part A Trust Fund operates like Social Security retirement insurance. It is a self-financed stand-alone plan. Its revenues come almost entirely, like those of Social Security, from employer and employee payroll contributions of 1.45 percent each, interest payments from Treasury bond investments, and, since 1984, Social Security benefits taxes. The Supplementary Medical Insurance Parts B and D Trust Fund, however, operates very differently. They are only partially self-financed with their revenues coming primarily from general taxes (over 70 percent) and secondarily premiums paid by participants (26 and 17 percent for B and D, respectively). See Table 7.1.

Although Social Security is an autonomous self-financed program separate from the general federal budget that does not add to deficit spending or the national debt, the same cannot be said of Medicare Parts B and D. Over 71 percent of their support comes from general taxes. This is not a bad thing since spending on healthcare should be a high priority for government spending. But it does indicate that the program is more vulnerable to being harmed by politically motivated underfunding than Social Security retirement benefits.

It is undeniable that the United States has the highest per capita medical costs in the world and that they tend to rise much faster than the general cost of living. These realities continually place strains on the Medicare program as well as private insurance. Medicare, like

TABLE 7.1: Sources of Medicare Revenues and Expenses by Parts A, B, and D, 2018 ($billions)

	Part A		Part B		Part C		Total	
Payroll taxes	268.3	87.5%					268.3	35.5%
Interest	7.1	2.3%	2.5	0.7%	0.1	0.1%	9.7	1.3%
Benefits taxes	24.2	7.9%		0.0%		0.0%	24.2	3.2%
Premiums	3.6	1.2%	93.3	26.4%	15.8	16.6%	112.7	14.9%
Federal taxes	1.6	0.5%	253.2	71.6%	67.8	71.1%	322.7	42.7%
State payments	-	0.0%		0.0%	11.7	12.3%	11.7	1.5%
Other	1.8	0.6%	4.6	1.3%		0.0%	6.4	0.8%
Total	**$306.6**	**100.0%**	**$353.6**	**100.0%**	**$95.3**	**100.0%**	**$755.7**	**100.0%**
Expenditures	$308.2		$337.2		$95.2		$740.6	

Source: *2019 Annual Report of the Boards of Trustees of the Federal Hospital Insurance and the Supplementary Medical Insurance Trust Funds* (Washington, DC), Table II.B1, 10.

private insurance, can partially compensate by establishing reimbursement rates for Part A (hospitalization) and Part B (doctor visits and other provider services). However, lobbyists for the pharmaceutical companies succeeded in prohibiting Medicare from negotiating Part D prescription drug prices.

Medicare private reimbursement rates tend to be lower than those of private insurance. This helps to slow the rising cost of healthcare, but at the same time, for the same reason, more than a quarter of primary care physicians do not accept Medicare for new patients.[6]

Administrative bloat is one of the drivers of the high cost of private healthcare. A study of a North Carolina healthcare system with 1,600 physicians revealed that for every physician, there was $99,581 in annual insurance billing costs.[7] A clear advantage of Medicare is that its administrative overhead costs are dramatically lower than those for private insurance plans. Administrative overhead for its Part B fee-for-service plan, for example, is only 2.2 percent of total costs compared to 12 percent of premiums for private insurers.[8]

The Limits of Medicare

From an ideal point of view, retirees (along with everyone else) would have insurance that covered 100 percent of all health costs. There would be no out-of-pocket expenses. As valuable and appreciated as Medicare is to those who rely on it, it falls far short of that ideal. It does not cover many health issues, including dental, visual, hearing, foreign care, and long-term nursing home care. For each Part A hospital or other stay, patients must pay a deductible of $1,408 (as of 2020). There are limits to hospital stays. Patients have to pay steep costs after sixty days. It requires an annual deductible of $198 and a copay of 20 percent for Part B services. It does not pay the full cost of prescription drugs. What Medicare does not pay can result in considerable, often bankruptcy-causing, out-of-pocket expenses. Fortunately, this is not the case for most members. But it is a risk. Also, there is a regular monthly premium cost of $144.60 (for Part B for most members in 2020). Medigap and Medicare Advantage plans may reduce or eliminate such financially catastrophic risk, but they vary significantly in how much they do so, and they don't do so for free.

Medicare estimates that the average annual out-of-pocket cost for a person in good health on traditional Medicare is $7,850.[9] That is 32.4 percent, nearly a third, of the average median personal income of $24,224 of the Medicare-age population.[10] And those are averages for people *in good health*. For those not in good health, the costs can be considerably higher. No one thus should assume they are home-free regarding health insurance when they reach age 65. Everyone should be, however, and this is where union and employee benefit issues come in.

The gaps in Medicare coverage have led to the growth of sup-plemental plans, which cover 81 percent of traditional Medicare participants. Employer-sponsored policies cover 30 percent of par-ticipants. Medigap private insurance plans are paid for directly by 29 percent of participants. A further 22 percent of participants are eli-gible for dual coverage by Medicaid. The remaining 19 percent have no supplementary coverage. Like most private health insurance, sup-plementary policies vary significantly in terms of costs and benefits. Medigap plans' annual prices range between $816 with a high deduct-ible and $5,388. Plans for dental, visual, and hearing care are extra.

Given the current Medicare system, it is clear that supplemental coverage is needed and a concern for the future well-being of all employees. It is an issue for unions that negotiate on their behalf. Once again, no one should assume that once they've reached Medicare eligibility, they are in the clear regarding health insurance. Current Medicare falls far short of providing needed comprehensive benefits in the same way that Social Security retiree benefits fall far short of giving enough retirement income to maintain pre-retirement stan-dards of living.

There are two roads to resolving the issue. The first would be to fix Medicare so that it left no one financially vulnerable. This is, by far, the best solution. Fixing would mean expanding the health condi-tions covered to include dental, visual, and hearing. It would mean having Medicare cover 100 percent of all costs, effectively ending the annoying and expensive system of copays, deductibles, and premiums. It would mean having Medicare cover long-term nursing home care.

Employer-Sponsored Supplemental Retiree Health Benefits

The second road to resolving the issue is for unions to bargain for stretching employee health benefits into retirement where they don't exist or defending and improving them where they do. Unions should bargain for supplementary plans to cover what Medicare does not. There are two models for such supplemental plans. The first is for retirees to receive a supplemental employer-paid plan and for the employer to pick up the costs of Medicare Parts B and D premiums. The second is for employers to enroll, at their expense, retirees in Medicare Advantage plans that offer full coverage.

Many employees have adequate supplementary retirement health benefits. But many do not. This indicates both the unfairness of the distribution of retiree health benefits and that it is possible to have them. The first questions are how to pay for them and who should pay. We can start with the premise that the benefits should be paid for by current workers as insurance for their years in retirement. That spares retirees the expenses of healthcare when their incomes have dropped and their health expenses increase. This is the same model as Medicare Part A Hospital Insurance that is paid for by the 1.45 percent payroll tax on employers and employees. If Medicare expanded to cover all health costs, it would be just a matter of calculating how much the payroll tax would have to increase. It is the same type of calculation for determining how much would be needed to be withheld from current payrolls to finance supplementary health insurance for retirees. The results of collective bargaining would determine how much of that employers and employees would pay, respectively.

Every company that has such a policy also has to determine when employees become eligible for the benefit. Most require a set number of years of employment with the company to vest in its retiree health benefit.

Such systems work well for long-term employees but not for short-term workers who leave before vesting. They pay into the insurance but never become eligible for its benefits. That problem can be partially mitigated by refunding the contributions into a Health Savings Account, which the departing employees could later use to purchase private Medigap insurance or a more generous Medicare Advantage plan.

The sad reality is that very few retirees enjoy employer-sponsored supplementary insurance. Most pay out of pocket for it. According to a Kaiser Family Foundation study, the percentage of large firms (two hundred or more workers) sponsoring supplementary insurance dropped from 66 percent in 1988 to 18 percent in 2018; and those plans have become more limited in coverage. State and local government employers are an exception, with 68 percent sponsoring supplementary retiree health plans.[11]

Unlike accrued retirement income benefits that cannot be cut or eliminated, most employers are free to reduce or eliminate supplementary retiree health benefits even if employees have paid into such plans during their working years. Employers have had little financial incentive to continue sponsoring supplemental insurance. Unlike active workers, keeping retirees healthy has no positive impact on profits. On the contrary, paying to keep them healthy has a negative effect since it is an expense rather than an investment. Employers thus have every incentive to reduce or eliminate retiree health costs, and they have.

Medicare for All

There are parallels between Social Security and Medicare. Both social insurance programs are the largest source of insurance against their respective risks for the retiree population. But both fall significantly short of adequately protecting against the threats. As discussed, retirees from average-income careers (who have always had average incomes) receive monthly a Social Security check that works out to about 41 percent of what their working paycheck had been. That, in turn, works out to be just 59 percent of the 70 percent replacement income that retirement experts assume that people need. This leaves them 41 percent short. Medicare recipients have insurance that covers about 69 percent of expenses on average—not including dental, vision, and hearing, which it does not cover. This leaves them 31 percent short for the services that Medicare covers and a lot shorter for other services that they may need.[12] In both cases, expanding the programs could significantly reduce or eliminate the shortages.

In the case of Medicare, the leading Medicare for All proposals call for not just spreading the program to those under 65 but also for significantly improving it to eliminate the gaps highlighted above—eliminating copays and deductibles and covering dental, vision, and hearing. This would be the cleanest and most effective course of action. As with current Medicare, a combination of dedicated payroll and general taxes could finance it. Unlike Social Security, there is no cap on labor income taxed for Medicare. But, as with Social Security, investment income—the primary source of income for the rich—is currently spared Medicare taxation. Taxing those considerable earnings would provide a significant source of the new revenue that would be needed to finance such an improved Medicare for All program.

PART II

EMPLOYER-SPONSORED PENSION PLANS

8

The Pension Gold Standard

Aside from Social Security, which covers nearly every working person in the United States, there are over 50,000 other
defined benefit pension plans with some 60 million participants as active or retired workers.[1] These include private-sector
plans covering auto, airline, and telephone workers and public sector
plans covering federal, state, local, and military employees. While the
number of people covered by employer-sponsored pension plans has
declined dramatically in the private sector and conservatives have
attempted to take them away from public sector workers as well, such
plans have by no means approached extinction. They remain a vital
part of the retirement policy world, depended upon by millions of
teachers, cops, soldiers, and others to top off Social Security earnings
enough to provide living-income retirements. Pensioner incomes
play their part in stimulating the economy. Were they to vanish over-
night, we would enter into a new Great Depression.

Yet there's something I often notice when I meet people of
retirement age who seem to be financially comfortable. While not
overflowing with money, they do not have money worries. They are
satisfied that they have enough to do most of what they want. After
a while, it comes out that they are living on a good pension and their

Social Security. They don't advertise that they have a pension, especially if they were public employees. It's almost as if they feel guilty about it. I interpret this to mean they've bought into all of the anti-pension, especially anti-public employee pension, false propaganda that is so much a part of the current media and public climate in general. It is the inverse of pension envy, guilt for having a pension. In its best reading, it is survivor's guilt for not having fallen victim to the retirement crisis suffered by others.

In a situation that I know well, the Yankee Institute, a Cato Institute-affiliated conservative-libertarian foundation in Connecticut, celebrated a state employee retiree with a defined contribution 401(k)-like plan that paid a much lower retirement benefit than the state employee pension plan.[2] "I don't have to encumber my fellow taxpayers for the rest of my life to have a decent retirement," said the retired state employee. In fact, as we will see presently, taxpayers paid higher employer contributions for his 401(k)-like plan than they paid for the state's pension plan.

To be sure, I also know many retirees with pensions who are not shy defending what they've earned. No one should feel guilty about having a pension unless they feel an overwhelming moral obligation to support as much as possible the investment houses of Wall Street with their retirement savings.

How Pensions Work

Pension systems are referred to as *defined benefit* plans because there is a specific, predictable, and guaranteed benefit—pension payment—that employees earn if they meet specified conditions. In the most typical pension plan, the pension amount increases the longer someone works, and the higher the salary. The 401(k)s and other employer-sponsored savings plans, in contrast, are referred to as *defined contribution* plans. Instead of having predictable pension amounts, they only have set contributions, usually percentages of salary such as 5 percent, to be made by employers or employees. The plan does not specify what the contributions will generate as retirement incomes.

Placing contributions into collective rather than individual accounts carries enormous advantages for retirees in defined benefit (DB) pension plans. In virtually all cases, a dollar invested in a DB pension plan will deliver significantly more retirement income than one invested in a 401(k).[3] The fundamental reason is that collective plan members share risks. First, in the language of insurance, there is the risk of living a long time, a *longevity risk*. I unequivocally can say that living a long time is a good thing, assuming that you're reasonably healthy and enjoying it. But the danger here is that you will make it to 90 but then run out of money when you're least able to get a job to support your remaining years. Pension plans solve this problem by setting pension amounts according to average ages of death and then pay the pension until you die, which can be before or long after the average death age. The average age of death for someone who makes it to retirement at age 65 is just over 85, according to Social Security data.[4] With that basic fact, actuaries know that the pension funds they advise must have enough money in them to pay out benefits for just over twenty years. They can then calibrate and recalibrate contribution rates and assumed rates of return on investments to make sure that the necessary funds are or will be there.

If you live to the ripe old age of 99, you "win" by this system of the short-lived subsidizing the long-lived since you receive payments for fourteen years after the average age of death and after what your contributions earned for the system. On the other hand, if you die before or shortly after retirement, you "lose" by this system since you will have paid more in than received. Is this game of actuarial winners and losers fair? Unequivocally yes! The fundamental goal of a retirement system should be to support people in retirement, however long or short that is. That's what a pension system based on actuarial averages does. Besides, no one resents, after death, having supported longer-lived pensioners with their contributions. And no one before death should begrudge that possibility. The value of mutual responsibility forms the foundation for pension plans—all for one, one for all. The goal is to provide retirement security for all, long or short as those lives may be.

Many would object, protesting that if they die early, they would prefer their excess contributions to go through inheritance to family members rather than longer-lived pensioners who they may not even know. As understandable as this individualist ethic is, it undermines the fundamental goal of pension plans to maximize support in this life rather than provide gifts from beyond the grave. All of that said, there are pension plan designs that try to meet both goals by making excess contributions of short-lived members inheritable. This, however, results in lower pension checks.

While Social Security is our national pension plan, it is not the subject proper of this chapter. And though for one in four retirees Social Security is their sole source of almost all of their income, it is not supposed to be.[5] For most people to maintain their pre-retirement standards of living, they also need employer-sponsored retirement plans. Generally, people take for granted that their jobs include Social Security as a retirement benefit. Most reserve the notion of a retirement benefit for a plan that their employers directly sponsor. Up until the 1980s, for the majority of workers, this was a pension plan. Then we went through the severe retirement transformation in the 1980s when private employers who had retirement benefits beyond Social Security shifted from pension to 401(k)-like plans massively. Some local, state, and federal government employers have also moved to 401(k)-like plans, but not nearly as many.

As of 2018, 13 percent of private and 77 percent of local and state public employees had pension plans. Overall, 22 percent of civilian employees, excluding federal government ones, have pension plans, a proportion that continues to decrease.[6] The federal government's approximately two million employees have pension plans along with Social Security coverage and the Thrift Savings Plan, a defined contribution retirement savings plan. However, their occupational pension component replaces less pre-retirement income than did an earlier system before 1987 reforms.

Most private pension plans are *single-employer* plans. This type of plan makes sense for workers likely to spend most of their careers at one company. But in many lines of work, such as trucking and entertainment, workers frequently change employers. In such work, employers may offer a joint *multi-employer* plan so that employees can continue accruing retirement credits as they shift from employer to employer.

Virtually all employer-sponsored retirement plans, whether defined benefit pension or defined contribution savings, invest contributions in stocks and bonds, which is a risky business. The stock market goes up and down. Some stocks gain—or lose—value more than others. Predicting which will do what is always a gamble. In addition to such *investment risk,* there is a subsidiary *timing risk.* Investing in a particular stock just before it takes off in value is much better than making it when its value will remain flat for some time or decline. There is no sure way to estimate when that time is. For those with defined contribution plans, retiring when the market is up is much better than retiring when it is down, when accumulations have declined, such as during the 2008 Great Recession.

Pension plans absolve their members of these risks. Professionals make the investments, thereby avoiding types of risky investments made by individual amateur investors. No one's pension size depends on how the market is doing the year they retire. How the size is determined remains the same from year to year regardless of how the market is doing. Pension trustees do have to be mindful of market behavior and adjust investments accordingly to make sure that in the long run, pension revenues (contributions plus investment returns), are sufficient to pay out pensions. The key phrase here is "in the long run." If a person begins to draw a pension during a down market, plan managers have the luxury of knowing that the market will eventually go up enough to cover the overall pension amounts. Those with individual accounts do not have that luxury. If they retire when their investments have lost great value during a down market, they are stuck. The down market will decrease the amount they can withdraw as retirement income.

The risks of pension plans are, in theory, shared by all members. In practice, members of the vast majority of pension plans do not experience risks. If the market tanks, it is a problem for the plan managers to resolve. I remember during the 2008 recession that when the market lost over half its value people in pension plans seemed utterly oblivious to that fact. Those who retired that year had not the slightest worry that their pension check would be smaller. Those of us, however, who were in retirement savings plans were continually worried about what was going to happen. Our 401(k)s, as the bitter joke had it, had become 201(k)s. Almost everyone who could delay retiring did so, hoping that the market and their investments would come back enough so that they could afford to retire.

Everything I've discussed about risk so far in this chapter assumes solvent, reasonably well-funded and managed pension plans. The vast majority are that, contrary to the media scare stories on outlier pension plans that have serious solvency problems. We will return to that topic presently.

Don't Be Tempted by Lump Sum Payments

Pensions are regular payments to retirees to provide income for the rest of their lives. Some pension plans allow members to instead take a one-time lump-sum payment upon retirement. Unless your doctor has told you you're about to die, receiving a lump sum payment is almost always a terrible idea. It may be tempting to suddenly have control of an amount of money that most people have never had in their lifetimes. A lump-sum payment provides instant wealth as opposed to a steady, secure income. But though you can survive on income without wealth, you cannot survive on wealth without income. The lump-sum wealth will have to be turned into income to pay for food, housing, clothing, medical care, and other living expenses.

Is there a way to turn the wealth into income that exceeds what the pension payments would have been? The answer almost always is no. You could, of course, withdraw large amounts for the first few years of retirement that exceeded what the pension payments would have been. But then you would soon run out of money and be left with no income. Could you figure out how much to withdraw to keep cash coming in for the rest of your life? There are any number of financial advisors who will try to convince you that they can manage your wealth so that it will deliver handsome payments. If this appeals to you, be very careful. Following is a true horror story, one to make you weep.

Several years ago, a Portland, Oregon, public school system retiree hired financial advisor Shayne Kniss to help him with retirement planning. The retiree would seem to have had no need for Kniss's services. He already had a guaranteed life pension coming from his years of public service. But Kniss talked him into cashing out the guaranteed pension and turning the resulting $729,000 into an investment account in his Iris Capital firm. Kniss confidently estimated 8 to 12 percent returns, which would have been higher than the guaranteed pension payments.

For the first few months, regular $3,500 checks arrived. You can guess where this story is going. But then they stopped. Iris Capital was tanking. Most of its $5 million capital, collected from fifty people like this public school system retiree, had been invested in a shaky real estate flipping operation that was collapsing.

In the "you can't make this up" category, as the real estate investments were falling apart, Kniss found an attractive new destination for what was left: he started a business in Oregon's newly legal recreational marijuana market. What was left went to pot, literally.[7] Like the real estate investment, the pot investment turned into a bust.

It is doubtful that Kniss's clients will get any of their money back. They will have to entirely depend on much smaller Social Security payments for the rest of their retirement years.

The obvious solution to protecting pensioners from this type of financial manslaughter is not to allow them to cash out their employer-sponsored plans, just as they cannot cash out their Social Security benefits. Social Security, fortunately, is beyond the reach of financial operators like Kniss. So far, to my knowledge, not even the most ardent Republican foes of Social Security have suggested making its earned benefits vulnerable to cash-outs encouraged by self-interested financial advisors. The pension plan I am in has a lump sum cash-out provision, as do many others. This provision should either be removed or strictly regulated to avoid fast and loose financial advisors from manipulating retirees into cashing out. Employees and their union representatives should also be wary of attempts to add such cash-out provisions, often under the deceptive claim—or in some cases well-meaning but confused motive—of adding financial control and flexibility to defined benefit pension plans.

Most Americans are not vulnerable to losing pensions in this way for the simple reason that most no longer have them. They instead have 401(k)s and IRAs. But they too are vulnerable since those account balances are also targets for financial operators and outright swindlers. Indeed, another Kniss client was a retired teacher who invested her $495,000 life savings in Iris Capital.

It's easy to blame the victims for their gullibility. Kniss was able to convince them that he knew what he was doing and that he was honest. One client reported thinking, "Wow, this guy is really on top of things; he really cares about me."

We don't know whether Kniss was a swindler who took other people's money or was simply irresponsible with it. Either way, he got control of their money, from which he made a living. He could only have done that by winning their confidence.

This reminds me of when I worked at a university with a 401(k)-type plan. A representative of the financial company managing the plan visited us regularly for "counseling" on our investments. I questioned whether some of the advice was more in the interest of the company administering the plan than us. A colleague responded, "Oh, but George is such a sweetheart." Being perceived as a sweetheart helps any salesperson close deals, not to mention swindlers winning over marks.

It's also easy to assume that this is an outlier experience, hardly typical of what we would expect from financial advisors. The vast majority of financial advisors believe they're providing useful services to financially unsophisticated clients.

I would rather blame an evolving private retirement system in which both small and powerful financial interests target American retirement savings for profiteering. The Kniss operation in that respect falls within a broader category that includes financial firms extracting large fees to manage 401(k) accounts, hedge fund operators gaining control of public pension funds, and insurance companies profiting from annuity sales.

Pension Benefit Formulas

Every DB pension system employs a *formula* to determine the size of the benefit. It is critically important to understand these formulas to know what lies ahead for employees when they retire. The U.S. Bureau of Labor Statistics lists four main types of benefit formulas along with the percentages of employees having each (see Table 8.1, below). I will add a fifth type, adjustable pension plans, for reasons to be made clear.

1. Final Salary Plans. In this formula, there are three determinants of pension amounts: number of years of employment, a multiplier, and size of final salary. Each is important for determining the size of a given pension. Assume a twenty-five-year employee with an $80,000 salary in a pension plan with a multiplier of 2 percent for each year. If the employee retires that year, the pension will be $40,000 (25 x 2% = 50 percent of $80,000 = $40,000).

TABLE 8.1: Percentage of Employees Participating in Defined-Benefit Pension Plans by Type of Benefit Formula, 2014

Traditional Defined Benefit		
	Final salary	34
	Average salary	8
	Dollars x Years	21
Shared-Risk Plans		
	Cash balance	30
	Adjustable pension	-
Other		7
Total		100

Source: Adapted from Richard Works, "Trends in Employer Costs for Defined Benefit Plans," *Beyond the Numbers: Pay and Benefits* 5/2 (February 2016).

Years Worked x a Multiplier x *Final* Salary = Pension amount
(Example: 25 years x 2 percent = 50 percent of Final Salary)

If she waits a year to retire and she receives a 5 percent raise for that year bringing her salary up to $84,000, her pension will be $43,680 (26 x 2 percent = 52 percent of $84,000 = $43,680). That's a 9.2 percent rise in the pension. Even if there were no raise, the pension would go up to $41,600, 4 percent higher than a twenty-five-year pension.

A second way to increase the years of service and thereby pension amount that does not require working longer is through the purchase of service credits. There are pension plan programs that allow participants to use outside funds to purchase additional years of service. Though up-front costs are often steep, these are most usually good deals in terms of the extra pension income they will yield. It is unlikely that participants will find better ways to invest this money if they have it. It is an excellent way to use funds accumulated in supplemental 401(k)s, individual retirement accounts, and other retirement savings accounts. If a pension plan does not have the opportunity to purchase service credits, union negotiators and employers should attempt to add it.

The costs of service credits are usually set by actuaries so that they are neutral or beneficial to plan financing. The prices of the extra credits are equal to or greater than the liability in terms of increased pension payments. At the same time, the increase in pension payments for the participants is well worth the price. It is a win-win for pension plans and participants.

Purchase programs may put limits on the number of years that can be purchased. They may require proof that the years purchased were during the performance of a particular type of labor—for example, schoolteachers being allowed to buy time only for when they taught elsewhere. From an actuarial point of view, though, there is no reason to place any limits on the purchase of service credits so long as the prices balance the extra pension incomes. Union negotiators and employees in these situations should attempt to remove as much as possible the limitations.

The critical variable for determining the generosity of the overall pension formula is the size of the multiplier. These vary greatly. A 1 percent multiplier is below average in terms of generosity, producing for a twenty-five-year employee a pension income of 25 percent of final salary (25 x 1 percent = 25 percent of final salary). Many state employee pension systems have a 2.0 percent multiplier. In that case, a twenty-five-year employee would receive a pension of 50 percent of the final salary (25 x 2.0 percent = 50 percent of final salary). This plus their Social Security, if they have it, would provide a high retirement income that would easily replace the major part of their pre-retirement income.

Employees may seek to inflate the size of the final salary by taking on paid overtime and other means shortly before retiring so that there is a lot of extra income in the last year or years. This practice is informally known as *spiking* and frowned upon by plan managers and actuaries. It places a load on the pension fund since the spiker's pension will exceed her or his contributions. For pension funds to remain solvent, revenues—contributions + earnings on investments—must balance benefits.

Plan managers have various ways to control spiking, such as through counting only base salaries and not extra income. They can also limit the amount of additional pay included in final salary calculations. While spiking benefits employees who can do it, it places the entire pension plan solvency at risk. For that reason, union negotiators and employees have a greater interest in controlling the practice than in allowing individuals to take advantage of it. This argument, admittedly, can be difficult to make to potential beneficiaries of the practice.

2. Average salary plans. A career average plan is like a final salary one, except that the pension is a percentage of the average rather than final salary.

Years of Work x Multiplier x *Average* Salary
(Example: 25 years x 2 percent = 50 percent of Average Salary)

Career average salaries are almost always much less than final salaries. As a result, career average pension benefits are also much less. It is the final salary that most workers are most interested in maintaining as much as possible in retirement. Maintaining average salaries results in maintaining midpoint career salaries. Over a forty-year career, this would be the worker's often much lower salary at age 45 rather than at 65.

Final salary formulas are almost always more beneficial to employees than average salary ones because of the effects of inflation and raises. Whenever there is inflation, which occurs in most years, nominal salaries rise over time even if their buying powers remain the same. It is to the employee's advantage to have the inflated amount at the end of his or her career as the determinant of the pension amount rather than the much lower, less-inflated career average amount. The Social Security career average benefit formula (discussed in chapter3) avoids the inflation problem by indexing earlier incomes. Raises have the same effect of making final salaries higher than career average ones. However, it is also true that not all careers have significant real income raises over time. In some work careers, final incomes decline because laid-off workers are forced into lower-paid positions or drop down to part-time work.

3. Dollars x Years Plans. In a flat "dollars times years" benefit system, the pensioner receives a fixed dollar amount for each month or year of service. Retired members of the Chicago Symphony Orchestra, for example, receive a pension worth $2,314 for each year of service. Unlike final salary pensions, higher salary members, such as first chairs, do not receive higher pensions. Length of service is the exclusive determinant of pension amounts along with the dollar amount that the number of years multiply.

This amount, depending on the plan, can vary from year to year or month to month for a variety of reasons, including market conditions. Different years of service can add different amounts to the pension benefit. Depending on how much variance is present, it can be complicated to calculate any one employee's pension benefit. In all cases, it is in the worker's interest that the amounts per year keep up with rather than lag behind inflation.

Years of work x Dollar Amount = Monthly Pension
(Example: 25 years x $10 = $250 monthly pension)

4. Cash Balance Plans. In these plans, employers or employees make percent-of-salary contributions into a collective fund, as with any pension plan. But unlike percent-of-earnings pensions, participants are individually credited each year as if they had separate accounts like with retirement savings accounts. Some refer to them as hybrid plans because of the shared pension and personal account features. In cash balance accounts, participant accounts grow by dollar amount contributions, usually based on a percentage of salary, often along with a set rate of interest. Employees can track year by year the growth of their cash or percent balances. The ending size of career cash balances determines the amount of retirement income. By law, cash balance plans must have a life pension option for the distribution of their benefits. They also have a lump-sum option. Like other pension plans, cash balance pension payments come out of the pension trust fund. This distribution out of plan assets results in higher pension payments for retirees than having to purchase commercial annuities from outside life insurance companies.

Pension plan trustees and managers are responsible for all investments and bear the risks of those investments, unlike with 401(k) plans where investment decisions and their risks are the responsibilities of participants. Cash balance plans have portability advantages for job changers, unlike other types of pension plans. While plan features vary in this respect, in many they can roll their accumulations into other plans when they terminate employment, or they can leave them in place to withdraw as annuities upon reaching retirement age. It is usually not a good idea to roll hybrid balances into 401(k)-type plans, however. Doing so results in losing the very significant annuity advantages of defined-benefit plans. Moving them into another cash balance plan is reasonable. If one is not available, then the balance should be left where it is until retirement. Cash balance plans are flexible enough to handle varieties of work where there are erratic earnings and multiple employers such as in trucking.

Contributions + interest →Individually credited within collective fund → Individual pensions or lump-sum payments (Size of cash balance accumulated determines size of pension or lump sum)

Nebraska has a cash balance plan for state employees with the following features: Employees contribute 4.8 and employers 7.5 percent-of-salary to the fund, with each employee having a separate account balance. Each account is credited annually with a minimum of 5 percent interest, depending on investment returns. Upon retirement, employees have the option of taking their total balances as pensions or lump sums. They can also choose to take proportions of both. The state provides an online calculator to estimate pension payments. For a 65-year-old in 2019, it showed a payout rate of 10.54 percent without cost-of-living increases. A career cash balance of $100,000 would have paid a flat annual pension of $10,540. The comparable payout rate for a commercial life insurance annuity was dramatically less: 6.66 percent for males and 6.32 percent for females. Employees also have the option of taking their pension payments with COLA adjustments of 2.5 percent per year. In that case, the pension would have started at $8,678.

Cash balance plans preclude most of the advantages of spiking for employees. There is no incentive for workers to take on overtime or otherwise gain jumps in pay to inflate their pensions artificially. Any extra payments will add to their cash balances, but the addition will not be enough to increase their pension payments significantly. For example, take a twenty-five-year worker with a salary of $70,000 in a final salary plan with a 2 percent multiplier. If she manages through overtime to increase her salary to $80,000 for the last year, her pension payment increases from $35,000 to $40,000, a significant 14.3 percent increase. Let's assume, instead, that she is in a cash balance plan from which she is due an equal $35,000 annual pension, and she increases her final pay to $80,000. In that case, using the Nebraska contribution rate of 12.3 percent of salary from combined employer and employee contribution, her final cash balance would increase by $1,230 (.123 x $10,000). That extra amount would render an increased pension payment of $130 without COLA (.1054 x $1,230) and $107 (.0868 x $1,230) with COLA—far less than the $5,000 increase if there had been a final salary formula.

Cash balance plans can disadvantage late-career workers because their late-career promotions are not as valuable as those in final salary plans. The late-career promotion adds more contribution dollars to their balances, but those extra dollars do not have much time to grow from investment gains. With final salary plans, the extra promotion dollars translate much more directly into higher pension payments.

5. Adjustable pension plans. Sometimes called variable pension plans, these are a new type that has been in existence since 2012. As of now, though widely discussed as in-between alternatives to traditional pension plans and 401(k)-type plans, APPs cover very few workers. *Consumer Reports*, the product review magazine, changed from a traditional pension to this plan. In so doing, it shifted part of the plan risk from the employer to employees. Going the other way, Unite Here, Local 26, in the Boston area changed out of a 401(k) to this type of plan, shifting part of the risk from its hotel and restaurant workers to their employers in the multi-employer plan.

An APP guarantees a low "floor benefit," that is, minimum amount, based on either a percent of salary or flat dollar amount. If investment returns are favorable, the benefit will increase. If investment returns are negative, the worker will only receive an accrual equal to the floor benefit for that year.

The overall benefit is similar to that of a cash balance plan. In both, employers and employees share investment risks. The difference is in terms of the accrual unit. With cash balance plans, contributions plus awarded interest rates accrue each year. With adjustable pension plans, what accrues are fractions of retirement income expressed as percentages of final or average salaries or flat dollar amounts.

What we've been looking at are textbook examples of different pension benefit formulas. Their differences and calculations are straightforward. The real world of benefit formulas for actual pension plans is likely to be far messier and challenging to comprehend immediately. In the final salary pension plan I was in, there was one multiplier for income up to a certain amount and another multiplier for income above that. Also, that income line changed every year. I can offer my own mock rule of pension formulas: If a simple pension formula can be made more complicated, it will be made more complicated. The more complicated the benefit formula, the less transparent the plan. It is tempting to believe that pension managers enjoy making what is simple into something complicated to elevate themselves into a priesthood that controls access to vital information. My paranoia in this direction was fed by an experience when I was counseling state employees who were considering transferring from their 401(k)-like plan into the state's pension plan. They quite reasonably wanted to know two things: How much it would cost and how much it would benefit them. It took me about twenty minutes with some simple information from them and the use of online calculators to explain the costs and benefits. At the same time, a financial advisory firm was charging $700 to provide the same answers. It did it in the most complicated manner possible, producing twenty-page "individualized" printouts of tables that came to the same conclusions as my free service.

But let's give the pension managers the benefit of the doubt and assume they have honest actuarial fine-tuning motives for making the formulas complicated. They may, for example, be under the gun to reduce pension payouts in the fairest ways. Whatever the reason, employees and their union representatives, if they have them, should have access to online benefit calculators that are simple to use. Plan sponsors, at the least, should have available enough information about formulas so that participants can calculate individual benefits by hand.

With pension benefit formulas, the devil is in the details. This importance of details is true for both learning how to understand them and for evaluating how beneficial they are for employees. The same holds for understanding the impacts of proposed management changes.

The Employee Retirement Income Security Act (ERISA) of 1974 requires that private employers make available summary plan descriptions (SPDs) for their retirement plans. Most public employers, either voluntarily or because of state laws, also make SPDs available for their plans. The SPD is the first document to look at when studying a particular retirement plan. They contain information about eligibility, benefits, and costs of the plan.

Cost-of-Living Adjustments

Very important is whether a pension plan contains a cost-of-living adjustment (COLA). These protect against inflation risk. Since retirees will depend on the pension income for as much as twenty or more years, it is in their interest that the pension check keeps up with the rate of inflation. For example, for the twenty years between 1998 and 2018, the average annual inflation rate was 2.1 percent.[8] This meant that while the nominal number of dollars per check remained the same, the real value declined cumulatively by 4.3 percent. The real value of a $1,000 monthly pension dropped to $957. Adding up the declines for each of the twenty years due to inflation, it totals $6,005 in lost income. This loss was during a period of relatively low inflation. For the twenty years between 1973 and 1993, the average annual inflation rate was 6.1 percent, almost three times as high. The 1980 inflation rate was a staggering 13.5 percent. In 1974, 1979, and 1981, it was over 10 percent. The year 1973 was a horrible one for a pensioner to retire without the protection of a COLA. Those retirees would have seen their real monthly income for a $1,000 monthly pension decline over twenty years to $280 (!), with a total loss of $125,223—over half the pension's nominal $240,000 value ($1,000 X the 240 months in 20 years). There's no guarantee that high inflation will never return.

For that reason, all pension plans should include COLAs, even if that requires making initial payments lower.

Lack of a COLA should be an immediate red flag concern for employees and their union representatives. They should bargain for the plan to contain one, even if it requires higher contributions on the part of active employees. It is in their interest as future retirees, and it shows solidarity with current ones. No one should have to endure shrinking real income during retirement.

Pension plans vary considerably in how they calculate COLAs. Most base them in some way on the Consumer Price Index. I say "in some way" because the COLA may be a fraction of the CPI. The plan may also set limits on COLA increase even if the CPI is higher. Employees and their union representatives should pay special attention to management proposals for changes in the calculations of COLAs.

The Social Security COLA has been a model for employer pension plans. This is not to say that most plans follow Social Security on COLAs. Instead, it is to say that Social Security has a best practice, the principles of which are transferrable to employer pension plans. These are principles that employees and their union representatives can keep in mind during negotiations over COLAs. The first principle is that Social Security automatically sets the COLA amount annually. It does not require congressional authorization each year. Second, it increases or does not increase the COLA according to a known public measure of the rate of inflation, the CPI. Employees and their unions should resist management attempts to require annual authorizations of COLAs. They should also resist management being able to lower COLA increases because of years of low or negative pension fund investment returns. As implied above, if actuarial conditions worsen and thereby make COLAs less affordable for the fund, it is better to increase fund revenues, even if that requires increasing employee contributions, than to reduce the COLA benefit. Once management reduces such a benefit, it is difficult to get it back, and it will be at the expense of the vulnerable population of retirees.

Spouse Protection

When it comes time to retire, most pension plans allow a choice between single life and contingent annuitant payments. Single, sometimes called straight life payments, cover the pensioner alone. Rules for contingent annuitant payments establish that should pensioners die, their surviving spouses can continue collecting for life. The most common options are to have survivors receive 100 or 50 percent of the original pension amount. If there are survivor benefits, pension check amounts will be less than for single life payments to compensate for the extra payouts. Most couples choose the 50 percent option on the theory that it takes half as much income to support one survivor compared to a two-person couple. In return, the 50 percent option lowers the pension payment less than the 100 percent option. The cost of the 50 percent option in terms of reduced pension payments is surprisingly low, assuming the survivor is close to the same age as the pensioner. It would be a different story if a 65-year-old pensioner had a 21-year-old spouse (!). Then the actuarial cost to insure the spouse, as well as pensioner, would be much higher since she or he would most likely live and collect much longer past the death of the pensioner than the typical survivor. Plan managers can control that extreme possibility by requiring that survivors be of retirement age to collect.

Reforms to Improve Pension Plans

Every pension plan has room for improvements that benefit its participants. Unfortunately, due to the steady drumbeat of anti-pension news and commentary in the media, participants and their union representatives are more likely to be thinking defensively. They want to ward off attacks that would decrease or eliminate benefits and, in many cases, end the pension plans entirely. We'll look at that in chapter 10, but for now, let's think positively about what employees and unions can do to shore up retirement security.

Many of these suggestions are no-cost reforms to pension plans, which makes them easier to accomplish. The changes are not for higher-cost benefits but rather better ways to distribute existing benefits or allowing the purchase of higher benefits at cost. Getting individual retirement savings, such as in 401(k) accounts, into collective pension plans most often results in higher retirement incomes.

1. Create or Improve a Cost-of-Living-Adjustment. Every pension plan should contain a COLA. Having one protects against inflation risk. No pensioner wants to see the real value of her retirement income decrease because of raging inflation. Many, but by no means all, pension plans contain COLAs. There is a tradeoff to having a COLA. Initial pension checks will have to be smaller to be able to grow each year to keep up with inflation. How much smaller? The state of Nebraska's cash balance plan, cited above, gives pensioners the choice of taking their annuities with or without COLAs. That gives us a reasonable estimate of the difference since it is calculated by the plan's actuaries so that either choice will have an equal impact on the trust fund's solvency. (If I were a trustee of that plan, I would not allow such an option and require the taking of the COLA, just like Social Security does not have a non-COLA option. But this is another matter.) The COLA option results in an initial benefit that is 21.2 percent less than the non-COLA option. That difference will then decrease each year for ten years until the benefit amounts are the same. Then if the pensioner continues to survive and draw checks, his benefit will be higher than the flat non-COLA pension. Overall, after ten years, he would receive more total income. However, I don't think that the total figure amount should be the criterion for deciding which option to take. People should not be trying to estimate how long they're likely to live to make these types of decisions. What is important is the security of knowing that your real income will keep up with the rate of inflation, no matter how long you live.

Forgoing early income to have a COLA presents the same risk to pensioners as does the regular pension plan: if they die early, they will have had to live on less money than necessary. But that is an acceptable risk because its payback is known security of income. Having a COLA presents a risk to the plan trust fund. If there is excessive inflation beyond what plan actuaries had planned, plan solvency will be compromised. But that is an acceptable risk since the plan, unlike mortal individuals, has decades to make up for temporary excessive outlays.

Starting or increasing COLAs is not technically difficult. The most straightforward way is to actuarily calculate the necessary reduction in the flat payment amount—21.2 percent in the Nebraska case—and that becomes the starting pension amount for new retirees. The amount of the COLA can be indexed to an external measure such as the Consumer Price Index, as is Social Security, or have a constant annual increase, as is that of the Nebraska cash balance plan. For retirees who are already collecting, plan managers could give them the option of continuing with their flat amounts or taking a reduction in return for having the COLA. The age of the pensioner would actuarily determine the amount of individual reductions.

An advantage of creating or increasing a COLA that makes it easier to convince plan managers is that it does not result in any higher cost to the plan. It is just a different way of distributing already earned benefits.

2. Purchase Service Credits. Final salary pension plans work very well for long-term employees. They work less well for employees who have come to the plan relatively late in their careers and will have fewer years in it before retiring. A way to partially compensate for that is to allow employees to purchase service credits—additional years in the plan. Job changers may be carrying with them 401(k) account balances, which they could roll over into the pension plan in return for extra years of work credit. Service credit purchases are almost always to the advantage of the employee by paying off handsomely in extra pension income. At the same time, they place no load on the pension trust fund since the service credits purchased are at actuarial cost.

3. Rollover Outside Retirement Savings into Cash Balance Plans.
The purchase of service credits is not relevant for cash balance plans.

Years of work have no bearing on the size of their pensions. It is instead the size of the accumulated cash balance that determines the size of the pension annuity. This feature works well for long-term employees, as in the case of final salary plans, but less well for shorter-term end of career employees. They should have a way to roll over their 401(k) or similar accounts, if they have them, into the cash balance plan to be able to increase the size of their pension annuities. A dollar invested in a cash balance annuity will render much more income than one spent on a 401(k) commercial life insurance annuity.

4. Increase Multiplier for Final Salary Plans. As described above, there is a great variation of multipliers for final salary pension plans, from less than 1 percent to over 3 percent. It would be a hard sell to increase still further a multiplier in the higher range. But one in the lower range is worth examining. If a plan is overfunded, one way to use the extra funds would be to return them to workers in terms of higher pensions, which would be the result of raising multipliers. If a plan is not overfunded, it could increase either the employer or employee contributions or both, to finance higher benefits. Low multiplier plans most likely produce inadequate pensions. Employees and unions can thus frame arguments in terms of improving pension adequacy. There will undoubtedly be a tradeoff between increasing the pension benefit via an enhanced multiplier and pay raises. While here-and-now pay raises are always nice, long-term investments in pension adequacy may well have better payoffs.

9

Solvency

All pension plans must be properly funded and managed to be financially sustainable. There must be enough revenue going into the plan's budget or trust fund to cover pension payments coming out. If an imbalance occurs, then either the money going in has to increase or pension check amounts coming out decrease, or some combination of the two. For those reasons, responsible plan managers continually monitor and, when necessary, adjust pension funds. How they adjust them, by increasing revenues or decreasing benefits, is a story of labor-management struggles.

Every pension fund has two primary sources of revenue: contributions and returns on investments. Unlike Social Security, employer-sponsored pension funds receive more income from investment returns than employer and employee contributions. In 2018, investment returns accounted for 62 percent of state and local pension fund revenues.[1]

PAYGO and Prefunding

There are two basic ways to fund pension plans. Pay-as-You-Go (PAYGO in the shortened acronym) systems pay pensions from the current contributions of employers and employees. To a large extent, this is the way Social Security functions. Many state governments used to pay pensions as line-item general budget expenses.

PAYGO systems can function so long as there is as much money coming in as going out, and the employer is in business. But if the employer goes out of business or declares bankruptcy, the source of pension payments vanishes, and current and future retirees are left in the lurch. In 1966, car manufacturer Studebaker did precisely that. It went out of business with its PAYGO system unable to continue pension payments to current retirees and the accrued pension benefits of pre-retirement workers becoming worthless. This prompted Congress in 1974 to pass the Employee Retirement Insurance Security Act (ERISA). Among other stipulations, ERISA required private employers with pension plans to move from PAYGO to *prefunding systems*. State and local government pension funds, though uncovered by ERISA, also have moved from PAYGO to prefunding.

In prefunding systems, plan sponsors build up trust funds with contributions and investment returns so that there is enough to pay off all the accrued benefits to retired and current workers. PAYGO systems, in contrast, only need enough funds to make payments to current retirees. They do not also need, as do prefunded systems, enough to pay all of the not yet due payments to retirees for the rest of their lives or the accrued benefits of current workers. They do not need trust funds if they make pension payments out of general budgets.

Funding Ratios and Unfunded Liabilities

Funding ratios and unfunded liabilities are artifacts of prefunding systems. They don't exist for PAYGO systems. A funding ratio is the size of a pension trust fund divided by the total liability of the plan. A plan can be under-, fully, or overfunded, depending on whether its ratio is under, equal to, or over 100 percent.

Trust Fund Assets / Total Liability = Funding Ratio
(Example: $8 billion assets/$10 billion liability = 80 percent funded)

Prefunded systems with funding ratios of less than 100 percent have unfunded liabilities. They have fewer assets in their trust funds than necessary to meet all obligations.

$$\text{Total Liability} - \text{Trust Fund Assets} = \text{Unfunded Liability}$$
(Example: $10 billion liability – $8 billion assets = $2 billion unfunded liability)

The scary-sounding concept "unfunded liability" is grossly misunderstood. While elimination of unfunded liabilities is a goal of pension fund management, it is neither a requirement for the fund to function nor an indicator of insolvency or imminent collapse. A plan can work sufficiently well somewhere between the PAYGO minimum funding required to make current payments to pensioners and less than full prefunding so long as it has the revenue to make those minimum payments. At the same time, if it is trying to achieve full funding status, it will have to make extra contributions to make up for the unfunded liabilities. Once it reaches its funding ratio goal, it can reduce contributions considerably. In this funding quest, there is a continual hope by plan managers that investment returns will be large enough to offset the need to increase contributions.

In looking at any pension plan with unfunded liabilities, it is essential to determine the sources of those liabilities. There are several possibilities:

1. The move from PAYGO to prefunding. Once a pension system makes the change to prefunding, it instantly acquires an unfunded liability. Plan managers now have to acknowledge future liabilities as well as current payments due to retirees. To reduce or eliminate the liability, they have to create a trust fund into which they place enough assets to cover the additional liabilities beyond current payments due that the plan has taken on because of the accounting system change. A pension plan can thus go from fully solvent to significantly underfunded from one day to the next simply by adopting a different accounting method. There's still enough to make pension payments, but now more contributions or other revenues are required to lessen the newly acquired unfunded liability.

2. Underfunding. Actuaries estimate the contributions that employers or employees must make to keep a pension plan in balance. If an employer shorts those contributions, that is, pays less than needed, the deficit will accumulate over succeeding years. It is similar to skipping house mortgage payments and then having to pay them back in the future with substantial, mounting interest.

ERISA controls for private-sector pension plan contribution shorting by mandating an Annual Required Contribution. The ARC changes from year to year according to investment returns and other factors. Those changes can make budget planning difficult. Some have argued that ERISA's variable ARC requirements become an accounting burden and give private employers an incentive to terminate pension plans. The 401(k)-like plans then looked attractive because the employer's contribution percent of salary would not vary from year to year unless the employer wanted to change it.

In industries such as coal mining, far fewer workers are required now than in the past, meaning that fewer contributions are going into pension trust funds. A result is underfunding. With the drying up of contributions, there are not enough pension assets to continue supporting retirees drawing pensions. In many industries, companies go out of business frequently or declare bankruptcy, leaving pension liabilities unpaid. Corporate managers often carry out mergers and other machinations precisely to shed pension liabilities at the expense of worker beneficiaries. ERISA attempted to address these private-sector problems by requiring private pension sponsors to insure their pensions through the federal government's Pension Benefit Guaranty Corporation. The PBGC has functioned as intended, providing a backstop to the private pension system. But, ominously, it too is underfunded, especially its multi-employer pension plan program, with dire warnings that it could run out of money.[2] Any resolution of private pension solvency will require expanding sources and amounts of revenue for the PBGC.

Public sector pension plans operate in a different reality than those in the private sector. Government entities are much less vulnerable to going out of business or bankrupt. Despite its fiscal problems, it is unimaginable that the federal government would declare bankruptcy, much less go out of business. State governments, by law, cannot declare bankruptcy, though there are political and economic interests that would like to end that prohibition. Local governments in some states have been allowed to declare bankruptcy, but relatively few have. The 2013 Detroit bankruptcy, though significant, was still a rarity for cities.

Public pension plans also operate in a different reality than private sector plans because governments have more permanence. Private companies come and go, whereas there are always governments in place. Public pension plans have the advantage of having decades to make up shortfalls. There is much less assurance that private companies will still be in existence over such long terms.

State and local government pension plans, because ERISA does not cover them, do not have to make specific ARC payments. However, they generally monitor what ARC payments would be for accounting purposes. With state and local governments required to have balanced budgets but not to make ARC contributions, the temptation is great to short pension contributions. It is politically more feasible to shift money from a pension contribution to an immediate demand, such as school budgets, than vice versa. That kind of shorting is common and is the major source of public pension unfunded liabilities. The growing unfunded pension liability will not present an urgent problem as would be the case if teacher salaries could not be paid. The generosity of pension payments is not a significant factor, contrary to many accusatory media claims. Such underpayments don't affect the state or local government's ability to meet obligations to current retirees. They do, however, result in a mounting cost of future funding payments. The more such unfunded liabilities a state government has, the lower its bond ratings, which, in turn, make borrowing more expensive.

When governments short pension contributions, they essentially receive interest-free loans from pension trust funds with no fixed terms for being paid back. Those loans then accelerate unfunded liabilities, which politically motivated critics use unjustly to support narratives that call for cutting pension benefits to lower the liabilities. This basically is a call for governments to renege on repaying those loans from current and retired workers. It would be quite different if governments that shorted pension contributions were required to purchase interest-bearing bonds from the pension funds. The bonds would then add assets rather than liabilities to pension trust funds, and that would then eliminate an oft-repeated justification for taking away pension benefits.

An indirect way in which public employers have shorted pension payments has been to overestimate future investment returns. Whether intentional or not, it was common to estimate 8 percent returns when this was not a realistic assumption. In actuarial estimations of pension liabilities, the assumed future rate of return is referred to as the discount rate. That is, actuaries discount future liabilities by the assumed rate of return of investments. The effect of overestimating future investment returns was to underestimate unfunded liabilities and actuarily needed employer contributions. That accounting operation freed up money to spend on more pressing public needs.

There are thus two types of shorting—direct and indirect. The first is to make a lower contribution than what is known to be actuarily needed. The second is to make a lower contribution because what is required actuarily is underestimated. In either case, the pension fund is subsidizing other government spending.

3. Reduced investment returns. When stock markets decline, inevitably revenues to pension funds decline, resulting in decreased funding ratios. As we've seen, this is not a significant problem since collective pension funds have long-term time horizons to compensate for market return shortfalls.

4. Retirement incentive programs. During economic downturns, employers may have incentives to shed employees, such as teachers and civil service workers, who are reaching the tops of their pay scales and have job security. They cannot simply lay off or fire them, but they can give them an incentive to retire early. Such an incentive can be a grant of extra years of work credit for purposes of determining final salary pensions. This solves the problem of reducing the workforce size and cost for employers, and for employees, it is a good deal, one that allows them to retire early with a good pension. It is a seeming win-win. But it is at the expense of the stability of the pension fund. The employees are essentially receiving pension credits they did not earn in terms of contributions to the pension fund. The employers are unloading payment responsibilities from their current labor force budgets to pension trust funds.

It is also possible to use a variation of this strategy to pay off severed workers after corporate mergers. Instead of paying severance pay, which requires payment of Social Security and Medicare employer taxes, to longtime employees they cut, the employers can give employees extra pension credits or cashouts from trust fund assets. In essence, the employers will use pension assets to finance corporate restructuring instead of to assure retirement security for the affected employees. Telecommunications giant Verizon, which emerged out of the merger of Bell Atlantic and GTE (General Telephone & Electronics Corporation) in 2000, did precisely that. Verizon would later freeze its depleted pension plan for part of its labor force.[3]

Such retirement incentive programs are, for obvious reasons, very popular with workers. Union representatives are under strong pressure to support them. But they represent a fiscal irresponsibility that people concerned about pension solvency should resist. Any union that goes along with them will face future problems when union enemies use the resulting growth of the unfunded liability to pressure them into benefit concessions. They thus are not in the long-term interests of unions. They are also not in the interest of the majority who do not receive the free service credits. That majority most likely will be required to pay for them through increased employee contributions or other measures.

Normal vs. Unfunded Liability Costs

In evaluating the solvency of any pension fund, it is always necessary to distinguish between its *normal* and its *unfunded* liability costs.
Normal costs are the contributions that employers or employees must
make to keep a plan in actuarial balance. They do not include the
costs associated with past underfunding, movements from PAYGO
to prefunding, or retirement incentive programs. The normal cost
is the accurate measure of the fiscal viability of a pension plan. Any
adequately funded and well-managed plan should be able to avoid
accumulating costly unfunded liabilities (except for those associated
with the move from PAYGO to prefunding).

In the pension struggle I was associated with in Connecticut, it was
a great revelation when we discovered that our employer, the state of
Connecticut, was contributing *more* for the 401(k)-like plan than the
normal cost of its pension plan. Stories of how expensive the pension plan was were a constant theme in the press and in the human
relations departments of the state agencies that oversaw the distribution of salaries and benefits. But those were figures that conflated
the state's sizeable unfunded liability with the normal cost. Until the
1970s, Connecticut had run its pension fund on a PAYGO basis and
then switched over to prefunding. There were still a large number of
retirees collecting pensions who had spent their careers under the
PAYGO system. No money had been set aside for them, and so their
pension payments were a drain on the subsequent prefunding system.
The unfunded liabilities associated with those who had started their
careers under the prefunding system were much less. There were
still unfunded liabilities because the Connecticut legislatures and
governors over the years had shorted contributions to the pension
fund as well as sponsored retirement incentive programs that gave
out unearned service credits to encourage relatively high-salaried
employees to retire early.

Once we knew that the normal cost was less than that for the
employer contribution to the 401(k)-like plan, we could make a very
persuasive argument that allowing us to transfer to the pension plan

would save the state money. The state repeated that argument when the governor's office defended its economic policies.

10

Cutbacks, Freezes, and Bankruptcies

I n the 1980s, as corporations began substituting 401(k)s for pension plans, the generalized belief grew in the media that traditional pension plans were no longer sustainable. Supposedly, most were in poor financial condition with unpayable liabilities, as discussed in the previous chapter. That was true of some terminated plans but not all pension plans.

In fact, according to a provocative study by former *Wall Street Journal* investigative reporter Ellen Schultz, many large corporate pension funds were in excellent financial condition by being overfunded. The excess assets became tempting targets for raiding by overzealous managers and their accountants. As a result, many corporations terminated overfunded pension plans and swept the surplus assets into other uses. Congress in 1990 attempted to halt the practice by levying taxes on the excess assets. But that did not end it. Corporate accountants and lawyers exploited loopholes and found more creative ways to raid the pension funds. As late as 1999, there was still overfunding of corporate pension plans by a quarter of a trillion dollars. Another wave of plan terminations and raiding eliminated the surpluses, which were, according to Schultz, "sold, traded, siphoned, diverted to creditors, [and] used to finance executive pay, parachutes, and pensions."

By removing the cushion, the remaining plans became more vulnerable to stock market downturns, including the 2008 Great Recession. Then the corporations either reduced benefits or terminated their pension plans altogether.[1]

Corporate raiding of private-sector pension surpluses along with underfunding of public sector pension plans set the stage for a frenzy of managerial efforts to reduce pension benefits in some cases and terminate plans in others. The primary forms of both follow.

Cutbacks

1. Final Salary Averaging. Plan managers that seek to lower benefits for final salary pension plans can change the final salary size from that of the last year to that of the *average* of the final, say, three years. The more the number of years included, the lower the pension checks when the last years include pay raises. Table 10.1 (below) shows the effect of salary averaging on pension size. The data assume 5 percent annual salary increases. The higher the raises, the more harmful the impact of salary averaging on pension sizes. If there are no raises, there is no effect. Pension amounts remain the same since the salary amounts are the same. However, no union negotiator or employee would want to accede to a management demand for salary averaging because of an assumption of future flat salaries. Employees and unions should resist salary averaging since it will produce significant pension

TABLE 10.1: Effects of Final Salary Averaging on Pension Sizes

Number of Last Years Averaged	Salary	Average	Pension	Percent Pension Reduction
5	$80,000	$84,101	$42,050.63	4.8
4	$82,000	$85,127	$42,563.29	3.6
3	$84,050	$86,169	$43,084.38	2.4
2	$86,151	$87,228	$43,614.07	1.2
1	$88,305	$88,305	$44,152.50	-

Assumptions: 2.5 percent annual salary raises; PENSION FORMULA of Years x .02 x Final Salary.

reductions in the vast majority of situations. If a pension is actuarily out of balance, it is always better for future pensioners to increase its revenue (contributions or investment returns) than reduce pension check amounts.

2. Eliminate or Reduce COLAs. Cost of Living Adjustments, where they exist, are often a tempting target for pension cutbacks because, in pension law, they are not guaranteed, unlike accrued pension benefits. It is different if the COLA results from a binding contract. With many public employee pensions, governing bodies or legislatures control whether to grant COLAs to pensioners. What they give, they can take away. They can also be a tempting target for budget cutters since they don't immediately affect current employees, and pensioners may not think the cutback will be that significant. But any examination of the math will show that COLA reductions or eliminations greatly diminish overall lifetime values of pensions and should be resisted.

3. Increase Age of Eligibility. Any increase in age of eligibility to start collecting a pension is a cutback. If, for example, the eligibility age goes up by two years, pensioners will receive two years' fewer benefits, a decrease in the total amount of benefits collected over their lifetimes. There is less harm if the additional required work years are for higher salaries that increase the sizes of pension checks for final salary pension plans. But the increased benefit can be far lower than the amount lost to the foregone years of pension collection. There are other reasons to oppose raising pension eligibility ages as well, including, most important, that many people are less able, due to health conditions, to continue working extra years.

4. Shift Funding from Employer to Employee. If union negotiators and members must make pension plan concessions, the best, least harmful to their members' retirement income interests, is to agree to initiate or increase employee contributions. While no one likes to have to pay more for an employee benefit, having a real pension is, compared to a 401(k) plan, so valuable that the extra payment to maintain it is well worth the price. A dollar invested in a pension plan renders far more retirement income than one contributed to a 401(k) for reasons elaborated on in the next chapter.

Freezes

The worst thing management can do to a pension plan is to end it with no replacement. The second worst, and more common, is to replace one with a 401(k), which is like replacing a car with a bicycle. Employees and unions should resist these substitutions at all costs. A third possibility is to convert a final salary defined benefit plan to a cash balance plan.

Such conversions can take several forms. So-called *soft freezes* keep existing pension plans for current participants but not for new employees. *Hard freezes* stop pension plan credit accruals for current employees and do not allow new employees to participate. There are in-between possibilities in which existing members are allowed to continue accruing some but not all benefits. Delaying implementations of freezes for several years can also soften the blow. Typically, 401(k) or cash balance plans then replace the frozen final-salary or dollars-times-years pension plans.

Soft freezes meet less employee resistance than hard ones since new employees are not at the table to defend their interests. They must depend on the solidarity of current employees, which can vary greatly. They are also less likely to know of the harm done because it won't be the first thing on their minds when they get the new job, and their retirement will likely be decades away.

In a typical hard freeze scenario for a final salary pension plan, members receive the credits they have accumulated so far, which is required by law, but all new contributions go into a 401(k). For members of frozen final salary plans, this is damaging to their financial interests because later pension plan service credits are more valuable than earlier ones, as they represent claims on larger salaries. In my case, I earned 25 percent of my pension in the final five years, which were just 17 percent of my time in the plan. Some employees earn as much as half their pensions during those years. Because the last years of long-term employees cost final-salary pension systems proportionately more than earlier years, it becomes tempting for managers to lop them off through hard freezes.

With 401(k) contributions, it is the opposite. Earlier years are more valuable to plan members than later ones. While later career contributions based on higher salaries will be more significant, earlier contributions, even if smaller, carry with them compounded accumulations over many years, which grow to represent more considerable sums than original contributions. For example, $1,000 at 5 percent interest over five years results in $1,276, a gain of $276. But over thirty years, it results in $4,322, an increase of $3,332—far greater than the original contribution. For an employee with just five years left to retirement, new 401(k) contributions would have limited time to grow with compounded interest or stock market gains to make up for the loss of the pension plan accruals.

Here's an example (Table 10.2) of how badly a near-retirement employee with a final salary pension plan would fare under a hard freeze. First, let's see what the pension would typically be without any 401(k) conversion of the final five years. Assume a typical pension benefit formula of Years of Service x .02 x Final Salary = Pension Amount. Assume further that the salary after twenty years was $70,000 and then the employee received 2.5 percent raises for each of the final five years. That would bring the final salary up to $79,199 after twenty-five years, which would yield, following the pension benefit formula, a pension of $39,599.

Now, let's consider what would happen if the worker received a pension for the first twenty years and a 401(k) for the final five years. Her pension would be $28,000 (20 years x .02 x $70,000). Let's say that an amount equivalent to 12.3 percent of her salary, much higher than average, was deposited in a 401(k) account for the final five years and that she had a gain of 5 percent per year and was receiving the 2.5 percent raises each year. That would work out to a final accumulation of $49,936. With that amount, she could purchase at age 65 an average life annuity (like a pension) that would give her a yearly income of $2,342.[2] Her pension of $28,000 plus the 401(k) annuity of $2,342 would give her a retirement income of $30,342, far less than the $39,599 she would have received had she been able to stay in the pension for the full twenty-five years. To match the full pension income, she would have had to have accumulated $247,313 in the 401(k). That would have required a return on investment of 104 percent every year, somewhat like the odds of winning the lottery.

Converting to Cash Balance Plans

It has become common for employers to switch from final salary to cash balance pension plans, a change from a more favorable to employees type of pension plan to one less beneficial. This switch carries severe disadvantages, especially for long-term employees. For them, as stated, the last years are much more valuable for building up pension benefits than earlier ones. In cash balance plans, the contributions of earlier years are worth more for retirement income than those of final ones since they have time for compounding interest to add substantially to their values. These disadvantages, however, are less than conversions to 401(k) plans because cash balance plans still have the annuity advantages of defined benefit plans. Table 10.3 shows an example of a cash balance conversion, using the same assumptions for salary history, pension formula, contributions, and accumulations as the 401(k) conversion example in Table 10.2 (below). The difference is that the terms of the cash balance annuity are more favorable to

TABLE 10.2: Retirement Income Impact of Converting Final Five Years from Final Salary to 401(k) Plan

Years of Work	Final Salary		Frozen Pension + 401(k) Annuity			
	Salary	Pension	Pension	401(k) Accumulation	Annuity	Total
20	$70,000	$28,000	$28,000	$0	$28,000	$28,000
25	$79,199	$39,599	$28,000	$49,936	$30,342	$30,342

Assumptions: 2.5% annual raises; pension formula of Years x 2% of Final Salary; 12.3 % of salary contribution; 5% annual interest; 3% COLA with payout rate of 4.69% for 401(k) annuity.

the worker than the 401(k) annuity—8.68 percent versus 4.69 percent payout. This is because the cash balance annuity is issued from within the collective cash balance trust fund, whereas 401(k) annuities come from separate life insurance plans, which inevitably are more expensive. For early-career workers, there are still disadvantages of having cash balance rather than final salary pension plans, but they are not so severe as those of workers who face the conversions late in their careers.

There are two ways to effect a cash balance plan conversion. The first, which we have been assuming so far, results in the employee carrying two retirement plans. One includes the service credits in the original plan up to the date of conversion. Those will translate into a pension upon retirement based on the pre-conversion work career. The other will be the lump sum or annuity earned in the post-conversion cash balance plan. The second way is to convert the final salary pre-conversion service credits into a cash value, and then use that as an opening balance in the new cash balance plan. Plan managers calculate cash values in different ways, with multiple possibilities for short-changing workers. Employees and union representatives need to be especially vigilant. Managers often obscure how they make the calculations or present them as inevitable. During the 1990s, it was common to make the opening balance what it would have been if the plan had been in effect during the worker's entire career with the corporation—a lower figure than the actual annuity value, which included the more valuable final years. A pension law reform in 2006 prohibited the practice for cash balance conversions going forward. Upon retirement, the worker receives just one lump sum payment or annuity, that from the cash balance plan.

At the same time, conversions from final salary to cash balance pension plans are not as overall bad as conversions to 401(k)s. True, for late-career employees, as indicated by Tables 10.2 and 10.3, the damage is nearly as considerable. For new and early employees, the damage is less. They retain the advantages of defined benefit plans: guaranteed pensions, professional investing, and low costs of annuities issued from within the collective trust funds at actuarial value. A

TABLE 10.3: Retirement Income Impact of Converting Final Five Years from Final Salary to Cash Balance Plan

Years of Work	Final Salary		Frozen Pension + Cash Balance Annuity		
	Salary	Pension	Pension	Annuity	Total
20	$70,000	$28,000	$28,000	$0	$28,000
25	$79,199	$39,599	$28,000	$4,339	$32,439

Assumptions: 2.5 % annual raises; pension formula of Years x 2% of Final Salary; 12.3% of salary contribution; 5% yearly interest; 2.5% COLA with a payout rate of 8.68% for cash balance annuity.

subtle but essential advantage is that past accumulations are accruals that cannot decrease during periods of stock market declines.

Employees and unions confronted by management hell-bent on ending final salary pension plans should, of course, resist those terminations as much as possible. But they should also have backup plans if that is not possible. The worst outcomes are pension freezes with 401(k) conversions. The cash balance conversion lies in between and is not as terrible an outcome if late-career employees can be protected. It should be possible to negotiate a tipping point of years of service. Those with many years would keep the final salary plan until retirement. Those with fewer years would retain their accrued pension rights in the final salary plan while having their later years in the cash balance plan. Determination of how many years of service constitute the tipping point are questions of calculation and negotiation, both of which are possible.

Bankruptcies

Private employers can get out of paying pension obligations by declaring bankruptcy, thereby nullifying pension guarantees. State and federal sponsors of public pensions do not currently have that option. For this and other reasons, no state in the United States has ever failed to meet pension payment obligations in full. But because of the vigorous conservative anti–public employee pension campaign pursued by the Cato Foundation and others, there are lawyers, including some affiliated with the Democratic Party, who are continually developing legal challenges to state pension guarantees.

Cities and counties, unlike states, can declare bankruptcy and a few have. Detroit in 2013, as mentioned, was the most prominent. So too did the territory of Puerto Rico in a roundabout way in 2017, which required special congressional action. Some see in that congressional action a potential model for allowing states to do the same.[3]

When governmental bankruptcies occur, courts decide where and how much debt to liquidate. In addition to pension liabilities, governments also have outstanding bonds to banks that they took out to pay for such public projects as bridges and civic centers. Those bonds constitute debt liabilities in the same way as accrued pension credits. When these bankruptcies occur, there is always a fight between banks and pension plan members over who has priority of payment.

In the Detroit bankruptcy, pensioners had to take a haircut in having their payments reduced. New employees had it worse in that the pension plan was closed to them, leaving them with only a 401(k) and much lower support for their future retirement years. Many people observing the Detroit bankruptcy and subsequent pension payment reduction drew the false conclusion that the employees would have been better off with a 401(k) since those accumulations are currently untouchable during employer bankruptcies. The 401(k) may be safe from employer bankruptcies, but they are not safe from market declines in the same way that pension plan participants are. Also, no one will defend 401(k) holders in court if market dips reduce their retirement incomes in the same way that union lawyers fight it out with bank lawyers to protect pension benefits during bankruptcies. When the Detroit bankruptcy hearings began, there was the threat that city pensioners would lose as much as 34 percent of their checks. By the end, the loss went down considerably, to 4.5 percent, along with the loss of the cost of living adjustment.[4] It was still painful, but not nearly as much as it could have been, and workers had more income than they would have had had they been in a 401(k) all along.

By being union members of a collective plan, workers have access to resources that members of individual plans do not. Even when

401(k) participants are union members, and the plan is part of the collective bargaining contract, they are unlikely to get union help if market dips cause retirement income losses. The simple reason is that contractual guarantees to make civil legal claims do not exist. Pension plan members have a legally sound case to put forward during bankruptcies, 401(k) participants do not.

11

The Pension Wars

Pension battles are among the most significant forms of class struggles in the United States, Europe, and Latin America. Hundreds of thousands of people have taken to the streets in France to defend their national pension systems and in Chile to demand restoration of one taken away from them. In 2005, unions, senior groups, churches, and others mobilized to successfully stop President George W. Bush's attempt to partially privatize Social Security. Large and small battles over workplace pension plans are an omnipresent feature of labor-management conflicts.

No Best Buy Retirement Plan at Consumer Reports

Consumer Reports has a well-earned reputation for trustworthiness when it comes to the advice it gives readers about which products and services they should purchase. It carefully tests and ranks competing products. Those that are of high quality and comparatively low cost earn its designation of "best buys." The same cannot be said, however, for the retirement plan it gives its workers.

Until 2013, its union-represented employees had an excellent final salary pension plan. Then Consumers Union, the parent organization of *Consumer Reports*, froze the plan and replaced it with one of the new adjustable pension plans described in Chapter 8. The original plan had an accrual rate of 1.9 percent. For each year of employment, *Consumer Reports* employees would receive a pension worth 1.9 percent of their final salary. A thirty-year employee, for example, would receive a pension worth 57 percent (30 x 1.9 percent) of final salary. The new plan did not have a fixed accrual rate like the old one. Rather, the rate varied according to market conditions. This immediately meant that market risk was shifted from plan sponsors to plan members, as with a 401(k). However, unlike a 401(k), once the rate was credited for a given year, it could not later be reduced because of adverse market conditions.

Proponents of the adjustable pension plan explained clearly that accrual rates would go up and down. The actual range of the accrual credits was hypothetical since there was no actual experience with the plans yet. By 2018, though, there was five years' experience and the results were not good. *Consumer Reports* plan members received an average accrual of 0.91 percent, less than half the 1.9 percent they were receiving under the old plan.[1] They were losing over half their pension benefit.

According to several people with background knowledge of the plan's development—who did not want their names used—*Consumer Reports* management started the 2013 negotiations by demanding that the old plan be frozen and replaced by a 401(k). Negotiators from The Newspaper Guild, which represented *Consumer Reports* employees, did not think the old plan could be saved. At the same time, they did not find a 401(k) as an attractive replacement. After much research, they settled on the untried adjustable pension plan. The Newspaper Guild was also involved in the *New York Times* negotiations, which also resulted in adoption of an adjustable pension plan. For the union representatives, the adjustable pension plan was the best or least bad alternative under the circumstances. It had the advantage over a 401(k) of producing an actual pension. I would add, as discussed earlier, that a pension coming directly from a defined benefit plan, which an adjustable pension plan technically is, would be a better deal for retirees than a comparable annuity bought through a commercial provider.

When I cited the very low average accrual rate of 0.91 percent, one person stated that was because of unusually low interest rates in the plan's first five years and that *Consumer Reports* management had insisted on contributing no more than 5 percent of salary to the plan. The *New York Times*, in comparison, was contributing 6.6 percent of salary.[2]

A second person stated that he had expected interest rates to return to normal levels by 2015. In fact, they had continued to decrease, leaving him mystified. I asked him what the accrual rate would be under the best of circumstances, that is, if and when interest rates returned to normal levels. He estimated 1.2 to 1.25 percent. That would still be considerably less than the steady 1.9 percent of the old *Consumer Reports* plan. What is more, better accrual rates would have to be unusually high to make up for the years of extra-low ones. In addition, the old plan's accrual rate was of final salary, whereas the adjustable pension plan's would be of current salary, which is much lower.

There's no question that the adjustable pension plan was a better deal for employees than the 401(k) that *Consumer Reports* management wanted to impose. The union did what it could to salvage the situation with it. But in the end, it was management's victory, and *Consumer Reports* employees were left with much worse retirement security than they had under the old plan. The adjustable pension plan could have been a more acceptable substitute for the final-salary pension plan they had if management had been willing to fund it with a higher rate of contributions. Management could have easily done that without increasing its total retirement benefit costs. It could have redirected contributions it was making to an existing supplemental employee 401(k) into the adjustable pension plan to make it more robust. Not only did it not do that, it shifted one percent of salary that had gone into the old plan into increased funding for the 401(k)s instead of the new adjustable pension plan. Management did not follow the advice so often offered in its magazine to invest in a product or service—in this case retirement plan—that would deliver the greatest bang for the buck. Good advice to offer readers but apparently not to use when dealing with its employees.

Jeff Bezos "Rescues" the Washington Post *at the Expense of Its Employees*

For eighty years, the Graham family owned the *Washington Post*. It developed a defined benefit pension plan that covered, as of 2008, its nearly one thousand employees. It included everyone from editors and reporters to the truck drivers who delivered the papers to newsstands. Like other owners of private businesses, though, the Graham family succumbed to the trend and closed the plan to new employees—a soft freeze—in 2009. Veteran employees were unaffected. For new employees, a cash balance plan was substituted. Employees would still get a defined benefit pension, but it would be less favorable than the one it replaced.

For reasons that had nothing to do with either pension plan, the newspaper had financial difficulties. In 2013, the Graham family put the *Post* up for sale. If the paper was bleeding red, the final salary pension fund was a different story. Not only was it not in trouble, it was overfunded to the tune of 140 percent. Its trustees had followed an exceptionally successful investment strategy. Also, the Graham family, in a generous gesture of support for its workers, had made a substantial extra contribution to the fund. The family wanted veteran workers to have the stability and security of the promised pension they had earned. Nevertheless, the newspaper was failing financially even if the pension fund was thriving, and they wanted out.

If some banks are too big to fail, some newspapers are too important to fold. The *Post* was one of them. True, there were other newspapers in Washington, but none with the reputation of the *Post*. Someone or some corporation was needed to save it. That someone turned out to be Jeff Bezos, the founder of Amazon and the richest man in the world. He bought the newspaper on October 1, 2013, for $250 million.

There was a collective gasp from many people. Would he do to the newspaper business what he had done to the brick-and-mortar bookstore business? Fortunately, the worst fears did not bear out. He infused the newspaper with needed new capital and hired new reporters. The *Post* emerged from the sale stronger. Many of its employers see Bezos as having saved their jobs.

But at what cost? The Amazon business model is to sell as cheap and fast as possible to impatient customers looking for low prices, an online version of Walmart. What would that look like if applied to the newspaper world? It would mean paying *Post* employees less and the first target would be their retirement benefits.

In 2015, Bezos hard-froze the highly successful overfunded pension plan, replacing it with a far less adequate cash balance plan. He also closed the 2009 cash balance plan. The new plan, called the Secure Retirement Account, was dramatically less generous than the final salary pension plan and less generous than the 2009 cash balance plan.

Why did he do it? He certainly did not need to. Since the longtime final salary pension plan was significantly overfunded, it did not cost Bezos more than a minimum amount to maintain for years, possibly less than was being put into the new cash balance plan. Since there had been no new members accruing benefits in it since the 2009 soft freeze, it was even less expensive to maintain. Fredrick Kunkle, a *Post* reporter and union negotiator, asked Bezos that question at a public forum.[3] He responded that he didn't believe in cash future liabilities. His response was more of a non-response. Kunkle found it indicative that, in a room that included many reporters, no one followed up or pressed Bezos on the matter.[4] Not even reporters were aware of how significant the issue was. It involved millions of dollars collectively and hundreds of thousands of dollars of lost retirement income to some individual retirees. One would think that reporters would be aware of retirement cutbacks that harmed members of their profession.

Without direct knowledge of his motives, we can only look at possible reasons. For that, we can look at the history of corporations freezing overfunded pension plans. In all cases, they involve monetizing the pension fund by getting access to the overfunded part—the surplus—to use it for other purposes than providing retirement benefits. Freezing a pension plan does not necessarily mean terminating it. It means that there will be no more accrual of benefits. The plan will cease having new liabilities. The fund will then amortize—literally and figuratively—its existing obligations, that is, pay off accrued retirement benefits. The surplus part of the pension plan can continue to grow in a tax-favored manner from investment returns. Among the things that companies can do with surpluses are to use them to offset the costs of other benefits. In the past, this has included paying health benefits, which reduces a company's loss to the bottom line. More nefariously, it could mean merging the executives' deferred compensation liabilities into the pension fund from which they would then be paid. What originally was a fund set up for ordinary workers would be used to finance perks for highly paid executives. It's also possible that the surplus could be held in reserve so that should Bezos purchase a company with an underfunded pension plan, the plans could merge so that the *Post*'s surplus would offset the unfunded liabilities of the new company.

Without access to the actual motives of Bezos and those who designed the freeze for him, we do not know which of the above or some other possibility was the real motive. What we do know is that the result significantly reduces the retirement income of *Post* employees. Converting from a final salary to a cash balance plan will not be as bad for employees as switching to a 401(k), but they will still lose future retirement income.

Veteran employees, whose final years are much more valuable in pension accrual than earlier ones, will take an especially steep retirement income reduction. What all employees will suffer in common is that benefits will not accrue as fast. Put differently, to obtain the same retirement income as the previous final salary pension plan would have provided, they will have to work many more years.

For its own employees, Amazon has a 401(k) with just a modest 2 percent employer match, less than half the corporate average of 4.7 percent.[5]

The Gravedancer's Wife

In March 2019, the one hundred musicians of the world-class Chicago Symphony Orchestra went on strike for seven weeks, the longest in its

128-year history. Management wanted to hard-freeze their defined benefit pension plan and replace it with a 401(k). The funding ratio, according to management, was dangerously low, threatening the financial stability of the CSO. The musicians, represented by the American Federation of Musicians – AFL-CIO, had quite a different take. True, their dollars-times-years pension plan was underfunded. But that was entirely the fault of management. For years it had been underfunding the plan to siphon the difference to a building fund. By ERISA law, it had to contribute a minimum amount each year, which it did. But while ERISA law required it to make this annual required contribution (ARC), it did not require it to make enough of a contribution to provide long-term financial stability of the pension plan, let alone provide for future increases in retirement benefits. This practice was especially important for the CSO plan since members only accrued flat-dollar benefits until higher amounts to keep up with inflation were negotiated in new contracts. The pension, once received, was also flat without a cost-of-living increase. It was a classic case of managers deciding that they had a better use for the money needed to properly fund a retirement plan. It would then become a self-fulfilling prophecy used to justify terminating the plan.

Steve Lester, a bassist for forty-one years, had long been active in the union. He was chair of the negotiating committee and had served as a union-appointed trustee for the pension fund. He believes that management's underfunding was premeditated—not only to use the money for the building fund but also because management had been intending to eventually terminate the pension and substitute a 401(k). From management's point of view, there was no need to properly fund the pension plan.

Marilyn Katz, who worked on communications and political strategy for the union, saw the pension struggle in a still broader context in which the ultimate dystopian goal of management was to convert the musicians into contract labor in the new gig economy.[6] They would be paid a set amount for each concert/gig, like Uber drivers. Management would not be responsible for providing health or retirement benefits, and there would be no employment security.

Management would be free to replace veteran players with more talented new applicants. The logic of the best person for the position might sound appealing, but it would completely undermine the harmony in both the musical and personal sense needed to maintain the quality of an orchestra. Musicians need to be both skilled individual players and capable of working with other orchestra members. Having players change constantly would be a recipe for discordance. But management seemed tone death to that concern.

Management announced the hard freeze during spring 2019 contract negotiations. The negative reaction from the musicians was instantaneous. It touched off the strike. Conductors usually stay neutral during orchestra strikes. But CSO conductor Riccardo Muti, who understood the musical as well as financial stakes, said, "I'm with the musicians," and joined the picket line.[7] It would be an epic struggle pitting world-class musicians against world-class wealth in a board of trustees made up of individuals representing some of the most powerful financial interests in the country. Helen Zell, chair of the board, is the wife of real estate magnate turned corporate raider Sam Zell, known in the corporate world as "the grave dancer."[8] He thrived by taking advantage of the misfortunes of other investors. He bought their distressed assets and was able to make them profitable for himself. With a fortune of $5.6 billion, he ranks 114th on the *Forbes* list of the wealthiest Americans.[9]

To garner public support, the orchestra, conducted by Muti, gave twenty free concerts, drawing in Black, Latino, schoolchildren, and other communities, many of whose members could not afford the prices of regular concert tickets. It was enormously successful and won the relatively high-salaried strikers support from Chicagoans who had much lower incomes.

Management, though, refused to budge. It rebuffed all attempts, including testimony from retirement experts, brought in from around the country to persuade it to keep the pension plan. According to Lester, it was clear that management entered the negotiations determined to impose the 401(k) on the musicians. It had no interest in compromise solutions such as hybrid plans.[10]

It is useful to look at major symphony financing in the United States to understand the attitude of management. Ticket sales account for only a minority of the funding of performing institutions: 32 percent of the CSO's $73.6 million 2018 operating budget.[11] The balance comes from contributions, overwhelmingly from wealthy individuals, families, and foundations. Not surprising, the Zell family, through its family foundation, was the CSO's lead contributor, explaining why Helen Zell landed the position of chair of its board of trustees.[12] It is different for counterparts in Europe where the arts receive much higher tax-funded public support. Public subsidies, for example, make up 60 percent of the Vienna State Opera budget. Logically, the board of directors of an orchestra such as the CSO has members who answered to their rich contributors, just as a corporate board of directors represents the interests of owners. It is further logical that if in the private corporate world 401(k)s had replaced pensions, it would seem proper for the CSO's board to do the same with its retirement plan. The board members might appreciate the value of music, but they came from a different world more in tune with the interests of high finance, which have benefited considerably from the management and control of 401(k) retirement plans. These were men and women quite accustomed to firing employees and cutting their benefits. They undoubtedly also shared the corporate belief that any worker, no matter how skilled, is replaceable.

The strike forced the cancellation of twenty-seven regularly scheduled concerts. As it wore on without resolution of the central pension issue, it threatened to force the cancellation of the entire next season's performances. The board, most likely, was willing to let that happen. None of its members had personal income at stake, and a long strike could benefit the CSO financially since there would be no need to pay salaries and benefits. A prolonged work stoppage would harm the musicians much more. They were receiving some strike pay from their union, but that replaced only a minuscule amount of their regular incomes.

The protracted strike was averted when both sides agreed to have Mayor Rahm Emanuel broker further talks. What he helped to hammer out was enough of a tentative agreement to bring the musicians back to work. There was an agreement in principle to replace the pension plan with a 401(k). But many details remained to be worked out. To say it was a reluctant agreement on the part of the musicians would be an understatement. It was a case captured by the Latin phrase *coactus volui* (it is his wish, although coerced). Management agreed to delay implementation of the freeze, which would help veteran members. Interestingly, it agreed to make up any retirement income losses by the switch for the veteran musicians. How that would occur was unclear. This was an upfront admission that the new 401(k) plan would result in a benefit reduction. New members received no such guarantee. Veteran union members were well aware of the danger of a two-tier retirement plan between them and new members. They succeeded in getting management to agree to set up a study group with them to develop ways to remedy the shortcomings of the 401(k) plan for new members as well as for themselves. By my estimation, new members who served twenty-five years with a 401(k) plan would receive as much as 42 percent less in retirement income than if they had been in the pension plan the full time.

Dubious Free Choice

In 1980, Joy Lindsey started a new job as an English as a Second Language instructor at Houston Community College. At the Human Resources office, she picked up her new office keys and filled out forms for a parking pass and health insurance. Then she came to the form for her retirement benefit. It required her to make an irrevocable choice between the Teachers Retirement System, a defined benefit pension plan sponsored by the state of Texas, and a defined contribution Optional Retirement Plan. She didn't know what to do. She asked the HR employee for advice. He said that the ORP plan was better because its investments had outperformed those of the TRS. That settled it and she signed up for the ORP plan.[13]

Twenty-five years later, a number of co-workers that had begun when she had were retiring. She was fifty-nine, a little early to retire.

But so were a number of them around that age. Feeling somewhat burned out by the job herself, she decided to join them. She then investigated what her retirement income would be and was shocked to learn that it would not be nearly enough to meet her monthly expenses. Making matters worse, Houston Community College did not participate in the Social Security system. She received no Social Security credits for the highest earning years of her career. Her Social Security check would be minimal, based only on contributions from earlier, lower-paying jobs.

Lacking the income to fully retire, she began a series of part-time jobs. Meanwhile, she was hearing from co-workers who had retired at the same time that they were not having to take part-time work. Instead, they were making plans to travel abroad for extended vacations. How was it possible for them to afford that comfortable retirement lifestyle and not her? The answer, she found out, was simple. They had opted for the pension plan when she had taken the individual savings and investment account option. Despite having the same incomes and years of service, they had pensions that rendered far more retirement income than her 403(b) retirement savings plan.

She was learning the hard way that 401(k)-like plans are not nearly as good as traditional pension plans. But hadn't the HR person back in 1980 advised her that the opposite would be true? Indeed, the HR person had repeated what a lot of people thought, who themselves had been influenced by the rosy sales pitches of the financial services industry that profits off retirement savings plans. In telling her that ORP investments were doing better than TRS ones, he sounded knowledgeable, giving reasonable advice. But that comparison was irrelevant since the TRS pension benefits were based on years of service and salaries, not stock market returns. To be fair, HR clerical staff are often asked questions that they are not trained to know how to answer and they have no backup experts to whom they could refer new employees. That's a role unions, if they exist, could play since pensions are often a central benefit of union membership. But at the time that Joy Lindsey began, there was no union at Houston Community College.

Free choice sounds like a universal positive. Who wouldn't want it in the abstract? But it's one thing when it's possible to have an informed free choice and quite another when it isn't, as was her experience and that of others who had to make irrevocable loaded choices between retirement plans they were ill-equipped to evaluate.

Most people in Lindsey's situation who realize that they would have fared much better in a pension plan assume that there is no way to reverse the decision. If they ask HR staff, they are quickly reminded that it was an *irrevocable* choice. But this is not exactly true. There have been a number of successful struggles, most led by unions, to allow people to switch to pension plans if their employers offer them. We'll look at some of them in chapter 16. Still, the vast majority don't know this and make do with what they have.

When I spoke to Lindsey fifteen years after leaving Houston Community College, she was in her mid-seventies and still working to make ends meet. She was bitter about the unfairness of receiving a much lower retirement income than colleagues with similar positions and years of experience. Her life was a continual struggle. She had the advantage of good health. She had made a virtue out of necessity in that she did not mind being frugal. For a number of years, she tried different investment strategies to maximize the income from her retirement savings account and had had some success. She thought she was getting close to the point that her Social Security plus retirement savings incomes would be enough to cover her monthly expenses. Any future tanking of the stock market, however, would push her back into the red.

I didn't ask her whether her adult children had pitched in to help. I do know from correspondence with other retirees with low incomes from 401(k)-like plans that this is often the case. A woman who had read some of my critical writings about these types of plans wrote: "Up until I retired, I didn't really know what went wrong with my retirement plans and assumed that it was somehow my fault although I have always been a saver and had put in an extra $100/month to my 403(b) as long as I was a full-time employee. It meant a lot to me to know that my predicament was not just the result of poor planning on my part. When I run into former colleagues who also retired, I find that they are in the same boat. One has gone back to work full-time and another, a good bit older than me, is working two jobs." Another 401(k) retiree wrote of having felt guilty about having to get support from her adult children. She and her children had assumed that the blame was hers for coming up short and needing help.

A Dangerous Precedent

Defined-benefit pension plans are supposed to have guaranteed payments. If their trust funds run into shortfalls, it is up to the fund's trustees to find ways to make them up. The Pension Benefit Guaranty Corporation, created under the Employee Retirement Income Security Act, is the backstop for the private pension system. It functions as insurance with private pension plans required to make regular premium payments. If a fund goes bankrupt, the PBGC takes over payment, usually at a reduced amount, of owed pensions. ERISA tries to avoid that by requiring private pension plans to prefund benefits, while at the same time making insurance payments to the PBGC to cover remaining bankruptcy possibilities. Pensions remain at least partially guaranteed. 401(k)s and other retirement savings plans, in contrast, have no guarantees at any level.

Up to 2014, a private pension sponsor could only get out of future obligations by either declaring bankruptcy or freezing the pension to new benefit accruals. It had no way to maintain the same failing pension plan without making up all of the losses itself. If it maintained the pension plan, it had to maintain the same payments to pensioners and accrual credits to active workers covered by the plan.

In 2014, Congress enacted legislation that modified part of this system by giving multi-employer plan sponsors a new option: to make up losses by reducing payments to pensioners. It modified just part of the system because it covered only multi-employer plans rather than all private pension plans. Usually unions, such as the Laborers International Union, the Teamsters, and the American Federation of Musicians, sponsor pension plans for industries where workers typically go from job to job and employer to employer. Construction workers build for different developers. Truckers drive for different shipping companies. Musicians play at different clubs. There are approximately 1,400 multi-employer pension plans with ten million participants in the United States.[14] About one-third are in trucking and mining.[15] They cover just over a quarter of all defined benefit pension plan participants.[16]

The Multiemployer Reform Act of 2014, among other provisions, allows pension plan trustees to petition the Treasury Department to lower pension payments if the plan trust fund is in danger of running out of money within fifteen years or, in some cases, twenty years. They must file, in the technical language of the Act, "critical and declining status" notices, that is, briefs that the trust fund is in critical danger with a declining balance that will result in it running out of money to pay pensions. The Treasury Department then evaluates the application to authorize or deny the sought cuts. The intention of the pension cuts is to financially restabilize the plan so that it can survive into the future. It also provides an alternative for sponsors to pension freezes.

There is a limit to how much trustees can reduce pensions—110 percent of the amount guaranteed by the PBGC. If, for example, a retiree had a $10,000 annual pension that the PBGC fully guaranteed, plan trustees could only cut the pension to $11,000 (110 percent of $1,000). It is significant that the maximum pensions that the PBGC guarantees for multi-employer plans are far lower than they are for single-employer plans. This means the potential for draconian pension cuts is far greater for multi-employer plan participants under the MPRA provisions than if similar legislation existed for single-employer plans.

While people often erroneously believe that most pension plans, especially those sponsored by unions, are teetering on the brink of financial collapse, most multi-employer plans are in fact unaffected by the legislation because they are financially stable with no need to make cuts to achieve survival. The PBGC projects that only about 10 percent of multi-employer plan participants are in plans that are in danger of running out of money.[17] In the first five years of the Act, trustees for thirty-two plans covering nearly 600,000 participants filed "critical and declining status" notices. By far, the Teamsters Central States Pension Fund with 411,000 participants was the largest. Of those, the Treasury Department authorized pension reductions for seventeen plans covering 95,000 participants, just 0.2 percent of participants in all multi-employer plans.[18] It denied the Teamsters Central States Pension Fund application. Nevertheless, this breach of the inviolability of pension guarantees was a dangerous precedent that labor unions fought a losing battle to stop in Congress. Many pensioners feared that they too were vulnerable to losing part of their payments in the future, causing them to be nervous about the finances of their plans. Knowing that most participants are safe from pension cuts provides no solace if you are in the minority that are not.

Among them was Kelly Stillwell, for twenty-five years a construction worker and Laborers Union activist in Las Vegas. He was approaching retirement and depending on his union-sponsored multi-employer pension when he heard that Congress was debating that bill. He had worked for a number of different construction companies in the Las Vegas area, all of which had contributed to his union-sponsored pension plan over the years of his career. Now he feared that he might not be getting as much of a pension as he assumed was coming and what he needed. He talked to fellow participants about his fears. He made inquiries through his union. He tried to get information from the plan trustees.

Was his pension vulnerable? It was unclear. The answer was not easy to find. But after a great deal of effort, he determined that his pension plan had a 52 percent funding ratio, which was less than the 65 percent ratio that permitted plan trustees to file for "critical and declining status." He thought they were in real danger and stepped up his campaign among fellow participants. When Congress passed the Multiemployer Pension Reform Act, Stillwell put up a website with pension information for people in his situation (www.retiredunionworkers.org).

So far, the trustees have not filed for critical and declining status and have not announced any intention to do so. Stillwell thinks that the attention he drew to the issue may have discouraged them from pursuing that strategy. However, he remained wary of what could happen in the future now that trimming pension rights is an option.[19]

Running a Pension Fund Into the Ground

Adam Krauthamer is president of 802, the largest local of the American Federation of Musicians. AFM has locals across the country, from the show business capital of New York to the movie capital of Hollywood and all points, large and small, in between where musicians ply their trade. In New York City 802 members play in multiple venues, from jazz clubs to Broadway shows, symphonies, and operas.

He grew up in that area. His father was a schoolteacher and, like him, a union member. He remembered that his father thought that the pension he was earning was the most valuable benefit of union membership. That had allowed him to look forward, as he was working and raising his children, to one day being able to retire with adequate income.

Krauthamer always remembered his father's appreciation of the union-negotiated pension benefit as he began his own career as a freelance French horn player for Broadway shows. Like his parents before him, he was accruing credits in a union-negotiated pension plan. This was a multi-employer plan tailored to the working realities of most musicians who go from employer to employer—in his case, from Broadway show to Broadway show.[20]

One day, Krauthamer received an ominous letter from the pension plan's trustees. They were warning him and other participants that the plan would likely soon be in critical and declining condition and that they would have no choice but to use the provisions of the Multiemployer Pension Reform Act to apply to the Department of the Treasury to reduce benefits. The letter came out of the blue. Previous trustee letters had assured members that the plan was in good financial shape. The letter ended with especially ominous advice:

> Many of you have asked "What can we, the participants, do now?" Given our financial status, we are faced with the reality

of the one-dollar benefit multiplier as the basis for any benefits earned in the future. This means that while the AFM-EPF pension you receive will still be important, for many the benefit will be a modest one. A modest pension emphasizes the importance of having a comprehensive retirement strategy that includes a personal savings component to supplement the AFM-EPF pension and Social Security benefits.[21]

After years of assuring him that the pension plan was stable, they were now telling him it was not and he should start a savings plan instead. Krauthamer, with his family pension experience, was alarmed. He was not the only one. There were a lot of other musician members who noticed. Getting a pension was a big part of the value of being in the union. Concerned questions poured into the trustees, forcing them to sponsor a series of meetings around the country to explain what was happening to the pension fund and to defend their plan to file for permission to reduce benefits to token amounts.

The American Federation of Musicians & Employers' Pension Fund had 50,000 participants. But there was great variation in how important or consequential the pension plan was for each of them because of the nature of the performing musician business. For people like Krauthamer and about half the plan members, it was their entire career. For others, it amounted to no more than a part-time job. They might have day jobs and perform weekend gigs. There were many who spent only a few years or less playing for money and then went on to more financially stable careers. All had accrued at least some credits in the plan, but only about half were depending on it for consequential retirement incomes. Those for whom the pension income would be token didn't bother to open the trustees' letter, much less voice concerns about it. That allowed the trustees to take the public attitude that only a minority were concerned.

This division between plan members who are depending on the pension benefits for a substantial part of their retirement incomes and those who aren't is true for nearly all multi-employer plans, whether in construction, music, television, Hollywood, or performing music.

It was a division that became an important part of the Multiemployer Pension Reform Act. To block pension cuts under the act, a majority of pension plan participants must vote in opposition. Typically, in such elections, non-voters are the largest or nearly the largest blocks. Those are the part-time or temporary members who have little financial stake in the plan. The majority of the members for whom the plan is consequential can be opposed to the cuts but their no votes don't add up to a majority of the participants.

At the AFM-EPF meetings for participants, the trustees blamed the fund's financial problems on the 2008 market crash that had taken with it a sizeable amount of plan assets and demographic and industry trends that had reduced the ratio between active and retired participants.

Krauthamer and a number of other attendees weren't convinced. They began to meet, which led to the formation of Musicians for Pension Security (MPS). Its mission: to seek out information about the pension fund, educate participants, and try to stop trustee efforts to reduce benefits using the Multiemployer Pension Reform Act. They began distributing a newsletter and set up a website (www. musiciansforpensionsecurity.com), which I think is a model for this type of organizing. It is filled with easy to navigate information. In time, they were able to engage up to 20,000 of the 50,000 plan participants. That would make a great majority of full-time musicians for whom the pension plan was vital for retirement income. As their voluntary organization grew, it became clear that money was needed to hire outside actuarial, legal, and investment experts. That led to fundraisers and putting a donate button on the website. Participants responded with enough money to finance the needed expenditures.

They found that though it was true enough that the plan trust fund had a declining balance, there were questions about the trustees' explanations for the losses and, certainly, questions about whether pension cuts were the only solution. If the 2008 market crash and demographic trends were the causes of the losses, as the trustees maintained, why were peer plans, such as that for the American Federation of Television and Radio Artists and the Canadian affiliate of the AFM, which had also gone through the 2008 crash and had the same demographic conditions, able to recover quickly and now be in good financial shape? The only possible conclusion was that the AFM-EPF trustees had botched the recovery with poor investment planning. They also found that their plan had unusually high administrative expenses, including a $422,000 salary for one trustee. And that trustee had received large raises despite poor investment performances.

The revelation of the trustees' poor investing led two plan participants, independent of MPS, to sue the trustees for breach of fiduciary responsibilities. The judge agreed with the plaintiffs that the trustees had shown poor investment judgment. The suit was settled with the trustees not admitting fault but being required to pay a $27 million settlement, which came from insurance carried by the trustees. After legal costs, about $16 million went into the pension trust fund.[22]

Another fundamental question was why the trustees seemed to be dead set on reducing benefits as the only way to stabilize the fund. It might be defendable to reduce very generous benefits. But that wasn't the case with the AFM-EPF pension. Its accrual rate had already been decreased by three-quarters since the 1990s. Why were the trustees not backing legislative efforts in Washington to reverse the pension cut provision of the Multiemployer Pension Reform Act and finding alternative sources to make up the shortages?

That the trustees saw pension cuts as the only way out became clear when they took the first opportunity to apply for them through the U.S. Department of the Treasury. At the time of the letter to members, the pension fund was on its way to, but not at, the critical and declining status to be eligible to apply to Treasury for cuts. One of the metrics for the critical and declining status is to have less than a 65 percent funding ratio. Two years later the plan slipped under 65 percent and the trustees immediately filed for cuts. Treasury denied the application on a seeming actuarial technicality regarding mortality assumptions. That denial did not prohibit the trustees from filing again, which it did the next year.

A Welcome Victory

As some plan trustees were busy trying to cut pension benefits, the potential victims were lobbying Congress to rescue the pension plans. Most efforts centered around the Butch Lewis Act. Lewis was a truck driver member of the Teamster Central States Fund who stood to have the pension he had worked decades for slashed by over half. He rallied fellow participants and they began lobbying Congress to block the cuts. Especially galling to them was that the Teamsters had often sacrificed needed raises so that the money could be used to support the pension fund. And now it wasn't going to be there for them. On New Year's Eve, 2016, he died of a massive stroke. His wife, Rita, thought it had been brought on by the stress over the pension cuts. She then took over leadership and became the dynamic face of resistance to the unfair cuts. She herself faced an even bleaker financial future with her husband gone. Her survivor's pension ($2,500 a month, 75 percent of Butch's pension) would drop to $1,400 if the cuts went through. That would not be enough for her to afford to stay in the house they had lived in for decades.[23]

The Butch Lewis Act would have mandated that the federal government subsidize loans to the pension funds as an alternative to cuts. The Act gathered significant congressional support, but not enough to overcome Republican control of the Senate and White House during the Trump presidency. Then a lot of unexpected things happened. In 2020, the Covid-19 pandemic threw the country into a public health crisis. Democrats prevailed in an unusually close presidential election and took back, just barely, control of the Senate. That allowed the new Biden presidency to pass a $1.9 trillion American Rescue Plan relief package. Little noticed was that the rescue plan included the Butch Lewis Emergency Pension Plan Relief Act. Unlike the original version, it included $86 billion in grants rather than loans to rescue distressed multi-employer plans. The cut benefits of about 100,000 pensioners were restored. Those approaching retirement would get what they were originally promised.

Rita Lewis was thrilled at the news in a call with Senator Sherrod

Brown (Dem.-Ohio), the Act's chief sponsor. She repeated the mantra of the lobbying campaign, "a promise is a promise is a promise." Kelly Stillwell, the retired Las Vegas construction worker, wrote on his website, "VICTORY VICTORY VICTORY." The Pension Rights Center, which had been a key backer of the lobbying campaign, wrote, "Time to celebrate!" The Musicians for Pension Security wrote on its website to members, "With your help, pension relief is now a reality!" It called on them to be ever vigilant going forward to make sure that their pension fund remained healthy.

What happened was what is supposed to happen but often does not. People fought back against an injustice—cutting their promised pensions. They lobbied their political representatives in Congress for relief, and relief was delivered. Stripped to its bare bones, victims of an injustice organized to put pressure on political officeholders to use government resources to democratically remedy the situation. Quite often, the injustice is palpable enough and the victims get organized, but the political step is blocked. In this case, it took two unexpected Democratic Party victories in U.S. Senate elections in Georgia to tip the balance enough, just barely at that, to make possible the passage of the Butch Lewis Emergency Pension Plan Relief Act.

This, in turn, would not have been possible had the victims not organized to fight back. It is unlikely that the Democratic Party members of Congress would have acted on their behalf as they did had they not been collectively pressured to do so. The existence of the pension injustice alone would not have been enough to move them to effective action. In this case, the victims were members of a collective pension plan. That gave them an inclination to work together since they were members of a common plan. It is a theme that we will return to in this book—that pension plan members are more likely to act collectively to defend themselves than members of individual retirement account plans.

PART III

EMPLOYER-SPONSORED RETIREMENT SAVINGS PLANS

12

Origins of the 401(k)

I n 1890, business tycoon Andrew Carnegie was a trustee at Cornell University. He was shocked to find out how low the pay of professors was and that they did not have pensions for their retirement. Carnegie thought that he could solve that problem with an endowment of $10,000,000 to finance pensions at colleges and universities. Carnegie enlisted twenty-five educators to become trustees of the Carnegie Foundation for the Advancement of Teaching that would administer the pension plan. The pensions, which began in 1906, were free to faculty members who had served at least fifteen years and had reached age 65. Their pensions would be half of their final salaries. It was an exceptionally generous defined benefit plan. The multiplier could be as high as 3.3 percent, much higher than the vast majority of final salary defined benefit pension plans today. It was innovative in that the pension rights followed the professors if they moved to another university within the participant universities, which grew to ninety-six. In that sense, it was a multi-employer plan with the portability of pension benefits.

But within a very few years, by 1915, it was clear that the plan was not financially sustainable. The endowment was not enough to generate sufficient revenue to finance the pensions. In 1923, the benefit formula changed to a less generous one. In 1931, the plan was closed to new entrants. The Carnegie Foundation made good on its promises for the free pensions to those already in the plan. It continued to pay them in full down to the 1990s when the last of the original beneficiaries died. Altogether, it paid out $87 million in the money-draining operation. Meanwhile, beginning in 1915, the foundation leaders had been at work designing what would become the Teachers Insurance and Annuity Association (TIAA) to solve the retirement problem.

Primarily the Carnegie Foundation, backed by the Carnegie Corporation, was looking for a way to get out of new pension obligations without abandoning the quest for faculty retirement benefits altogether. It wanted a new system that both benefited faculty and was financially sustainable. To make it viable, it would need ongoing contributions and not just depend on income from an endowment. To benefit faculty, it would have to carry over the principle of portability. It could be enhanced portability if more colleges and universities joined the pool of retirement benefit sponsors.

TIAA Pioneers a Model

What emerged after much planning was TIAA. Its full name indicated its approach: the Teachers Insurance and Annuity Association. It had the following components:

Teachers and their employers would each make contributions.

The contributions would purchase deferred annuities, redeemable in lifetime incomes upon retirement. The greater the value of the deferred annuities, the higher the retirement income. (Deferred annuities are annuities that begin making payments to their owners in the future, whereas immediate annuities make payments immediately. In theory, deferred annuities should offer much higher payments since they have time to accumulate increased values through investing.)

Teachers could keep adding to their TIAA benefit as they moved from university to university so long as the new university also sponsored a TIAA plan.

Each participant had an individual account that contained the deferred annuities whose current values were known and reported.

This approach formed the prototype for what would later become the 401(k). But it would have to evolve further before it entirely resembled it and similar retirement savings plans.

TIAA started as a nonprofit corporation, a status that allowed it to build up considerable faculty trust. The assumption was that even though it was a private corporation, its profits would be reinvested in higher benefits for participants rather than distributed to stock owners.

In 1952, TIAA expanded into stock market equity investing. Up until that time, all of its investments had been in bonds. To carry out that part of its business, it created a wing named the College Retirement Equities Fund (CREF), and the overall company renamed itself as TIAA-CREF (In 2016, it reverted to its original singular TIAA name). This was the beginning of weakening the annuity component of its retirement plan. Contributions were no longer strictly dedicated to producing lifetime income annuities, like pensions, upon retirement.

The company grew considerably over its early decades as more colleges and universities joined. It also expanded outside of colleges and universities to hospital, government, and nonprofit employees. As of 2017, it was one of the largest money managers in the world, with nearly $1 trillion in assets that it managed for its five million participants.[1] Its portability feature was especially attractive. Also attractive was that it was supposedly nonprofit and presumably more trustworthy than Wall Street–aligned money management firms.

While TIAA started and was for nearly seven decades a not-for-profit company, it lost that status in 1997. TIAA did not widely announce to participants this change to a for-profit company, and many continue to believe that it is still nonprofit. TIAA now advertises itself as having a "nonprofit heritage."

As a corporation, TIAA has ownership shares. Its Board of Overseers owns all of the shares. But unlike other corporations, these overseers are not free to publicly trade the shares on stock markets.

Nor do they have individual ownership of them. The TIAA charter states that the function of the Board of Overseers is to hold the shares for the interest of the company and its participants. It is to distribute profits to the participants as higher interest payments. But several recent legal actions have contended that TIAA also distributes profits to its top management as multimillion-dollar compensation packages and to its over 5,000 sales agents as bonuses.[2]

How Good Is TIAA Today?

TIAA has escaped much of the increasing criticism of 401(k)-type plans. Many academics with TIAA-administered plans are unaware that it is a 401(k)-type plan, thinking that the growing criticisms of 401(k)s do not apply to their situations.

TIAA enjoyed relative immunity from criticism for two reasons. It was assumed, albeit erroneously, to be a nonprofit company that operated exclusively in the best interests of its participants because it did not have shareholders. And precisely because it was the plan of so many highly educated professors, it was presumed to be good because, surely, they must know what they are doing. (In fact, as I found out after counseling hundreds of higher education professors and administrators, very few of them had more than a superficial understanding about how the plans worked or realistic estimations of what to expect in terms of retirement income.)

Yet TIAA participants fare no better in retirement income than other 401(k)-type plan participants with other financial services industry companies such as Prudential, Vanguard, and Valic.

Like other companies, TIAA charges third-party administrator fees to manage investments, fees that come out of the account balances of its participants. This is a major problem for all participants in 401(k)-type plans. As a competitive company, TIAA advertises heavily to convince participants to contribute more, to maintain its hold over existing accounts, and secure new business. The costs of the advertising come out of the accounts of participants. These costs are at the expense of their future retirement incomes.

Among the places where TIAA prominently advertises is in the publications of the American Association of University Professors, the organization that represents a large percentage of its participants. AAUP, not surprisingly, does not take a critical stance toward TIAA, seeming to treat is as a fixture of university life as normal as the English Department.

TIAA's top managers and trustees have joined the general corporate trend of increasing their already high pay packages, which diminishes more assets to provide retirement incomes. In 2018, CEO Roger W. Ferguson Jr. received a compensation package worth $24,200,000. Four other top managers received over $6,000,000. Its fifteen Board of Trustees members, which include nine outside corporate executives and six academics from Harvard, Cornell, Princeton, Yale, Howard, and Illinois, received base compensations of $310,000 with $20,000 to $25,000 extra payment for chairing board subcommittees. For attending meetings outside of their regular schedules, they received $2,000 per session.[3]

Like other financial services giants, TIAA defends the high compensation of its top managers and trustees as being necessary "to attract, retain, motivate and reward employees who possess the knowledge and experience we need to conduct our business."[4] In other words, because other financial services companies pay mega-salaries to top executives, TIAA also has to in order to get the top people. So much for it representing an alternative nonprofit philosophy.

Annuities were a crucial part of TIAA's original approach to retirement planning. They were supposed to mimic the lifetime incomes of the Carnegie Foundation's free pensions. When it was a nonprofit company, one would assume that TIAA could have offered annuities to its members on better terms than those provided by for-profit life insurance companies. Whatever the case with that, one might also assume that its "nonprofit heritage" might make its annuities at least less if not a lot less expensive than those of other commercial life insurance companies.

I put this assumption to the test by requesting by phone from TIAA what $100,000 would yield in lifetime monthly income for an

174 THE LABOR GUIDE TO RETIREMENT PLANS

age seventy retiree. The answer was from $642 to $666. I then compared that to three online commercial quotes. They were from $625 to $651, virtually the same.

I then compared those annuities with what was available on a truly nonprofit basis. The defined benefit Teachers Retirement System, operated by the State of Connecticut, sells annuities to its members. A $100,000 annuity for a seventy-year-old would yield $793 in lifetime monthly income, significantly more than the TIAA annuity. Because the Teachers Retirement System does not have the overhead costs of advertising, high executive compensations, and other expenses that TIAA has, it can charge its members significantly lower costs for annuities. In fairness, the Teachers Retirement System can also offer higher payouts because it has equity investments that yield more than the bond investments that the annuity parts of TIAA and other life insurance companies are restricted to by law. However, the general point holds: TIAA's annuities, despite its "nonprofit heritage," are no better for retirees than those of other commercial life insurance companies. It is not an alternative worth seeking out.

Origins of the 401(k)

The central feature of a 401(k)-like plan is tax deferral. It allows participants to avoid paying income taxes on employer and their own contributions until they start withdrawing the savings when they retire. This tax deferral carries advantages. If a worker has a salary of $80,000 and receives an additional employer contribution of 5 percent or $4,000, total compensation is $84,000, all of which would have been taxable before those plans. But with the inauguration of them, the extra $4,000 was not taxable in the year it was received, along with any additional contributions made by the worker. Let's say the worker also contributes $4,000. This means that instead of $84,000 being taxable, only $76,000 would be taxed that year. Assuming a 10 percent tax rate, this would be a savings of $800. The savings might be higher if the reduction in taxable income resulted in having to pay a lower marginal tax rate since we have a progressive tax system where higher incomes pay higher rates. The Internal Revenue Service also defers taxes on any investment returns from such retirement savings accounts. Total tax payments are not only deferred but also reduced. When participants retire, they pay taxes on just what they withdraw during the retirement year. Since retirement income, in most cases, is less than working income, they will be paying lower marginal tax rates.

In essence, the federal government subsidizes through loss of potential tax revenue participants in tax-deferred retirement savings plans, such as 401(k)s. The amount of lost tax revenue is in the range of $150 billion yearly. It also subsidizes the financial services industry indirectly since the tax deferral feature encourages employees to save in those accounts, which generate industry profits. It is similar to the effect that the home mortgage interest deduction has on increasing the prices of houses that buyers can afford and also the profits of the real estate industry. Tax revenue lost through the mortgage interest deduction is approximately $30 billion a year, much less than that lost from tax deferrals on 401(k)-like contributions.[5]

TIAA plans have had the tax deferral feature since their beginning in 1918 (legally formalized in 1942). But those plans only covered college and university employees, and the tax deferral only applied to what the employers and employees were required to contribute to the plans. The origins of the 401(k) plan have to do with adding new categories of workers who were eligible to have tax-deferred retirement savings plans and increasing the amounts of money they could voluntarily put in them.

In the Technical Amendment Act of 1958, Congress added the 403(b) provision to the Internal Revenue Code. That allowed college employees to voluntarily set up additional tax-deferred retirement savings accounts into which they could contribute up to 20 percent of their incomes. Subsequently, government and nonprofit employees would become eligible for 403(b) accounts. Other pre-401(k) increases in tax-deferred retirement savings plans included Keogh plans for small businesses and their employees in 1962 and some further extensions of eligibility under the 1974 ERISA act.

All of the tax deferral options after that for TIAA-type plans were assumed to be supplemental to primary retirement plan vehicles, which were mainly traditional defined-benefit pension plans. They were a way to financially encourage employees to build up the third leg of the proverbial three-legged retirement stool of Social Security, a pension, and additional personal savings.

The 401(k) section was added to the Internal Revenue Code via the Revenue Act of 1978, taking effect in 1980. It regulated tax-deferred profit-sharing plans that had been in existence since the 1960s. Employers had developed the profit-sharing plans to replace bonus plans. The problem with the once-yearly bonuses before Christmas was that they were fully taxable. That was a special problem for executives and other highly paid employees when the then marginal tax rate on extra income was as high as 75 percent. An executive could lose $15,000 of a $20,000 bonus to taxes. The Treasury Department, without congressional authorization, had allowed employers to resolve that problem by setting up an alternative way to give bonuses that were tax-deferred. The profit-sharing plans that replaced bonuses required that at least half the amount given to the employee went into a tax-deferred savings account. The rest, or fractions of the rest, could be received as taxable income or added to the deferred tax retirement savings account. Higher-paid employees were more likely to take advantage of this provision to put it all in tax-deferred retirement savings. They had a less immediate need for the extra pay for Christmas expenses.

Congress added the 401(k) provision both to assert its authority over the Treasury Department on taxing matters and to address the discriminatory way in which the tax subsidy was favoring higher-compensated employees, which it defined as the top third. The 401(k) provision placed limits on but did not end the discrimination.

The existence of the 401(k) led many benefits lawyers and consultants to conclude that it potentially gave employers great latitude to go beyond profit-sharing plans to set up more ambitious supplementary retirement savings plans. Many companies, including JCPenney, PepsiCo, and Johnson & Johnson, developed proposals.

In 1981, the Internal Revenue Service during the Reagan administration developed regulations for 401(k) plans. They allowed payroll deductions to fund them. After the release of the rules, several corporations began to set them up. At this point, they were still being established alongside existing defined-benefit pensions as supplementary savings vehicles. In addition to the profit-sharing plans, which were now transformed into 401(k)s, there were also other after-tax payroll deduction savings plans that similarly changed to 401(k)s.

In record time, corporations would move from having 401(k)s as supplements to defined-benefit plans to substitutes for them. This was entirely an employer prerogative that required no special legislation. As always, it was their choice to have or not have any type of employee retirement benefit. Closing out pension plans had to follow laws and regulations, but those were apart from the laws and regulations about 401(k)s.

Accountant Ted Benna was one of the pioneers of the 401(k) development that transformed private sector retiree benefits. Today he has somewhat mixed feelings about what he helped to wrought. He is critical of the fees charged for administering the accounts. He thinks the addition of multiple investment options added complexity that resulted in higher fees. He would prefer limited simple choices. He would also like at least 90 percent of plan accumulations to be automatically annuitized upon retirement to provide certainty of life incomes as do pension plans.[6]

13

Saving Up to Spend Down

All retirement savings plans—401(k)s, 403(b)s, 457s, Individual Retirement Accounts, and others—go through two phases. Their *accumulation* or saving phase takes place during work years. Workers save and invest part of their wages or salaries. The *spend-down* phase occurs when they use their accumulated funds to provide income for retirement living expenses. I will start the discussion counterintuitively with the second phase, the spend-down, for reasons that will become clear.

401(k) Retirement Income Options

Few participants in 401(k)-type plans have thought through how their savings accounts will produce incomes once they retire. To the extent they pay attention at all, they focus on the growing balances of those accounts. There is an act of faith that somehow their savings discipline will produce an adequate retirement income.

Ideally, as was the original idea behind retirement savings accounts, account accumulations would seamlessly turn into life annuities upon retirement. The account balances would be annuitized. TIAA, the pioneer in the field, in its early days made the connection between accumulations and annuities clear to participants. The TIAA side of the fund contained deferred annuities. Participants invested their money in annuities that made regular payments for life upon retirement. That connection began to loosen when TIAA added the College Retirement Equites Fund (CREF) side of the fund, wherein participants could now invest in equities as well as deferred annuities. Equities don't have any automatic way to be turned into life incomes upon retirement.

By the time 401(k)-type plans had become the dominant type of retirement plan in the 1980s, annuitization had become a spend-down option that very few retirees chose. There are several reasons. The first owes to the nature of commercial annuities sold by for-profit life insurance companies. They are expensive because, in addition to administrative costs, they also have costs associated with profit needs and advertising. A brochure describing occupational retirement plans in the Netherlands (where, by law, annuities are strictly nonprofit) explains the different prices of for-profit and not-for-profit annuities.

> In the Netherlands, the average [annuity] costs amount to about 3.5% of the contribution. This means that almost all the contribution goes toward building up pension benefits. The situation with life insurance companies who offer individual annuity insurance is quite different. These organizations incur marketing costs in addition to administration costs. Furthermore, commercial insurers are expected to make a profit. As a result of this accumulation of costs, a life insurance company can spend 25.7% of the premiums on matters other than building up pension benefits.[1]

Over the last several decades, annuity costs have accelerated. The average price to purchase an annuity for an age 65 male that would have a payout of $1,000 a month rose from $104,999 in 1986 to $180,180 in 2019. For the same age female, the cost increased from $130,565 to $189,753. The average payout yields decreased respectively, from 11.4 to 6.7 percent and 9.1 to 6.3 percent.[2] Put differently, annuities became 71.6 percent more expensive for males and 45.3 percent more costly for females.

Compounding the problem for females is that they suffer discrimination in the annuities market. The sellers of commercial annuities,

TABLE 13.1: Average Cost of Immediate Life Annuity with $1,000 Monthly Payout, Age 65

	Male	Female
1986	$104,999	$130,565
1990	$113,636	$120,831
1995	$129,249	$137,969
2000	$120,598	$131,718
2005	$155,690	$168,890
2010	$158,479	$169,205
2015	$185,874	$198,807
2019	$180,180	$189,753

Source: Calculated from *Annuity Shopper Buyer's Guide, 1986–2019.*

mainly life insurance companies, charge women higher prices than men due to their longer average life spans. In 2019, average annuity prices for women at age 65 were 5.3 percent higher than for men. Defined benefit pensions and Social Security, to the contrary, use blended longevity assumptions.

Annuity costs rose primarily because interest rates decreased over the same period. Life insurance companies, by law, must invest what they receive from annuity sales in bonds since they yield guaranteed interest payments. In contrast, there are no guarantees that equity investments will increase in value. Added to that are the typical high costs of private life insurance company commissions, advertising expenses, and overhead.

With annuities becoming more expensive, investment advisors began telling clients it was better not to annuitize. Instead, retirees should keep investing—guided by the advisors' fee charging advice, of course. They could make periodic withdrawals from the accounts for their living expenses. But how much could they withdraw? Withdraw too much, and retirees would run out of money before death. Withdraw too little, and they would have to live on less income than necessary.

There is also a tradeoff between maximizing retirement income and having accumulations available for inheritance. If accumulations are annuitized, there will be more for living expenses but nothing for estates. If the withdrawal rate starts at the industry 4 percent rule of thumb, there will be less for living expenses but likely some amount left over for inheritance.

How Much Needs to Be Accumulated in 401(k)s?

The simple answer to that question is: "enough to finance retirement." But how much is enough? Another possible response is enough to bridge the gap between what Social Security will provide and 70 percent of final income—the rule of thumb of retirement advisors. If Social Security provides 41 percent replacement income for the median worker—who has always had a median income—then the 401(k) would have to provide at least 29 percent of final income (70 percent minus 41 percent).

Let's run those numbers. The median income for full-time workers approaching retirement (age 55–64) is $54,756.[3] Twenty-nine percent of that equals $15,879. Following the 4 percent withdrawal rule, obtaining that amount would require an accumulation of $396,981 (.04 x $396,981 = $15,879). But, as we saw in chapter 3, many, indeed probably the majority of median-income workers at retirement did not start their careers as median-income workers. They started at lower incomes and worked their way up. They will, following the Social Security benefit formula, receive less than 41 percent of their final income. For every percent point less than 41, they will have to have a percent point higher of replacement income from their 401(k) or similar plan. If they started as minimum wage workers, their Social Security income would replace 31 percent rather than 41 percent of their final salary. To make up the difference, their 401(k) would have to yield 39 rather than 29 percent of their final income. To do that, they would need a much larger accumulation of $533,871. Either way, the needed accumulation is several times the average that participants have who are approaching retirement. According to a U.S. Government Accountability Office study, 52 percent of households inhabited by age 55 and older adults have no retirement savings. Of the 48 percent that do, the median amount is $109,000.[4] That median amount would be worth, following the 4 percent withdrawal rule, an annual retirement income of just $4,360.

Some retirement advisors use as a rule of thumb that one should have a goal of accumulating a 401(k)-portfolio worth ten times the size of the final salary. The problem with a single multiple of last salary goal is that Social Security replaces different amounts of pay according to total career earnings and averages. There is no one multiple of salary figure accurate for everyone.

Table 13.2 (page 183) gives some idea of retirement need among different income classes.. The figures range between as low as $85,857 for low-income workers to $1,597,592 for workers at the top of the Social Security taxable range. The multiples of the final salary range between 3.7 and 12.6. Unfortunately, the further you are from retirement, the more difficult it is to estimate how much accumulation will be needed. It is difficult to predict what the final salary will be, given the unknown impacts of future inflation, raises, job changes, or job losses. And all of that is without the vast unknown of what future market behavior will be.

Why 401(k)s Deliver Less Retirement Income than Pensions

The 401(k)-type plans have one clear and one possible advantage over most employer-sponsored pension plans. Like Social Security, they are portable, though in a more complicated manner. Social Security is a single system. Contributions from any job participants have during their careers go to it, a unitary destination, where Social Security credits their contribution records. The 401(k) contributions from different jobs may go to various financial services companies. The result is that while workers have a single Social Security account, they may have multiple 401(k) accounts. Merging them into one can be difficult or impossible. They have total accumulations from them, and in that sense, the systems have portability, but the accounts may reside at different financial services companies. It is similar to the healthcare system, where there are multiple insurance companies with varying

TABLE 13.2: Accumulation Ranges Needed to Achieve 70 Percent Retirement Replacement Income (Combined with Social Security Income) in 401(k)-type Plans

Final Income		Replacement Percent Needed	Accumulation Needed	Multiples of Final Salary
Low	$23,308	14.7–18.5	$85,857–$107,800	3.7–4.6
Middle	$51,795	29–39	$375,514–$505,001	7.3–9.7
High	$82,872	36–45.5	$745,848–$942,669	9–11.4
Maximum	$127,061	42.9–50.3	$1,363,729–$1,597,792	10.7–12.6

Note: Table assumes 4% initial withdrawal upon retirement and subsequent withdrawals of 4% + rate of inflation. Final Income taken from Social Security figures in chapter 3, Table 3.1.

types of plans as opposed to a single-payer system like Medicare.

For those for whom it is important, 401(k)-type plans build wealth that is inheritable if the participant dies before expending all of it. But the inheritability feature inevitably reduces retirement income.

The primary disadvantage of 401(k) and other retirement savings plans is that in almost all cases they produce significantly less income than equal contributions and time invested in defined benefit pension plans. It is, of course, possible to have a higher income from 401(k)-type plans as a result of investing more money and time in them. It is also possible to have defined benefit pension plans with formulas that render meager pensions. But the general point remains that a dollar and a year of work time invested in a 401(k) plan will deliver far less retirement income than the same money and time spent in a defined benefit pension plan.

There are several reasons why 401(k) plans produce less retirement income than defined-benefit pension plans:

Lack of risk-sharing. Since no one knows precisely how many years they will survive in retirement, they have no way of knowing how much to withdraw from their savings accounts for living expenses. They run the double risk as mentioned earlier of either withdrawing too much and running out of money or removing too little and having less to spend on expenses than necessary. Pension plans solve those problems by paying amounts according to group longevity averages.

Those who live longer than average receive payments that are higher than they otherwise would be. The flip side of that is that those who live fewer years than average receive less than they otherwise could have. One might think that the latter category of those who live fewer years than average would, therefore, be better off in 401(k)-type plans so that they won't have to subsidize those who live longer than average. But that income advantage of living fewer years—which of course is not an advantage anyone would seek—is not enough to overcome the other disadvantages that follow.

Burden of market risk. All investment risks are assumed by participants in 401(k)-type accounts. If market values decrease, so too will the value of their portfolios. It will be their problem. With defined benefit plans, investment risks are assumed by plan sponsors, not personally but through the use of plan assets. Market decreases do not impact accrued benefits. Some defined benefit plans, primarily cash balance ones, have variable accrual rates according to market conditions. But under no circumstances are they allowed to decrease already accrued benefits. The 401(k)-type plans, to the contrary, have no fixed accrued benefits. Their future benefits are always vulnerable to dropping during market downturns. Existing account balances are not guaranteed to last. They can decrease and with them so too will future retirement incomes.

Timing risk. When individuals make investments affects the sizes of accumulations. An investment made just before a stock soars in value will render much more than one made after it has leveled off. Participants in plans, even if they had crystal balls to know when stocks are about to jump in value, have little control over the timing of their investments. With pension plans, timing issues smooth out so that they don't adversely affect individual participants.

When people leave work presents a second type of timing risk. If they retire just after a steep market downturn as opposed to during a period of significant market gains, it will adversely affect the size of their retirement income. Individuals with the same amount of contribution and years of making contributions can thus have very different retirement incomes depending on these timing issues.

As a result of the 2008 Great Recession, accumulated values of 401(k)-type plans dropped by a third and more. That was a problem for all participants, but especially so for those about to retire. They had to choose between deferring retirement in the hope that their portfolios would regain value or retire with far less retirement income. If they decided to keep working, they had no way of knowing how long it would take for their account balances to recover to pre-recession levels. Members of pension plans did not face the same losses or uncertainties. The recession did not alter their predictable retirement incomes.

For people about to retire who are dependent on 401(k)-like accounts, it's one thing if a stock market plunges sharply but then bounces back quickly. There are many examples of that happening. But it is quite another if it takes years to recover. On September 3, 1929, the Dow Jones Industrial Index reached a high of 381. But then it began to plunge sharply as the Great Depression took hold. It bottomed out on July 8, 1932, at 41, after losing 89 percent of its value. It then took over twenty-two years to recover, on November 23, 1954, to its pre-Depression level. Had someone with one of these retirement savings accounts been planning to retire in 1930 at age 65, he would have had to defer his retirement until 1954 at age 89, assuming that he wanted or needed the income afforded by the value of his September 3, 1929, portfolio. No market downturns since have matched in severity or duration the plunge that accompanied the Great Depression. But there have been two long-term events that presented problems to people dependent on these types of savings and investment retirement accounts. In January 1966 the Dow Jones reached a high of 994. It then began to slide to a low of 578 in December 1974, losing 42 percent of its value. It temporarily recovered its pre-slide value in February 1976 but then began to slide again. It didn't recover for good the lost value until September 1978. The plunge and recovery took a total of twelve and a half years.

The 1990s witnessed rapid stock market growth, with the Dow

Jones reaching a high of 11,561 on January 18, 2000. But then the tech bubble burst and market values began to plunge, bottoming out at 7,702, after losing 27 percent of their value, in July 2002. Full recovery of pre-slide value occurred in May 2006. The plunge and recovery took just short of six and a half years. But it was a very short-lived expansion that reached its high point a year and a half later in October 2007 when the Dow topped out at 14,096. Then began the plunge to 6,547, over half of its pre-plunge value, in March 2009. Full recovery took until March 2013, a loss of nearly five and a half years.[5] All of these examples indicate that individuals dependent on retirement savings accounts may not be fully in control of when they can retire.

Administrative and investment fees. All retirement plans have administrative costs that are at the expense of benefits. The 401(k)-type plans, though, have administrative costs that are far more than those of defined benefit plans. Part of the reason for that is whereas defined benefit plans have an incentive to minimize those costs to be able to pay out guaranteed benefits, 401(k)-type plans have an incentive to maximize the costs and fees since they are a significant source of the revenue of the companies that administer the plans. These companies seek out opportunities to charge fees for every possible service they provide in managing the accounts. These inevitably include record-keeping fees and can also include commissions, legal fees, and multiple other types. Usually, the fees are a percentage of account balances. Fees inexorably are incurred regardless of whether there is any service provided. Consider the example of a worker who leaves an employer and does nothing with the account after leaving, with no new investment choices or even contributions added. The company managing the account will still deduct fees. The deductions add up and can claim as much as 20 percent and more of the account's potential accumulated value, which in turn means a loss of that percent of potential retirement income.

Another fundamental contradiction is that though it is true that the more employees contribute early the more they will gain over the subsequent years, it is also true that more will be drained off by the financial services companies that administer the accounts. Assuming a thirty-five-year career with a 2 percent average wage increase, and a 5 percent average investment return, 1 percent average administrative and investment fees would drain off 18.5 percent of the total accumulation. On the face of it, the 1 percent fee does not seem like much. But by being charged against the account balance year after year, it adds up.

Total fees, which include those for administering plans and those resulting from purchases and sales of stocks and bonds within them, vary from .37 percent to 1.42 percent, according to one estimate.[6] In general, the larger the plan, that is, the more participants and assets it has, the lower the fees. Another calculation placed the average administrative cost at .46 percent and the average investment fee at .48 percent, for a total of .94 percent.[7]

Overhead costs, including management salaries and advertising. Top CEOs of financial service companies that manage 401(k) and other retirement savings accounts receive annual compensation packages in the tens of millions of dollars. Many other managers below them also receive a million dollars and more compensations. Other forms of compensation excess go down further in the managerial hierarchy, including bonus payments, as with the TIAA example cited in the previous chapter. All of this excess compensation comes out of the contributions and market gains of the individual accounts they control and therefore reduces retirement incomes. Advertising costs are another huge expense that comes out of participants' accounts. Because it is a competitive business, there is a continual struggle to attract new and hold on to existing customers. Though participants pay for it, they receive no benefit from the advertising. It does nothing to increase the values of their accounts. It results in only a drain from them.

Lack of professional investing. Participants in retirement savings plans are in charge of investing their money. On the surface, it sounds good to be in control of your retirement plan and be able to invest when and in what you want. It would seem that having an investment choice provides the flexibility necessary to meet particular retirement needs. And Americans now have more choice than they've ever had with their retirement plans. It was given to them by the private sector's massive shift from traditional pensions to 401(k)-like plans. With traditional pension plans, participants have no direct say over the investment of plan assets. With 401(k) plans, they have much more say. Having the freedom of choice sounds like a universal value that no person would want to relinquish, especially when it comes to something so crucial for their future as a retirement plan.

But freedom of choice has not brought more retirement income or security. Few people have the inclination, time, or skill to manage their retirement accounts capably. When it comes to investing, most participants in 401(k)-like plans are amateurs. Many attempt to compensate by engaging financial advisors, a growing cottage industry fueled by the 401(k) industry. But advice comes at a substantial price, usually a percentage of assets, that significantly compromises accumulations, and it is often given more in the interest of the advisor than the client.

The financial services industry answer to this undeniable reality is to preach the need for what it calls financial literacy to make every citizen able to navigate Wall Street's turbulent waters. The educators, of course, are to be drawn from the financial services industry for a price. But even if that could be accomplished and would significantly help, which is doubtful, do we want a nation of citizens for whom the highest goal of education is to be obsessed with making and tracking personal investment decisions?

The more choices retirement plan participants have and exercise, the more manipulations the financial services industry must make— and the more fees it can charge. Similarly, the more complicated and tailor-made or individualized an investment strategy, the more likely the participant will have to bear the cost of an investment advisor. For the vast majority of people, the best retirement plans are those that do not force them to choose among options that are not understandable, transparent, or predictable in terms of their consequences.

The 401(k) transformation has flooded the investor market with millions of amateurs, a development that has redounded to the advantage of major Wall Street firms. Consider professional gamblers' preferences. What would they prefer? To walk into casinos filled by just a few professional players like themselves or to walk into casinos filled with many novice gamblers? It is the same for Wall Street's professional investors. They, like professional gamblers, are good at taking advantage of the amateurs' mistakes and taking their money.

Strategies for Dealing with 401(k)s

As much of a critic as I am of 401(k)-type plans, I would never advise people to boycott them if those were the only type of plan available. One should try to maximize what is possible from them. This means to participate in them where there is a choice. Here are some strategies:

Employer matches. In many working situations, employers match contributions, almost always expressed as percentages of salary. The average employer match is 4.7 percent. Employers, however, have complete freedom to change or, indeed, suspend the size of their matches, if they have them. During the 2008 Great Recession, 18 percent of companies with a thousand or more employees either reduced or suspended their matches. The good news is that 75 percent of them reinstated the matches once the recession ended. The bad news is that a full quarter made the reductions or suspensions permanent. History repeated itself during the Covid-19 recession twelve years later with companies, such as La-Z-Boy and Bassett Furniture, suspending or reducing matches.[8]

If an employer matches up to 5 percent, employees should contribute the full 5 percent. The reduction in their take-home pay will be less than 5 percent because it is tax-deferred. Then a contribution equal to 10 percent of their salary will be deposited in their retirement account. Their money will more than double. If they don't participate, they allow the employer to keep the 5 percent. One should always be aware that there is a distinction between total compensation, which includes the value of health, retirement, and other benefits, and take-home pay, which is total compensation less deductions of taxes and fringe benefits. That's where employer matches come in. It is penny-wise and pound-foolish to maximize take-home pay by not participating in a retirement savings plan to avoid the employee deduction. The deduction is a form of savings. Though it cannot be spent right away like take-home pay, it will be available when needed in the future, assuming that the investment maintains or increases its value.

Not all employers offer matches. Many contribute nothing to retirement benefits. Instead, they sponsor voluntary plans financed entirely by employee deductions. Employees should participate in those types of plans, even if they don't have employer matches. The more money they can accumulate in them, the more personal capital they will have to finance their retirement. Also, they will have capital available should specific reforms or other opportunities become available to enhance their retirement incomes.

Start early. The earlier in their careers that employees begin contributing to these accounts, the higher the total accumulations. This is not just because of the obvious, that they will be making more total contributions if they start early. It is also because of the way that mathematical compounding works. Assume that an employee contributes $1,000 in the first year of participation and then contributes $1,000 for all subsequent years. In reality, he or she would be much more likely to be contributing a percentage of salary than a steady amount. But the math is easier to see with the constant amount assumption. Assume further that the employee receives an average 5 percent gain on the investment each year. Again, the reality is that the increase will bounce around with no fixed year to year gain, and there will be some years with losses. But, again, let's keep the math simple. At the end of year two, the employee will have accumulated two years' contributions of $1,000 = $2,000 plus the gain of $50 over one year of investment ($1,000 x .05). The total is $2,050.

Note that in year two, there is a $1,000 contribution plus a $50 investment gain. The other $1,000 was what accumulated at the end of year one. Now, for year three, it will be the same $1,000 contribution, but the gain will be more since it will be .05 x $2,050 rather than .05 x $1,000. The third-year investment gain is thus $102.50, which is more than double the second-year increase. That's the so-called magic of compounding. While, in this example, the contribution remains the same from year to year, the investment gain increases each year significantly. By the sixteenth year, the investment gain is higher than the contribution.

The point of this exercise in mathematical compounding is that for 401(k)-type plans, the time that contributions have to accumulate can add more value to the overall accumulation than the amount of the contribution itself. This is good for people who start early but not useful for those who start late. It is challenging to make up low or nonexistent early career contributions with larger late-career ones. All of this, of course, assumes a steady market of steady gains. The reality is quite different. But the assumption of steady gains is useful for seeing the importance of time in accumulation and the need to start in retirement savings plans as early as possible.

The fundamental contradiction is that during the early parts of careers, employees generally have lower salaries with more significant percentages of them needed for housing, food, child-raising, and other basic necessary expenses than in later years. Despite that reality, workers should put what they can in those plans so that it will have time to accumulate.

Index fund investing. One way to lessen losses from fees is to invest in index funds. The basic idea of an index fund is that it is a mutual fund of investments designed to closely match the performance of a particular stock market index, such as the Dow Jones Industrial Average or Standard & Poor's 500. Designers base those indexes on hypothetical samples of investments whose overall performances they believe to be representative of the market as a whole. It is the same principle as public opinion polling, where a carefully selected sample will have a high probability of having the same characteristics as the entire population. Pollsters can use samples of as low as one thousand respondents to predict election results for countries with millions of voters. Index funds are a sample of investments that are either the same as those in the index being copied or designed to match them. The term for this is passive investing because the investments simply follow whatever is in the index.

The other approach, active management, results in higher fees because it requires much more work. Investment managers must continually choose what to invest in and when to buy or sell stocks or bonds. The goal of active management is to produce returns that are higher than the market averages that are provided by index funds. Although it is undoubtedly true that they succeed some of the time, it is also true that other times they do not. From a retirement plan participant's perspective, an actively managed fund would have to not only consistently return more than an index fund, it would also have to return enough more to cover the extra fees charged. Investing in index funds, though, will not protect anyone from sharp drops in whole markets.

The 4 percent rule. It's time to explain the 4 percent withdrawal rule in more detail. William P. Bengen, a California financial planner, first outlined it in a 1994 article.[9] He had analyzed stock market returns going back to 1926. Unlike many advisors who use assumptions about future market behavior, he looked at the actual historical experience to try to calculate how much a retiree could safely withdraw from his or her retirement savings each year and not run out of money. He further wanted the withdrawal amounts to keep up with inflation. For that to happen, the portfolio balances also would have to keep up with inflation. Retirees would have to keep investing their accumulations to make them grow enough.

Bengen believed it was a fallacy for advisors to base advice on average market returns because of timing risk, which had a double impact on retirees. First, there was still the risk of when work-ers made investments during the accumulation phase. This risk continued to operate in the spend-down period because retirees needed to continue investing for their balances to grow enough to support withdrawals that kept up with inflation. Second, there was a new timing risk of when they began to withdraw funds for living expenses. If they withdrew and spent them during a down market, their balances would decline much more than if they took them out during up markets. Also, from 1926 to 1976, there had been three stock market "events" of unusually steep declining values: two associated with the Great Depression and one with the 1973–74 recession. Moreover, it was one thing to suffer steep stock losses during a deflationary period, like that of the first Great Depression decline, and quite another to bear losses right before a period of runaway inflation, as occurred after the 1973–74 recession. The latter was much more damaging.

To control for timing risk, Bengen traced portfolio values for people who retired and began withdrawals for each of the fifty years from 1926 to 1976. His primary question was how long the portfolios would last at different withdrawal rates. His conclusion became the origin of the 4 percent rule. Retirees who started withdrawing that percentage—more in subsequent years to take inflation into account—for each of those initial years between 1926 and 1976 had their portfolios last a minimum of thirty-three years. Most had portfolios that lasted fifty or more years. A 65-year-old retiree would be able to keep receiving inflation-indexed money until at least age 98.

His 4 percent rule had these components:

- Invest in 50–75 percent common stocks with the remainder in intermediate Treasury bills.
- Rebalance the portfolio each year to maintain those investment proportions.
- Withdraw 4 percent of the total portfolio value for the first year of retirement.
- For subsequent years, withdraw a dollar amount equal to the first year's withdrawal. Withdraw an additional amount equal to the rate of inflation for that year times the initial withdrawal amount.

Bengen later increased the initial withdrawal rate to 4.5 percent but then had second thoughts in a 2012 article after the experience of the Great Recession.[10] He became less certain about how long a portfolio would last at that rate of initial withdrawal. He then began to recommend more complicated investing strategies to keep such portfolios afloat long enough.

The 4 percent rule would seem to be a reasonable spend-down strategy if the singular goal is to assure there is a high probability that reliable inflation-indexed income will last throughout retirement. Note well that the condition for the income lasting that long is that the portfolio continues to be invested in stocks and bonds as he advises.

The Internal Revenue Service's Required Minimum Distribution (RMD) bears a superficial resemblance to the 4 percent spend-down strategy. It requires holders of tax-deferred retirement savings to withdraw 2.55 percent of their balances at age 70 and a half. The withdrawal percentages increase each subsequent year up to ages 115 and older (!), when the withdrawal required is 60.5 percent of balances.[11] But there are two significant differences between the RMD and the 4 percent rule. The RMD is silent on how retirees are to invest their portfolios. And its subsequent year required withdrawals are percentages of account balances rather than equivalent to the first-year withdrawal plus an extra amount to take inflation into consideration.

People who wanted to follow the 4 percent rule while taking the RMDs could calculate it each year and then compare the result to the RMD. If the RMD were higher, they could put the difference in a post-tax investment account. If it were smaller, they could withdraw the difference for spending money.

14

The Lone Ranger of the 401(k)s

J erry Schlichter grew up in the 1960s in a small town in southern Illinois. The early 1970s found him in law school at the University of California at Los Angeles, where he joined picket lines to support union strikes. After law school, he returned to Illinois, to East St. Louis, to work on civil rights cases. His commitment to labor and social justice issues would, by the early 2000s, carry him into a David and Goliath struggle over injustices embedded in 401(k) plans. The *New York Times* would later call him "the Lone Ranger of the 401(k)s."[1]

He was the founding partner of a small St. Louis firm, Schlichter Bogard & Denton, which handled labor, civil rights, and personal injury cases. In the early 2000s, he began receiving more and more inquiries from workers concerned about their 401(k) plans. They didn't know whether they would have enough in the accounts to retire and worried about fees they were paying. Schlichter did not know much about 401(k)s or the fees within them but decided they were worth investigating. That led him and his partners, in his words, to a deep dive into the issue for a year and nine months. He admits that the first book he purchased was *401(k)s for Dummies.*

He also spoke to a lot of people for guidance, including a longtime benefits consultant who had witnessed the displacement of defined benefit pensions by 401(k)s. The consultant observed that at the beginning of the development, employer representatives organized conferences on the new 401(k) plans. But then, as mutual fund executives saw the amount of assets moving into 401(k)s, they began to take over organizing such conferences and control the agendas. People who had no fiduciary responsibility were telling fiduciaries what and how to think about 401(k)s. Mutual fund companies, of course, wanted their investment lineups placed in plan options.

Schlichter's deep research dive produced two significant findings that left him astounded. The Employee Retirement Income and Security Act (ERISA) covers 401(k)s in addition to private sector pensions. For 401(k)s it states that employers have a fiduciary obligation to ensure that plan fees are reasonable and investments offered participants are prudent. *Reasonable* and *prudent* are the key terms here for legal purposes. For the first twenty-three years that employers moved retirement benefits from traditional pensions to 401(k)s, there had not been a single legal challenge brought against unreasonably excessive fees or imprudent investment options.

The second significant finding was that the Department of Labor, which regulates 401(k)s, had also failed to initiate actions against excessive fees or imprudent investment options. The DOL was exercising benign neglect regarding 401(k)s. It paid much more attention to regulating defined benefit pension plans. This finding was consistent with my own experience with the state employee retirement system in Connecticut. It had a board of trustees that included representatives of management and state employee unions. Although it oversaw the state's 401(k)-like defined contribution retirement plans as well as its defined benefit pension plan, in reality it spent almost all of its time with the latter. It was only when members of the defined contribution plans began to challenge the adequacy of its benefits compared to those of the pension plan that it began to devote more time to the issue.

In Schlichter's words, it was as if all of this employee money was being kept in a dark closet with no effective oversight or regulation.[2] There was no incentive for employers to do it. Company bottom lines did not depend on how their employee 401(k)s plans were doing. No CEO or other top manager's bonus depended on 401(k) performance for employees. There was complete neglect.

Uncovering injustices that are harming people does not automatically mean that lawyers can do anything about them through legal action. There has to be an angle of legal vulnerability. And someone or entity that is legally vulnerable. In these cases, the legal vulnerability was that ERISA mandated that employers who sponsored 401(k) and other private-sector retirement plans had a fiduciary responsibility. This meant employer plan sponsors had to make the interests of the participants paramount over those of its own company or companies that it contracted to administer and invest participant funds. The financial services companies that were making money from the plans were pretty much off the hook since they did not have any fiduciary responsibilities to participants. In the eyes of the law, they could make their bottom-line interests paramount over those of plan participants. But employers who sponsored plans had fiduciary obligations. They were not off the legal hook even if the main culprits, the financial services companies that made money from the plans, were.

Having a legal case, however, does not necessarily mean that you have the legal resources to prevail. Schlichter knew it would not be easy. He and his small firm would be going up against some of the largest corporations in the country, all of whom had considerable legal liability insurance for their retirement plans. This meant they had an unlimited amount of access to high-powered legal firms that would fight to prevent the opening up of these new lines of litigation. To mount an effective legal battle, Schlichter and his partners took out a massive line of credit, using their homes as collateral. It was exceedingly risky, and they knew it.

In September 2006, they mounted lawsuits over 401(k) excessive fees and imprudent investments against twelve of the most powerful corporations in the country, including Lockheed-Martin, Kraft, John Deere, and International Paper. The response was ferocious. Insurance giant AIG led the large insurers in fighting the cases. The top representative of AIG told Schlichter that they would never pay anything on the cases. They didn't care what they had to pay their attorneys. They were determined to kill the cases in utero and financially destroy Schlichter and his firm. It was essential to avoid a successful precedent for such employee challenges to 401(k) sponsors. Corporate power and determination had discouraged any previous legal challenges.

The scorched earth policy worked in the beginning. Federal judges dismissed three cases, with the dismissals upheld on appeal. Schlichter's position was that the judges needed to dig deeper into the facts rather than taking only a surface look.

The filing of the cases did, however, catch the attention of the Department of Labor, tasked with regulating retirement plans. The DOL asked Schlichter to come to Washington to explain what he was doing and what he had found. He gave the DOL representatives examples of fiduciary neglect, plans with over a billion dollars in assets accepting fees that were equivalent to plans with much fewer assets under control. As in much of commercial business with quantity discounts, financial services companies extend fee discounts to their larger customers. The sued companies were accepting fees, which came out of employee accounts, that were as much as four times what they should have been. They were either unaware that lower fees existed or did not care. The DOL response, discouragingly, was that they saw nothing wrong with employees in billion-dollar 401(k) plans not getting the advantage of the plan sizes to obtain much lower fees.

If plan sponsors were not exercising their fiduciary responsibilities on behalf of their employees, it was clear that neither was the government using its regulatory obligations. According to Schlichter, "Had the government brought two or three cases at the outset, decades of excessive fees would not have occurred." If the government had brought the cases, nobody would have tried to put a firm like his out of business for the effrontery of daring to challenge a significant financial services industry interest. This would have been a statement that companies could not get away with allowing fee gouging.

After judges dismissed the first cases, another finally went to trial. ABB is a Swiss-owned electrical company that moved into the U.S. market in 1989 with the purchase of Westinghouse-owned T&D.

For workers in its home country of Switzerland, ABB has a defined benefit pension plan as a result of Swiss government regulations.[3] In 1992, it began a 401(k) plan for its U.S. workers. ABB maintains pre-existing pension plans for legacy workers, that is, those who were in those plans before it adopted the 401(k) model. For new employees, the 401(k) is the only option, including new employees from corporate acquisitions. When ABB bought a General Electric company, Industrial Solutions, in 2018, workers were able to keep their jobs but lost their union-negotiated GE pension plan. For time going forward, they only had the ABB 401(k).[4]

Schlichter filed suit (*Tussey v. ABB*) on December 29, 2006, alleging that ABB had allowed its 401(k) plan administrator to charge excessively large record-keeping fees to participants, allowed high-cost and poor-performing investment options in the plan, and had used the plan to subsidize some of its own costs. The case went to full trial and through several appeals until a final settlement, over twelve years later, in March 2019. ABB spent over $50 million to defend itself.[5] It settled for $55 million and was ordered by the court to reform its 401(k) plan.

Tibble v. Edison was a case that Schlichter asked the Supreme Court to take as the first and only 401(k) excessive fee case in its history. In a rare unanimous opinion, the Supreme Court ruled in favor of Schlichter's clients that 401(k) plan sponsors had a fiduciary responsibility to select and maintain prudent investment options for participants. This included removing options that had become imprudent. In the words of the Court, a retirement plan "trustee has a continuing duty—separate and apart from the duty to exercise prudence in selecting investments at the outset—to monitor, and remove imprudent trust investments. A fiduciary must discharge his responsibilities 'with the care, skill, prudence, and diligence' that a prudent person 'acting in a like capacity and familiar with such matters would use.'"[6]

After these victories, it was clear that the cases had legal merit. The AIG threat that it would make sure they would go nowhere had been faced down and overcome. The same person who made the threat to put him out of business later told Schlichter that AIG would now look at each case on its merits. The litigation also educated judges and the Department of Labor about fee issues. It's an excellent example of how lawsuits are often necessary to get government regulatory agencies to act. The DOL subsequently began to investigate and bring its own excessive fee cases.

However, an unintended consequence occurred. As fees were lowered because of these cases, financial services companies developed other profit-seeking activities to compensate for the lost income. TIAA developed an aggressive sales campaign targeting high-accumulation participants with new services, including wealth management, IRAs, and life insurance. Schlichter's firm has filed suit against several universities for shirking fiduciary responsibilities by allowing TIAA to use confidential information from employee accounts for these sales campaigns. In one egregious example, with overtones of farce, a TIAA sales representative tried to get a longtime professor with a high balance to purchase life insurance. But the professor said she didn't need it because she did not have children. She only had a dog. Upon hearing this, the sales representative then tried to get her to purchase life insurance to provide for the care of the dog if she died first.

As of 2019, the law firm had won $425 million for participants minus legal fees. While the compensation for past damage was small on a per person basis, the settlements obtained more valuable court-ordered reforms to those and other plans going forward, including securing lower fees. Multiple federal judges across the country have stated that Schlichter's work has saved American workers and retirees over $2 billion annually in their retirement savings. Plan sponsors are also on notice that they are legally liable for upholding their fiduciary responsibilities. According to Schlichter, fiduciary duties now are understood, as opposed to being ignored by many plan sponsors.[7]

Yet, even with the awards from lawsuits, plan participants continue to suffer other 401(k) disadvantages so that they do not achieve equal benefits for equal contributions and years of work with defined benefit pension plan participants. Successful lawsuits offer some relief but not enough to resolve the problem. Participants will not be able to sue their way to achieve defined benefit pension plan retirement income standards. This does not mean that legal challenges are not worth pursuing. In the absence of a way to move into a defined benefit pension, maximizing possible accumulations through eliminating excessive parts of fees and other corporate misdeeds is in the interest of plan participants.

I asked Schlichter what he thought would be the ideal retirement plan. He thought back to his family experience. After his father, a civil servant airline mechanic, died, his housewife mother lived from his pension. This income arrangement was exactly what she needed. As he put it, "She no more would have been able to figure out stock selection than flying to the Moon." She didn't have to because she had a pension check automatically coming in every month.

From what Schlichter hears from clients and others, including executives as well as regular employees, what they want is certainty over the nature of their retirement. They don't follow the stock market. They don't want to. They don't understand it. To them, stock market investing just seems like rolling dice. It's too risky.

Sclichter thinks the ideal system is Social Security or, if it's going to be a private employer's plan, a defined benefit pension plan where retirees have certainty. With these plans, there are no incentives for private entities to come in and pressure fiduciaries to go their way. With defined benefit pension plans, people know what they're going to get and when it kicks in. They can plan and have financial security.

Of 401(k)-like retirement savings plans, Schlichter thinks the Thrift Savings Plan for federal employees is the best, though not as good as a defined benefit plan. Its advantage is that its investment options are all very low-cost index funds. Participants do not have to pay as much in fees as they would if they were in a plan with actively managed funds.

——— 15 ———

Autopsy of a Retirement Plan

When I was still in a 401(k)-like plan and approaching age 65 after thirty-seven years of university teaching, I took stock of my future retirement income. I wanted to know what it would look like in terms of achieving the 70 percent of preretirement income that retirement experts state is necessary to maintain one's standard of living.[1] I ran the numbers for my Social Security and my employer's defined contribution plan, in which I had participated for thirty-one years. This 401(a) plan, which functioned in the same way as a 401(k), had at various times TIAA, ING, and Prudential as administrators.

Together, my projected Social Security and employee retirement plan would amount to just 43.5 percent of my final income. The monthly Social Security check accounted for 19.5 percent, the annuity income option for my defined contribution plan, 24 percent.

Something had gone terribly wrong. Despite having accumulated almost a half-million dollars, which is much more than the $109,000 median for people approaching retirement, I did not have enough to finance a retirement that would allow me and my family to maintain the middle-class standard of living that my $117,615 final salary as a university professor afforded.

I didn't expect much sympathy from others who earned or had saved less. I had a good job that supported a better standard of living than most, and I was about to lose some of that middle-class privilege.

I'm aware that, as a tenured professor, I had considerable relative privilege within an academic labor force with severe salary inequities. Faculty members holding contingent positions are far less likely to have any retirement plan at all. If they do have defined contribution plans, their contributions are likely to be lower and more of a sacrifice to make than those for tenured and tenure-track colleagues. Those with higher incomes can have higher savings rates that have less impact on their ability to afford housing, food, healthcare, and other necessary expenses. Nonetheless, there is a lot for others to learn from my experience. If I had a good income that wasn't going to turn into a good retirement, then anyone with a defined contribution retirement plan could be in danger.

But why my experience alone? Aren't there already studies of these plans? Yes, but they are studies based on projections, assumptions, and modeling or indirect indicators. TIAA, for example, claimed that "on average, participants in TIAA-administered plans are on track to replace over ninety percent of their income in retirement."[2] Why wasn't that my experience?

Despite decades of experience with these types of plans and trillions of dollars running through them, there is a dearth of available research about actual rather than hypothetical experiences. I suspect that the financial services companies that administer these plans have performance data they do not share with the public because the resulting retirement incomes are too depressing and contrary to their rosy advertising campaigns.

Coming Up Short

Retirement-account balances are like poker hands. Their owners treat them as closely held secrets. Co-workers are unlikely to discuss openly how much they have accumulated in their accounts. It's like asking people how much they have in their checking accounts: none of your business. The problem, though, is that it is the business of all of us to know what's going on with defined contribution plans.

Was I at fault? Had I not saved enough or made poor investment choices? Or was the game rigged against me and, by implication, anyone else participating in such plans? Was it possible that even if I had saved and invested more responsibly, I would have still ended up without enough retirement income?

I was not alone. Increasing numbers of Americans with defined contribution plans are coming up short for retirement, and this was especially true after the 2008 recession. James Ridgeway wrote a 2009 *Rolling Stone* article in which he recounted how miserably his plan was doing and lambasted the whole approach. He started with the bitter faux riddle: "What starts with 'f,' ends with 'k,' and means 'screw your workers'? That's right, —401(k)."

Lower Than Expected Social Security Income

For the autopsy, I am focusing on my defined contribution plan. But since Social Security is also a significant part of my retirement income, a few words about my experience with it are in order.

Social Security, unlike a defined contribution plan, as we know, is not a retirement savings plan. Instead, participants and their employers pay contributions into a social insurance fund to protect themselves from loss of income in retirement. The contributions go into a collective pool, out of which come benefits for individuals. They do not go into individual accounts like savings or defined contribution retirement plan accounts. Participants don't own their contributions. They accumulate instead guaranteed rights toward income replacement in retirement.

We also know that Social Security has a progressive distribution of its benefits so that lower-income participants have more of their pre-retirement incomes replaced than do higher-income participants. My salary put me in the higher-income category that, according to Social Security reports, has 27.1 percent of its income replaced.

This statistic immediately raised the question for me of why I was having only 19.5 percent replaced. The answer, I realized, was simple. My 19.5 percent was a percentage of my final salary, whereas Social Security's statistic is of the average of the thirty-five years of highest contributions. I quickly calculated my average career salary and found the replacement value of it, using Social Security's methodology, to be closer to 44 percent.

But having 44 percent replacement of a career average salary is still much less than having 44 percent replacement of my final salary. My replacement value of 19.1 percent of the final salary was so low because of my career pattern. For about twenty-four of my highest thirty-five earning years, my salaries were in the middle and, in some cases, low range. Then they began to take off sharply due to promotions to end in the high-income range. Had they been in the high income for the entire thirty-five years, I would have had a much higher replacement rate.

Examining my Social Security statement earnings record further revealed some sources of very low or nonexistent contributions. For eight years, I had public academic employers who did not participate in Social Security. Had contributions been made for four of those years, which would have been among my thirty-five highest-earning ones, my retirement income would have been higher. This lack of contributory years is similar to the problem caregivers face if they take time out to tend for children or other family members. I would have happily paid the contributions during those years, but I did not have that choice. My experience raises questions about whether Social Security should allow participants to pay concurrently or retroactively for non-contributing years.

Financial-service companies have taken advantage of the Social Security practice of expressing replacement rates in terms of average rather than final salaries. TIAA, the leading provider of retirement plans for academics, had an advertising campaign in which it claimed that more than 90 percent of its plan participants were on track to replace more than 90 percent of their income, combined with Social Security, in retirement. This claim makes it look like participants will clear the 70 percent hurdle with ease. The fact that these figures refer to average, not final, career income was in a fine-print footnote in the advertisement. They, like me, will come up far short of 70 percent of final income. Such marketing lulls participants into complacency during their working years. They are in for a rude awakening when they approach retirement with much less than anticipated income for the future and can do little about it.

Social Security vs. 401(k)s

Given my low rate of salary replacement from Social Security, would I have been better off if I had been allowed to invest its contributions through a 401(k)-like plan instead? The answer is a resounding no. The primary reason is that participants don't only get retirement income from Social Security. For the same contributions they also receive disability, survivors, and dependent insurance. Even if we leave those additional benefits to the side, people would not necessarily get more income through stock market investing.

A common claim of advocates of Social Security privatization is that private accounts deliver much higher rates of return for participants. The Cato Institute, for example, in its *Cato Handbook for Policymakers,* tells us:

> Social Security taxes are already so high, relative to benefits, that Social Security has quite simply become a bad deal for younger workers, providing a low, below-market rate of return. This poor rate of return means that many young workers' retirement benefits are far lower than if they had been able to invest those funds privately. However, a system of individual accounts, based on private capital investment, would provide most workers with significantly higher returns. Those higher returns would translate into higher retirement benefits, leading to a more secure retirement for millions of seniors.

But is that true? To test the claim, I compared my Social Security statement with my TIAA statement. Both listed the total contributions made by the employers and myself per year. The Social Security statement indicated my benefit at 66, the age of my full retirement. My TIAA-CREF statement had the total accumulation achieved that year.

My first-year Social Security benefit was 12.61 percent of my total contributions. The first-year TIAA annuity was 12.06 percent of total contributions—*lower* not higher than the return on my Social Security contributions as the Cato Institute so confidently claims. Remember also that as a professional employee I was in a relatively high-income category with a Social Security rate of return that is less than that of lower-income participants. For them, the rate of return for Social Security compared to private accounts would be much higher than mine, making it an even better deal.

Like the optimistic projections of the financial services industry whose interests it serves, the Cato Institute based its claim on before-the-fact overly optimistic assumptions of future market returns. I made my comparison on actual after-the-fact experience.

Autopsy of My Employer-Sponsored Plan

Now we are ready to look more in-depth at why my employer-sponsored 401(k)-like plan failed to provide nearly enough retirement income. I had saved my quarterly statements. I knew how much my employer and I had contributed. I knew how I had allocated the investments and how they had grown. With the help of a spreadsheet, I was able to trace the growth of my accumulation and map out alternate scenarios.

The original idea of that retirement savings approach, as we've discussed, was that the accumulations would seamlessly be converted to life annuities to mimic traditional pensions.

But 401(k)-like defined contribution plans have not turned out as originally anticipated in this respect. Most participants do not use their accumulations to purchase annuities when they retire but instead manage their money differently, for example, by continuing to invest while making regular withdrawals. Annuity prices are nevertheless useful for knowing what accumulations are worth in terms of potentially providing pension-like incomes for the rest of the annuitants' lives. They form the bases for retirement studies (such as those by the highly regarded Boston College Center for Retirement Research) that calculate potential replacement incomes with given accumulation sizes.

I reached the normal retirement age of 65 at the end of 2009. That was a particularly bad time to do so for anyone in a 401(k) or other defined contribution plan. Because of the 2008 Great Recession, the stock market had tanked, taking with it the prospects of those like me who were approaching retirement. My portfolio lost 19.1 percent of its value between October 2007 and April 2009, seven months before my sixty-fifth birthday. To make matters worse, annuity prices were increasing at the same time. It was a perfect storm for anyone who wanted to retire that year with a defined contribution plan and purchase a life annuity.

If I had had a crystal ball in September 2007, I would have moved all of my stock investments to bonds and money-market funds. Then, when the market began to recover in late 2009, I would have moved them back into stocks. But I did not have a crystal ball. I did have enough sense not to completely panic in 2008 when it became clear that the fall in stock prices was not part of a temporary cycle of ups and downs. I didn't sell and hoped that the market would come back.

It was not at all clear how long it would take for the market to regain its lost values. After the 1929 crash, as we know, the Dow Jones took twenty-two years, until 1954, to recover its value. If the recovery after the Great Recession had taken that long, I would have been 87 before my investments regained their value.

Fortunately for me, this time the market recovered from its losses a lot faster. By 2013 the Dow was back to where it had been five years earlier, before the crash. By the middle of 2012, I was back to where I had been in 2007, faster than the Dow because of the proportion of bonds that had not lost value in my accounts. Then I cashed out completely, but more about that later.

Were my problems the fault of timing, the bad luck of approaching retirement as the market was crashing? To test that possibility, I pretended I had turned 65 in 2007 when the market was at its high point. If I had been able to retire then, my sources of retirement income would have added up to a 47.5 percent replacement rate. That rate was somewhat higher than the 43.5 percent rate I was looking at two years later but still well short of the 70 percent needed to maintain my family's standard of living. It's worth pointing out that while the 70 percent replacement rate is the most often cited goal, there are other retirement advisors and experts who think it should be much higher.

Some investment experts advise gradually reducing stock ownership as you get closer to retirement age to avoid losses like the ones I experienced. They have designed target-date plans that incorporate this strategy. Nari Rhee, director of the Retirement Security Program at the University of California at Berkeley, estimates that target-date funds have an average 6.05 percent rate of return. If I had had my retirement savings in such a fund with that rate of return, I would have avoided losing value in the 2008 crash but come up shorter, replacing, combined with Social Security income, 40.3 rather than 43.5 percent of pre-retirement income. This was because, as we will see below, my actual average rate of return was higher than the 6.05 percent target-date fund assumed average rate of return.

The leading explanations for people who come up short with savings in 401(k)s and other defined contribution plans is that either they didn't save enough or they didn't invest what they saved wisely enough, suggesting that luck isn't a significant variable. Such explanations are undeniably true up to a point. If you save more, you will accumulate more; if your rates of return are higher, you will accumulate more. But they don't answer the question of whether it is realistically possible to do enough of either to reach the 70 percent replacement rate.

Still Coming Up Short with High Savings and Investment Returns

Was I saving enough? Between my employer's 8 percent of salary contribution and my 5 percent of salary contribution, I was putting away a combined 13 percent of my salary for thirty-one years. That is a savings rate nearly double the average 7 percent of salary saving in 401(k) plans.

If my 13 percent rate of savings had not been enough, how much higher would it have had to be to get me to 70 percent? I went back to my spreadsheet and inserted higher and higher rates of savings until my combined retirement income reached 70 percent of my final pre-retirement income. Reaching that level would have required an unrealistically high savings rate of 26.1 percent of salary, just over double my actual savings rate. Such a high rate of savings also would have exceeded the legal limits for tax-deferred contributions.

But even if I had been able to put in the excess savings in a fully taxable investment fund outside of my retirement plan, you can defer gratification only so much before you end up lowering your and your family's pre-retirement standard of living. The two big expenses of the middle-class family—the home mortgage and paying for college for children—present additional obstacles to saving for retirement. Although many of us consume more than we need to, at some point frugality crosses over from cutting out unnecessary expenses to going without necessities. Well before that point you are cutting out the small pleasures that make life worth living, such as an occasional movie or dinner out, not to mention vacation travel.

If I can't take the blame for not saving enough, perhaps the problem lay in how I was investing what I was saving. When I started in these plans in 1979, I knew next to nothing about investing. Confronting a decision over how to invest my money through TIAA, I clumsily reasoned that bonds were guaranteed and stocks a gamble. I preferred guaranteed returns, incorrectly assuming that it would work out to more or less the same accumulation in the end.

Eight years later, I read somewhere that stocks had much higher accumulations than bonds in the long run. I then changed my allocation, putting 65 percent in stocks and the rest in bonds and money-market funds, a mixture that remained for the rest of my career. The money accumulated in TIAA bonds had to stay there because the company, unlike all others, does not allow participants to move it into stocks except over a protracted period of ten years through a process that is somewhat difficult to set up. Although I was not committed enough to invest the time and energy into that project then, I probably should have made an effort to do so.

My approach to investing was thus haphazard and far from sufficiently diligent. To that, I plead entirely guilty. I didn't know much about investing then. But should retirement security depend on investing skill or luck? If retirement incomes are supposed to reward careers of hard work, then they should rely on numbers of years worked and the salaries during those years. This is how Social Security and traditional pension plans, neither of which require investing skill, determine retirement incomes. Some would agree that virtuous, provident saving should also determine retirement security. Adding investing skill or luck to that mix builds in an extraneous factor that has nothing to do with working or saving.

Enough of my excuses. How well did I do as an investor over thirty-one years? Using the spreadsheet, I entered my final plan accumulation and year-by-year contributions. Through that exercise, I was able to determine that my average yearly return on investments had been 7.1 percent.

How good or bad was that? The average rate of return on the Standard & Poor's 500 for the same years had been 8.1 percent. My rate of return was lower. The average rate of return for the S&P 500, however, is not the same as the average investor's experience, which is lower because of the costs of retirement company fees, commissions, and other profits. According to Dalbar, a financial research company, the S&P 500 grew by an average of 10.35 percent between 1986 and 2016. But the average investor had a return of only 3.66. Dalbar attributes the gap to investor errors, such as not holding funds long enough to realize full gains, as well as what it refers to euphemistically as fund expenses.

It appears I stumbled into a relatively decent rate of return. My 7.1 percent average rate of return was even higher than the 6.05 percent rate cited above that is assumed for target funds. Yet I still came up very much short.

More What-Ifs

What rate would I have needed to make it to the 70 percent replacement? Instead of my actual 24 percent replacement rate from the defined contribution plan, I would have needed a 50.5 percent replacement rate. That would have required an 11.4 percent rate of investment return on the amounts of my and my employer's contributions. Had I known how to beat the market so successfully, I could have quit my job to write a get-rich-through-stock-investing bestseller or become an advisor to Warren Buffett.

Altogether, to have reached the 70 percent replacement rate—to yield $82,330 annually from savings and Social Security combined—I would have needed to accumulate $1,046,074 in my defined contribution plan. That was $550,020 more than the $496,054 I had—more than twice as much. Since many financial planners attempt to estimate accumulations needed as multiples of final salaries, it's worth noting that this million-dollar-plus figure represents 8.9 times my final salary of $117,615.

Perhaps the problem was that I had not been in the game long enough to reap its rewards. I was thirty-four when I began my first job with a defined contribution retirement plan. That gave me thirty-one years to save and invest.

To test this possibility, I gathered my Social Security statements from before that first job with a defined contribution plan. Where there were non-contributory employers, I estimated the incomes.

I first appeared in the Social Security files at age 16 with a yearly income of $73 from a brief busboy job. I then pretended that I had been making 13 percent of salary contributions with a 7.1 percent rate of return from that job at age 16 and all my subsequent jobs until the time I began my actual retirement plan. That seems to be in line with the message of the financial services sector: it is never too early to think about, worry about, obsess about, and save for retirement.

The result was an accumulation of $10,416.84, which then hypothetically grew for another thirty-one years at the 7.1 percent return until I reached age 65 for a total extra accumulation of $87,339.28.

That gave me nineteen additional years for a total of fifty years to accumulate. I added the results to my actual accumulation. My defined contribution plan rate of replacement hypothetically went up from 24 to 28.2 percent. That, along with my Social Security income, brought me up to a hypothetical 47.9 percent replacement rate—still far short of 70 percent.

Getting Out of the Trap

Any way I looked at my situation at age 65, I was in deep trouble. My wife did not have enough income from her Social Security or employer retirement plan to compensate for my shortfall, and we still had a dependent daughter living at home. My options were either to take a vow of poverty for my retirement years or to strategize a way to be able to retire with enough financial security at age 70—or, in the worst case, never retire.

As a result of exceptional circumstances, I was able to get out of the trap I was in. Delaying my retirement and switching from my defined contribution plan to a defined benefit pension plan provided me with a much higher retirement income.

I was fortunate to be able to delay retirement. I didn't have a physically strenuous job that had worn me out, my health was good, and my job was secure. Also, for what it's worth, I didn't hate it. That, of course, is not the situation for everyone who comes up short at age 65.

Delaying retirement until age 70 carries significant advantages for Social Security income. Every year past the normal retirement age results in 8 percent higher income. The additional five years of work increased my replacement rate from 19.5 to 29.8 percent for the Social Security portion of my retirement income.

Five more years of accumulations in my defined contribution plan at my average rate of return would have lifted that portion of my replacement rate from 24 to 36 percent. I would still be short at 65.8 percent. It would take me until age 73 to accumulate enough to retire at a 70 percent replacement rate—all the time keeping my fingers crossed that there wouldn't be another stock market crash. I would have to keep up an aggressive investment strategy rather than tapering off into the security of bonds—which many experts recommend—as I approached my new delayed retirement age. The expert advice only works if you have enough, not if you have to make a mad rush to get enough.

Instead, as recounted in the Introduction, I was able to take advantage of an opportunity to roll my defined contribution money into my employer's defined benefit pension plan and essentially purchase an annuity at a much better rate than those available on the commercial market. The rollover raised my employer-plan replacement rate from 24 to 46.4 percent, much better than if I had left it in the defined contribution plan. The total replacement rate went from 49.6 to 76.2 percent, and I was able to retire.

Reversing 401(k)ization

4 01(k)ization," as good a word as any to describe what has happened, in its most direct sense means employers freezing pension plans and imposing far inferior 401(k)s as substitutes. In another sense, 401(k)ization involves owners and top managers not even considering the possibility of creating pension plans for their employees, reflecting a dominant narrative that equates retirement benefits exclusively with 401(k)-like plans.

Despite this depressing reality for retirement income security, there is a contrary reality that millions of people continue to be covered by pension plans, and each year many join new plans. In what follows, we will look at the latter, at how employees have managed in a contrarian way to move from 401(k)-like to higher-benefit pension plans. Some of these have been through individual actions. Others have required union muscle to effect.

Changing Jobs

One way to move from a 401(k) plan to higher-benefit pension plans is simply to find a new job that has a pension benefit. Having a pension benefit may compensate for a lower take-home salary. It depends on how long you will stay with the position. Having a pension plan for a short amount of time will not do much good since there will not be enough accrued credits to provide adequate retirement income. It also depends on how generous the pension plan is. But if you can move into a new, acceptable job with a decent pension benefit and stay with that job for the years until retirement, you should. If the new pension plan allows the purchase of service credits, that is, purchase of extra time in the plan, with 401(k) savings from previous positions, you should.

Changing jobs to get a pension plan is a workaround in a national system that is reducing their availability. It can be risky if the employer later freezes the plan before the job changer has retired. Public employer plans, in that respect, are less risky since freezes have been much more common in the private sector. But even these are not entirely without risk as there is a steady drumbeat of lobbying pressure from conservative and financial interests to extinguish all pension plans. There are no guarantees in that respect. Anyone with a pension plan will have to be extra vigilant and ready to oppose any attempts to end it. But it is still a substantial benefit that is well worth having and protecting.

The more likely situation, however, is one in which it is not practical or desirable to change jobs. Instead, it would be useful to change the nature of the retirement plan for the current position, in particular, to change from a 401(k)-type plan to a decent pension plan. There are several possibilities.

Reversing 401(k)ization

The first possibility deals with literal 401(k)ization, that is, when an employer terminates a pension plan and substitutes a 401(k)-like plan for it. This type of plan conversion is entirely comparable to when countries, under World Bank encouragement, privatized national social security systems. It is comparable both because of the privatization and because many countries reversed it (see chapter 6), and movements in other countries are trying to do the same.

In the United States, West Virginia (1991), Michigan (1997), Alaska (2005), and Kentucky (2014) ended final-salary pension plans for newly hired teachers and other categories of state employees. They substituted either cash balance pension plans or defined contribution savings plan. The National Institute for Retirement Security has studied the impact of those decisions.[1] Years of underfunding led to significant unfunded liablilites in the Alaska and Kentucky plans, and these became a justification for the termination of the plans for new hires. But once a pension plan ends for new hires, it does not receive contributions for them. Its funding ratio will fall even more, as it did in Alaska. Kentucky, to compensate, had to make extra contributions. Michigan's pension plan was overfunded at 109 percent when it was frozen. It has since dropped to 67 percent. Ending pension plans, in and of itself, does nothing to reduce liabilities.

It's difficult to precisely measure the losses to workers in retirement income because the states do not release information on account balances in defined contribution (DC) plans for those retiring. Some states, such as Connecticut, do that for pension retirees. Anyone can use the internet to look up the pension of any Connecticut state employee retiree. For Alaska, the NIRS study did include an estimate. It concluded that teachers in the defined contribution plan would receive about 39 percent of their final salaries. This is a low replacement rate because Alaska teacher retirees do not receive Social Security. It compares to a 76 percent replacement rate for teachers still in the Alaska pension plan.

In 1991, in reaction to underfunding issues, West Virginia soft-froze its teacher pension plan, placing new hires in a defined contribution plan. It also allowed members of the pension plan to switch voluntarily to the defined contribution plan. VALIC, which administered the defined contribution plan, sent salespeople into the schools to convince pension members to switch, arguing that they'd be much better off, and many did switch. By 2005, it was clear that precisely the opposite had occurred. Those who switched would have been much better off staying put. Only 105 out of 1,767 members over age 60 had accumulated balances of more than $100,000, which in itself would not afford more than a $4,000 annual income following the 4 percent withdrawal convention.[2] As a consequence, West Virginia then closed the DC plan and reopened the pension plan to new hires. After a concerted union campaign, in 2008, the state allowed people still in the DC plan the option of switching into the pension plan, which 78 percent did.[3]

What is interesting about the West Virginia experience is how much it parallels those of Argentina, Bolivia, and other countries that were able to reverse privatizations of their social security systems. In all of the cases, it was clear that private accounts produced much less retirement income than the defined benefit pension plans they replaced. West Virginia remains as a model for state employees in other states that froze their pension plans

Winning the Right to Transfer Plans

If West Virginia represents an actual reversal of shifting employees from secure defined benefit pension plans to risky defined contribution 401(k)-like plans, other states have given their employees the option to transfer plans. This opportunity exists as a possibility for any private or public employer that maintains both defined contribution and defined benefit plans.

What often discourages employees from even asking about the possibility of transferring plans are irrevocable choice provisions. If given a choice between types of plans when first hired, there is most often a written warning that the decision is irrevocable. For as long as they worked with that employer, they would have to stay in the same retirement plan. There are many reasons why this is unfair. New employees may not know much about the differences between the plans. People in benefits offices may have given them bad advice. Their circumstances may change later in their careers. Employees who come to believe that pensions would better serve them than the 401(k)-like plans they chose find themselves stuck as they stare at the irrevocable choice provisions. Often, they then give up hope of ever being in a real pension plan. But they should not.

As definitive as the word *irrevocable* sounds, there are ways around these provisions. The actual Internal Revenue Service requirements for defined contribution plans allow plan designs that give participants the option to change plans after specific periods or events. For example, New Mexico public university employees can choose between a defined contribution and a defined benefit plan when first employed. Those who choose the defined contribution plan are then given after seven years a 120-day window of opportunity to change their minds and shift to the defined benefit pension plan. Anyone with an employer who maintains both defined contribution and defined benefit plans and who would like to change from the former to the latter can start exploring ways to get the change window of opportunity feature added.

Still another way around irrevocability clauses is for an employer to open a new defined benefit pension plan and then provide a window of opportunity for members of the existing plans to switch to it. That was what happened in Connecticut with the campaign with which I was associated. The state created a new hybrid retirement plan with a robust defined benefit feature that we had the option of joining.

Massachusetts, in 2014, permitted members of its defined contribution Optional Retirement Program to transfer to the defined benefit Massachusetts State Employees' Retirement System. What was required was an act by the state—Section 60 of the Pension Reform Act of 2011.

Going to Court Over Eligibility

Many employers with both defined benefit and defined contribution retirement plans do not give new hires the option of which to join. New hires are told by HR staff that they are eligible for a 401(k)-like plan only. Most accept this determination at face value since it is coming from the HR office staff, and it is their job to know. After several years working in the job, an employee finds out that the employer's pension plan provides a much better retirement benefit. Too bad she wasn't eligible. She can only curse her lousy luck and resent those who were eligible.

But is she necessarily so doomed? Probably she is, but maybe not. Anyone in that situation should consult with an experienced pension attorney to see if the original eligibility determination can be legally challenged. You should never simply ask an employer or employer's representative.

Jim Kaplan had been working for about fifteen years as a half-time adult education teacher in Massachusetts. When hired initially, HR staff told him that while public K-12 teachers belonged to the Massachusetts Teachers Retirement System pension plan, adult educators were only eligible for Social Security coverage. Later, even though there was a union contract in force, management through a unilateral change without bargaining replaced Social Security coverage with an individual option to defer income taxes by contributions to a 457 plan, similar to a 401(k) plan.

Invoking labor law protections against a unilateral change by management, the union's attorney filed a case seeking restoration of Social Security coverage, and the union side won. The adult education teachers in the bargaining unit now had the option to regain Social Security coverage. All but one chose to do so. The one who decided not to rejoin Social Security later much regretted the decision as retirement approached. For a little more take-home pay, she had irrevocably lost the opportunity to enhance her retirement income significantly.

When I heard this story, it rang true with my own experience. When I took my Connecticut job and erroneously chose a defined contribution plan over the state pension plan, HR staff members told me that an advantage of it was that I didn't have to pay Social Security taxes. I knew enough then to see that it wasn't an advantage but did not know enough to challenge it. Three years later, unions in Connecticut did challenge it and won optional Social Security coverage like in the Massachusetts case. A significant number of employees, though, chose not to join Social Security—I did decide to join—and later, like the Massachusetts adult education employee, much regretted that decision.

In Massachusetts, after the Social Security victory, Kaplan was asked by the same union attorney whether he also wanted to challenge the determination that he was ineligible for the pension plan. He hadn't thought to do that, but why not? The union attorney then went to court and successfully argued that the state statute that governed pension plan eligibility did not exclude Kaplan and other adult educators like him. He was then able to buy back coverage for all of his previous years of employment by transferring funds from his 457 plan to the state pension plan. That, combined with Social Security, made a tremendous difference in his retirement income some twenty years later.[4] The moral of this story is that one should never take unfavorable eligibility determinations at face value. Verify, including with pension attorneys, to see if an appeal or other action could pay off.

Purchase of Service Credits

In all transfer opportunities, there should be provisions to allow transferees to use the funds accumulated in the defined contribution plans to purchase service credits (credit for time employed) in the pension plan. The number of years served significantly affects benefit amounts. This was explicitly allowed in the Connecticut and Massachusetts cases but is not permitted, although it should be, in the New Mexico one.

There are two general approaches to pricing the cost of service credits. In the "looking forward" approach, plan administrators consider the credits to be like a deferred annuity that will provide income upon retirement at the age specified by the plan, say 65. Actuaries then estimate—since there is no way to know what future salaries will be precisely—the price based upon the number of credits purchased, the age of the purchaser, and the present salary. That was the approach used in the Connecticut example. I knew someone who had to pay over one million dollars for thirty-five years of credits. He had it in his account and considered it money well spent since he would receive a much higher pension income than what the one-million-dollar balance would afford, about $40,000 a year following the 4 percent withdrawal convention.

Massachusetts followed the "looking backward approach." Transferees were required to pay a sum equivalent to past employer contributions plus interest to their defined contribution plans. Kaplan, the part-time adult education teacher, was able to buy back twenty years of service with his 457 plan accumulation. His cost was what he would have contributed to the pension plan during those years plus a 1 percent interest rate. It resulted in a minimal price that he could easily cover with his 457 funds, which had been growing at 4 to 5 percent annually. The interest rate was so low, less than increases in the cost of living, because the state of Massachusetts had kept it low to minimize what it had to pay job changers who left the pension plan and cashed out with lump-sum payments. The state used the same approach for service credit purchases in 2014 for employees who transferred from the defined-contribution Optional Retirement Program to the defined benefit Massachusetts State Employees' Retirement System, except this time with a higher rate of interest.

Between the looking forward and looking backward approaches, the former is more expensive for employees. The extra expense, however, of the looking forward approach is not so much as to nullify the considerable financial benefits in retirement income that it brings as leaving the money in the defined contribution accounts.

The looking forward approach figured into the factors that enabled the Connecticut reform victory. In addition to the state saving money on contributions as discussed above, it would also save money because of the looking forward method used for pricing our purchases of service credits. We bought in at full actuarial value. We paid the total cost of the liability the pension fund was assuming—the cost of our future benefits. Unlike participants already in the pension plan, we carried no unfunded liabilities. For we transferees, the state only needed to pay normal contributions going forward, which, as noted, were less than what they would be paying to the defined contribution plan. This infusion of new money into a struggling pension plan reduced its percentage of unfunded liability. This improved the state of Connecticut's credit rating and thereby reduced its bonding costs.

Indeed, according to one subsequent budget estimate, Connecticut saved $10 million a year because of the transfers.

Creating New Defined Benefit Pension Plans

Each year, even though there is an overall downward trend in defined benefit pension plan coverage, some startup and existing companies are choosing to sponsor new defined benefit plans. There are two types. The first are traditional final-salary plans. But here there is a large qualification. The new plans are mainly in established prosperous small businesses, such as legal, financial, and medical firms, where owners pay themselves high salaries. By setting up traditional defined benefit plans, the owners can defer much more taxes than they could with 401(k)-type plans. The new plans are mostly tax-dodging strategies and do not cover many workers. But at the same time, workers for these businesses, in addition to the working owners, benefit from having an actual pension plan, especially if they participate in the plan for many years before retiring. Federal law requires the working owners to cover their workers as well as themselves.

While these kinds of tax-dodging plans continue to pop up for a minority of small businesses, there are no larger firms creating them. There is nothing to prohibit their creation if owners and managers were genuinely concerned with the retirement security of their workers. If it was possible to create final-salary pension plans in the past, it is possible to develop them now; and if it is possible to create them in other countries, it would be possible to develop them once again in the United States. But the reality is that owners and managers see too many risk, tax, and planning disadvantages to their creation. For them, defined contribution plans are less financially risky and more predictable, even if that is at the expense of their workers' retirement incomes.

However, it is different for the second type of new pension arrangement, cash balance plans. They have grown despite overall pension plan coverage declining in the private sector. Between 2001 and 2017, the number of cash balance pension plans have grown from 1,337 to

23,520, a rate of growth that exceeds that of new 401(k) plans. They exist in all sizes of business, from those with just a few employees to giant corporations such as IBM, AT&T, and Boeing.[5] Whereas final-salary pension plans have decreased drastically in the private sector, cash balance pension plans have increased significantly.

Cash balance plans are attractive to employers because of their limited risk compared to final-salary pension plans, risk that they can more easily manage. They also carry tax advantages for employers since they allow higher tax-deductible contributions than 401(s). For that reason, the vast majority of employers that sponsor cash balance plans sponsor them alongside 401(k) plans to maximize tax deductions.

These employer advantages come at the expense of employee retirement incomes. Nevertheless, cash balance plans are better for employees than 401(k)s. With them, employees accrue account balances that cannot decline during market downturns as do those of 401(k)s. Cash balance plans are required by law to offer annuity options from within their collective funds as well as lump-sum payments to retirees. They thus are more like final-salary plans in that respect since there is the possibility of receiving an actual pension upon retirement.

Any employee or union local stuck with only a 401(k) plan should consider trying to get the employer to change it to a cash balance plan. It should be a relatively easy benefit reform to win since it carries advantages for the employer as well as for employees. The same can be said for the new adjustable pension plans.

PART IV

TOWARD BETTER RETIREMENT

--- 17 ---

What Is Needed

The American retirement system, like its healthcare system, is fragmented. There are multiple retirement plans with different features. There is enormous outcome inequality. People with the same career incomes, types of work, and years working end up with dramatically different retirement incomes.

At the same time, within all of those fragments, some plans work well for those who are lucky enough to have them. In what follows, I will summarize the principles needed for an ideal plan (see Table 17.1, page 229) and then see how they are present or not present in the major types of plans Americans have. None of the plans, as can be seen readily from the table, has all of the principles. Some have more than others. Also, the principles are not of equal value. If forced to choose, it would be better to have a plan that produces an adequate retirement income than one that was portable, that is, so long as one was able to stay with the same job until retirement, a big assumption. What works for one employee does not necessarily work for another.

Instead of a fragmentary system, as with healthcare reform, a unitary one would be better. That would be an overall system built around the essential principles in Table 17.1 to produce secure lifetime retirement incomes that allowed people to maintain their preretirement standards of living.

Social Security is the base of the American retirement system. It has generally functioned well in that role, though with room for improvement. It is the other parts of the system, provided mainly through employer-sponsored plans, that have not worked well. These were supposed to complement Social Security so that in combination Social Security and the employer-sponsored plans would provide adequate retirement income. It is the employer-sponsored plans that are entirely fragmentary. Though they work well for some workers, they do not work well for all workers. They vary from providing no income, because close to half of all workers do not have access to a retirement plan beyond Social Security, to providing only token amounts, to providing adequate amounts. They differ in how they are organized. And, with an increasingly mobile workforce where changing jobs throughout careers has become more commonplace than staying with one employer, the plans, if they exist, do not coordinate well.

To know what such an ideal unitary system would require, it is necessary to specify its ingredients. These features exist among the different types of retirement plans.

Adequacy

Adequacy means that a retirement plan delivers enough income so that its retirees can maintain their pre-retirement standards of living without having to worry about the years ahead. Although there is no universal consensus among retirement planning experts as to how much income that would be, the 70 percent of final pre-retirement rule of thumb is reasonable for a starting point. Given that health expenses rise with age, having access to affordable healthcare is vital if there is to be adequacy. Medicare provides mostly affordable access to healthcare for the conditions that it covers. The problem is that it does not cover conditions such as dental, hearing, and visual.

Adequacy, in an American context, mostly refers to the combined retirement income from Social Security and employer-sponsored plans. We can compare types of retirement plans that have the same rates of contribution and years of plan participation. Final-salary pension plans

TABLE 17.1: Essential Principles and Types of Retirement Plans

Principles	Social Security	Final Salary Pension	Cash Balance Plan	Adjustable Pension Plan	401(k)
Adequacy	No	Varies	No	No	Least
Pool Risks & Assets	Yes	Yes	Yes	Yes	No
Portable	Yes	No	Yes	No	Yes
Professional Investing	Yes	Yes	Yes	Yes	No
Guaranteed Benefits Based on Work Careers	Yes	Yes	Yes	Yes	No
Lifetime Income	Yes	Yes	Yes	Yes	No
Cost of Living Adjustment	Yes	Varies	Varies	Varies	No
Properly Funded & Well Managed	Mostly	Varies	Varies	Varies	No

produce the highest retirement incomes, 401(k)s the least, and cash balance and adjustable pension plans more-or-less in the middle.

Dropping the assumptions of equal funding and years of participation to look at particular plans, we can still say that final-salary pension plans have the potential to produce the most replacement income for retirees. The qualifier *potential* is necessary because the amount of replacement income depends on the generosity of the benefit formula. Participants in the California Public Employees Pension System (CALPERS) have a generous final-salary benefit formula, with a multiplier of 2.5 percent, as well as Social Security. Members of other final-salary pension plans can have much lower multipliers of 1 percent or less. Also very important is that not all participants in public pension plans also participate in Social Security. Their pension plan may be generous, such as those for California and Massachusetts K-12 teachers, but because their employer does not participate in Social Security, their overall retirement income is significantly less than that of employees who have both plans. Their generous public pension may not be generous enough to make up for the lack of Social Security income.

Cash balance and the new adjustable pension plans are at the second tier of potential adequacy. As in final-salary pension plans, the devil is in the details of the funding and benefit formulas. They vary according to employer contribution rates and credited dollars provided for accrual. For every dollar contributed, they will produce less retirement income than equivalent amounts contributed to final-salary plans due to investment performance tempering their accrual rates. Whereas final-salary plans have locked-in accrual rates, those for cash balance and adjustable pension plans decrease if market returns decrease. At the same time, they produce much more income than 401(k)s at the same contribution rates.

Flexible (adjustable) pension plans have only been in existence since 2013. No one has yet fully retired under one. We don't know for sure what their adequacy will be. My sense is they will produce retirement incomes similar to those of cash balance plans—not as good as final-salary plans but much better than 401(k)s.

The 401(k) and other defined-contribution plans produce the least retirement incomes, assuming equal funding and years of participation. They lack the advantages of risk pooling and returns suffer due to considerable administrative fees, commissions, and profit-taking drained off by the financial services companies that administer them.

Pool Risks and Assets

Final-salary, cash benefit, and flexible pension plans are different subspecies of defined benefit plans. All pool risks and assets, unlike 401(k) and other defined contribution plans that individualize risks and assets. It is precisely because defined benefit plans employ the social insurance principle of pooling that they can deliver higher retirement incomes.

Longevity is the first of the risks. It is not living a long life, which is a good thing, that is a risk. The risk is having the good fortune of a long life ruined by the bad fortune of running out of money to support it. When that risk exists, it is both an individual and a social problem. For individuals affected, no one wants to look forward to a drop in income when they are least able to go back to work. For governments, elderly poverty is expensive, requiring the provision of tax-supported welfare services. It is in the interests of individuals and governments that retirement income last until death.

The problem with depending on individual savings to finance retirement is that it is impossible to know how to pace the expenditure of those savings during retirement so that they last until death since no one knows exactly when death will come.

Defined benefit pensions solve longevity risk by distributing income for life rather than until the income runs out. This solution is possible, as we've discussed, by actuarially calculating the average age of death for the pool of people insured and then distributing each retiree's income on the assumption that he or she will live until exactly that age. Most will live longer or shorter lives, but all will receive incomes for their entire lives. Money saved from paying the short-lived for fewer years than average offsets money lost from paying the long-lived for more years than average.

The 401(k) plans could be without longevity risk if they embedded life annuities, but few do. Most 401(k) and similar retirement savings plan participants continue to invest their balances after retirement and make periodic withdrawals. The federal government, which subsidizes these accounts through tax deferrals, requires retirees to begin spending down these accounts when they reach age 70 and a half through taking out Required Minimum Distributions (RMDs).

Pension plans pool investment risks in multiple ways. If individuals are in pension plans, market conditions at the time of retirement do not affect pension sizes. Members thus are immune to the market timing risks of when they retire. While the collective trust funds from which the pension payments are drawn rise and fall with market conditions, they are organized such that surpluses during up markets offset losses during down markets, leaving enough to make consistent payments.

Members are also immune to the more hidden timing risk of when managers place investments. For individuals with 401(k)s, it is better to be young when markets are beginning to climb since the increased values will have longer to render accumulating returns. Starting with a long period of declining or flat markets will not produce as much long-term accumulations even if the overall average rate of return is the same.

The timing of when individuals enter and exit markets and invest while in markets all affect final accumulations. This type of timing risk does not affect pension plan members. There is timing risk for the plan as a whole but not for members within it.

The pooling of assets shields pension members from timing risks. It is similar to the principle of individuals diversifying investments to avoid the risk of being overly reliant on a single stock whose value, Enron-style, could collapse. Except in the case of pensions, the spreading out is of risks as opposed to investments.

Portability

With fewer employees spending full or nearly full careers with the same employer, it is all the more critical that they be able to consistently accrue retirement benefits as they move from job to job. Such portability occurs with Social Security, 401(k)s, and cash balance plans but rarely with final-salary pension plans.

Because final-salary pension plans are generally not portable, people who leave positions covered by those plans are at a disadvantage. Having a vested final-salary pension plan based on just five years and a starting salary in your twenties will not produce much retirement income forty years later, especially when considering the impact of inflation.

Multi-employer pension plans, such as those covering truckers, musicians, and supermarket cashiers, resolve the portability issue so long as the job changer goes to an employer who is also a sponsor of the same plan. But that is only a partial solution. The portability does not extend to employers who are not sponsors of that particular multi-employer plan.

Some final-salary state employee pension plans have reciprocity arrangements with other states that allow service credits from earlier employers to transfer to those of later ones. But these arrangements are rare.

Professional Investing

Professionals rather than individual members should handle investment decisions. For all retirement plans with the exception of Social Security, investment returns are the most significant source of their revenues. For that reason, it is to the advantage of plan members that professionals handle their investment. Few members have the knowledge to invest competently. Do-it-yourself investing is a recipe for bad investing in most cases. In addition, being required to make investment decisions is burdensome for most.

Guaranteed Benefits Based on Work Careers

The work career, not investing skill or luck of the participant, should determine the size of a retirement benefit, and that benefit should be guaranteed. It should be the responsibility of plan sponsors to organize the funding and management of plans so that they can meet their benefit responsibilities. It should also be their responsibility to make up any shortages that threaten their ability to make benefit payments. Every worker participating in a plan should have the assurance that plan managers will never make up shortages through benefit reductions.

The principle of guaranteeing benefits is what keeps plan sponsors honest and responsible. Like having to make payroll, they know they have to make pension payments. However, they have more incentive to make sure they can keep paying active rather than inactive, retired workers. Without the former, their businesses could not continue. Not paying retirees what they are due would not harm profitability. In the coldest capitalistic calculation, retirees have no value, and thus business owners have no purely economic motive to assure their pension payments. For that reason and others, retirees need to have guaranteed benefits.

The problem with 401(k) and similar individual retirement savings plans in this respect is that employer sponsors do not have the responsibility of having to guarantee that the plans will produce specified retirement incomes that reflect work careers. If retirees come up short, it is their problem no matter how long or how much they contributed to their plans.

It is important to emphasize that even if active workers make no payments to retirement plans and employers exclusively fund them, workers are still making the contributions, as contradictory as that sounds. When employers pay for fringe benefits, such as health and retirement plans, the costs come out of the worker's *total* compensation, which includes fringe benefit costs as well as salary payments. By receiving the benefit, the worker gets less take-home salary. The worker is contributing a part of her or his total compensation. That the worker is paying is true even if it seems like the benefit is a gift from the employer. Employers thus are using worker money and should be responsible for guaranteeing that those contributions, which amount to deferred compensation, will be returned as adequate retirement income.

The principle of guaranteed benefits applies firstly to accruals. Once they are credited, they should be permanent. It seems reasonable, though, that a plan could modify future accrual rates according to market returns, as do cash balance and adjustable pension plans, in the interests of assuring overall plan solvency. What should be guaranteed are the accruals once credited. It is like a savings account deposit in a bank. Once credited to an account, the bank has a legal obligation to return it to the owner upon demand regardless of the shape of the bank's overall balance sheet. It can credit the account with different rates of quarterly interest going forward, but it can't reduce the account once credited.

The principle of guaranteed benefits also applies to pensions already being distributed to retirees. They should have guaranteed for life amounts.

Lifetime Income

All retirees should have regular guaranteed income that begins when they leave work and lasts for the rest of their lives. Social Security is the model in this respect. Upon obtaining early or full retirement age, participants begin receiving a set monthly income that lasts for the rest of their lives, long or short as they may be. There is no alternative option to take a lump-sum payment.

Having a lifetime retirement income is crucial for many reasons. It provides certainty that there *will always* be income to live on when no longer able to work. Receipt of the monthly checks is automatic, absolving the retiree of any work necessary to produce them. This absolution becomes a more valuable feature when sickness or advanced age impairs people.

Pension plans like Social Security also have automatic life payments. The 401(k)s, however, do not automatically produce lifetime incomes. They could if they automatically became annuities upon retirement, but most don't. Converting a 401(k) accumulation into an annuity—annuitization—is only an optional course of action. It is not followed by most because of the expense of commercial annuities. Most 401(k) retirees continue actively managing investments, with or without advisors, while making periodic withdrawals for living expenses. Both ends—managing investing and deciding how much to withdraw—are full of uncertainties that add to the problems of daily life during retirement.

Life incomes provide structure for retirement. There are enough problems that accompany aging without having to worry about a haphazard income.

The principle in this book is that retirees should have steady sources of regular income. It does little good if that income is a miserly amount. Retirees need reliable monthly income that is adequate to cover their needed goods and services. The principles of life income and adequacy need to be combined to produce a favorable retirement income system.

Cost of Living Adjustments

All retirement income should keep up with inflation. Cost of living adjustments fundamentally guard against inflation risk.

Whereas Social Security has automatic annual COLAs, employer-based pension plans vary greatly over whether their benefit payments contain COLAs. If they do, they vary in how and when they calculate those COLAs. In most plans, COLAs don't carry the same guarantees as accrued pension payments and can be suspended, eliminated, or reduced.

For family financial stability, it is better to have an initially lower-paying pension with a COLA than an initially higher-paying flat pension. The income to which household expenditures are adjusted will keep up, at least partially, with inflation. With flat incomes, there will be a chronic experience of being financially squeezed as inflation eats away the purchasing power of the pension payment.

Properly Funded and Well Managed

It is vital to properly fund a retirement plan if it is to be capable of providing adequate income. For pension plans, contribution rates must be sufficiently high to ensure that trust funds grow enough to make all guaranteed benefit payments. Intervening between contributions and benefit payments are market returns. Increasingly, employer-spon-sored pension plans have become dependent on them. Social Security funds are to a much lesser extent since they contain Treasury bills and not equities. Because of the significance of market returns to employer-sponsored pension plans, plan sponsors must make sound investment decisions. There are a series of other managing issues as well.

Properly funding a 401(k) is virtually impossible. As mentioned in my calculations in chapter 15, it would take contributions to 25 to 30 percent of salary to obtain, combined with Social Security payments, a 70 percent replacement of pre-retirement salary. The average corpo-rate employer-employee contribution rate is around 8 percent. Some plans have contribution rates as high as 15 percent, but are still well short of what would be necessary. Pension plans, primarily because of risk-sharing, can generate sufficient retirement incomes for much lower contribution rates.

18

Retirement Security for All

I n the previous chapter I compared types of retirement plans that exist for Americans in terms of their advantages and disadvantages. In this chapter we will return to the country's overall retirement system. Popularly known as a three-legged stool, it is a system built around Social Security, employer plans, and individual savings. Of those legs or pillars, only the first—Social Security—is universal, meaning that virtually all workers participate in it. They participate in it because their participation in mandatory. Neither they nor their employers can voluntarily opt out, with very few exceptions. And it is a good thing that it is mandatory. Otherwise, elderly poverty rates would be much higher than they are. Social Security is the part of the American system that works best. But as important or fundamental as it is, it is not sufficient, as currently structured, to deliver adequate retirement income. Employer plans must augment its income so that together the two pillars produce adequate retirement income. The third source, of individual savings, is insignificant in most cases. Unlike Social Security, the second pillar is not mandatory. The decision of an employer to offer a retirement plan is entirely voluntary. Therein lies the largest source of the inadequacy of the American system. Employers are also free to offer inadequate retirement plans, another reason why the American system comes up short.

For sure, the American system works well for the minority of workers who have long-term strong pension plans. But what is needed is a system that works well for all workers, not just one that provides retirement security for some. There are two ways to achieve this: make Social Security a stand-alone system that delivers adequate retirement income or ensure that all workers have, in addition to Social Security, adequate employer plans.

Both options are consistent with how other countries have achieved high levels by international standards of retirement income adequacy for all their workers. The nine highest-ranking countries (Table 18.1, page 239) in terms of retirement income adequacy are Italy, Luxembourg, Austria, Portugal, Denmark, Spain, Argentina, and The Netherlands. (The United States ranks twenty-eighth.) These are the countries that have come closest to providing retirement security for all. Seven of the nine achieve high levels of adequacy with stand-alone single-pillar public social security systems. Two, Denmark and the Netherlands, achieve it with two-pillar mandatory systems of social security and employer plans. Denmark's employer system is defined contribution, the Netherlands' is defined benefit. There may be other pillars or sources of retirement income, but they, as in the United States, are far less significant.

Three Models of Strong National Retirement Systems

The international experience thus shows that countries can achieve retirement income adequacy either through building up single national pension systems or through diversifying sources of retirement income. The World Bank, the Organization for Economic Cooperation and Development, and other international agencies promote the second approach. Their reasoning is that building up second occupational pillars, especially with defined contribution plans, promotes national savings, capital formation, and is more economically sustainable. It is also consistent with neoliberal reforms of retirement provision, with private financial services industries being beneficiaries through privatization of retirement funds. The opposite argument

**TABLE 18.1: The Three Models of High-Adequacy National
Retirement Systems**

	Description	Examples
Single-Pillar DB	Mandatory defined benefit national pension plan	Italy, Luxembourg, Austria, Portugal, Spain, Argentina
Two-Pillar DB/DC	Mandatory defined benefit national pension plan plus mandatory employer defined contribution retirement savings plan with adequate contributions	Denmark
Two-Pillar DB	Mandatory defined benefit national pension plan plus mandatory employer defined benefit pension plan with adequate benefits	The Netherlands

Source for highest-scoring countries for total retirement replacement rates: Organization for
Economic Cooperation and Development, *Pensions at a Glance 2019*, Table 5.3.

for stand-alone systems is that they deliver retirement income more efficiently at lower cost since there are no private companies pulling profits out of them. In addition, they have national coordinated administrative apparatuses as opposed to the duplication of functions required by competing private firms.

All the international systems that have achieved adequacy have had a defined benefit pillar, either stand-alone or as part of a two-pillar system. But second pillars, as indicated for the minority of countries that have them, have been based on defined contribution or defined benefit principles. There are thus three international models for achieving retirement plan adequacy: stand-alone social security systems, the most prevalent; modest social security systems combined with generous defined contribution occupational plans; and modest social security systems combined with generous defined benefit pension occupational plans. We'll look at them in turn for their potential lessons for resolving the retirement crisis in the United States.

Single-Pillar Social Security Systems. In Italy, Luxembourg, Austria, Portugal, Spain, and Argentina there is a single national social security system that provides adequate retirement income for the great majority of retirees. Secondary retirement plans are insignificant. It would be as if Social Security in the United States provided close to double what it does now, and there would be no need for 401(k)s or other occupational retirement plans.

Most stand-alone government systems operate through pay-as-you-go principles. Current workers through their contributions collectively provide incomes for retired ones. It is an inter-generation compact that current workers have an interest in honoring because though they are providers now, in the future when they retire they will be on the receiving end as beneficiaries. The opposite approach, consistent with defined contribution second tiers, is to have current workers save up to fund their own retirement expenses, hence their designation as funded systems.

Single-pillar retirement systems, somewhat like single-payer health insurance systems, have a number of prominent advantages because of their unitary integrated desgns. As with Social Security, workers can go from employer to employer while staying within and receiving credit within the same system. Their benefit accruals are completely portable. As public not-for-profit systems, there is no leakage of worker contributions to shareholder dividend payments or other forms of profit-taking. As unitary national systems, there is no leakage of contributions to the expenses, including advertising, to maintain a competitive parity with other firms. When they retire, workers only have to deal with a single source of retirement income. With two-pillar systems, they have to deal with two or more. More, potentially, because in two-pillar systems, workers who have changed employers may have more than one second-pillar retirement plan. Employers have advantages as well. Instead of having to deal with all of the administrative complexities of making contributions to two different retirement plans, they have a single payment.

It is theoretically possible for an unfunded pay-as-you-go system to transition to a funded one. This occurred with many private employer-provided defined benefit pension plans in the United States, as we know, after the 1973 ERISA legislation mandated them to do so. Such transitions are difficult because of the problem of double payment. Current worker contributions have to finance both their future retirement expenses and the legacy expenses of current retirees. That problem has bedeviled many retirement plans making such transitions. National governments have generally opted not to make such transitions or to make them gradually because of the budgetary problems involved. Either approach theoretically works, with each having different advantages, disadvantages, and consequences.

Two Pillar with Defined Contribution Second Pillar. Through the 1980s, Denmark had a situation like that of the United States. It had a social security system that covered everyone. Unlike the United States, however, Danes did not have to pay into it or have work records. They just had to meet age and income requirements. But, like Social Security in the United States, it did not provide enough income. Some occupational groups, such as civil servants, had supplementary pension plans that made up the gaps. But most did not.

Government, labor, and industry groups then devised a system wherein labor organizations would negotiate supplementary retirement plans for the workers they represented. This was the period of growing neoliberal reforms in many countries. Denmark was not immune, despite its reputation as a Nordic country with extensive welfare state programs. Instead of expanding its already existing defined benefit social security PAYGO system, the Danes opted to make funded defined contribution plans, similar to 401(k)s, the norm. Very quickly, new contracts were negotiated that included the new retirement plans. By the 2000s, nearly 90 percent of the Danish labor force was covered by the occupational plans. Employers pay two-thirds of the contributions and employees one-third. What is more, the savings rate, while varying, is minimally 12 percent, much higher than the 9 percent average for employees who have 401(k)s in the United States. As a result, large amounts of savings have piled up in these accounts. They will provide—most people under the new plans have not yet retired—a much larger fraction of Danish retirement income than that provided by its social security system.

Denmark was able to adopt a defined contribution second pillar in large part because it was designing a new system for formerly uncovered workers.[1] It would have been an entirely different matter if those workers already had defined benefit pension plans. Replacing those plans with defined contribution ones would have met considerable resistance as well as presenting financial difficulties.

It is tempting to see the Danish system as a model for the United States since it relies on defined contribution personal savings and investment accounts like 401(k)s. It is unlikely, however, under present conditions that the United States could expand its 401(k) system to approach the comprehensiveness of the Danish system. In Denmark, retirement plans for the great majority of workers are negotiated by unions. In the United States, employers in most cases have the sole prerogative over whether and how much to support a retirement plan. The reason for the difference is the much greater rate of Danish unionization. In Denmark, 82 percent of the labor force is covered by union-negotiated collective bargaining contracts. The figure for the United States is a much smaller 11.6 percent.[2] The unions not only negotiate the existence of the plans, they are also involved in managing them through representation on boards of directors.

Danish companies are not free to withhold contributions during trying economic times as they are in the United States. None of these conditions were government mandated, but they have become the norms because of the strength of unions. They also seem to be generally accepted as norms by companies.

The Danes have perhaps the best example of a defined contribution plan system because of its nearly universal coverage, high rates of contributions, and union involvement to represent worker interests. Still, it is unlikely that it will provide as much retirement income as defined benefit pension plans.

Two Pillar with Defined Benefit Second Pillar. The Netherlands represents a second example of a two-pillar system that in combination provides a comparatively high amount of replacement income. The first pillar is a defined benefit social security system, the second defined benefit occupational pension plans. Unlike in Denmark, occupational retirement plans have covered most workers for many decades. There was no need to build a new system to extend coverage to them in the 1980s and 1990s.

The Dutch system earns high marks for sustainability because its component parts must be fully funded, and then some, at 105 percent. When market investment returns decline or expenses cause them to become underfunded, they are required to regain full funding within three years through increased contributions, benefit reductions, or some combination of the two. The ability to reduce pensions to those already retired is controversial. It means that pensions are no longer strictly guaranteed. Tempering pension cuts, which there have been in the wake of financial downturns such as that of 2008, is that they have been modest—not more than 2 percent—and the systems are geared to restoring the losses to pensioners once better financial conditions permit.

There are lessons to be learned, or at least considered, from the Dutch experience regarding improving sustainability of existing pension plans in the United States. However, it does not seem likely that the United States would reverse course and return to a defined benefit pension model for companies that had abandoned that model for 401(k)s, and then extend that model to the approximately half of the labor force that is uncovered by any type of retirement plan. What the Dutch experience does show is that it is possible to have adequate and sustainable defined benefit pension plans for all workers.

Toward a Unitary One-Pillar System Based on Social Security

The United States has a two-pillar system composed of Social Security and a mainly defined-contribution set of employer-sponsored plans. The clear implication of the most successful example of that model internationally, Denmark, is that the United States should make its second pillar mandatory or quasi-mandatory with adequate contributions. While technically possible, neither reform appears politically likely. The second pillar remains under employer prerogative except where, in the minority of situations, unions have the power to

negotiate collective bargaining arrangements. Even those employers who offer defined contribution retirement plans voluntarily do so
with the freedom to reduce their contributions. Caught between the
realization that consistent second-pillar contributions are necessary to
achieve adequacy and the reluctance of employers to commit to them,
the financial services industry uges individuals to take the responsibility instead. If their employers do not have retirement plans, they
should open their own Individual Retirement Accounts. But though
IRA contributions have grown, they have come nowhere near what is
required to provide adequacy. The voluntary second pillar of the U.S.
system, in short, is too weak to provide enough retirement income
supplemental to Social Security to achieve universal adequacy comparable to the two-pillar Danish and Dutch systems.

Since a second pillar of mandatory employer-sponsored plans with
adequate contributions is unlikely to occur, a more feasible alternative would be to have the mandatory first pillar, Social Security,
provide relatively more of the nation's retirement income. The more
that Social Security could provide adequate retirement income, the
less that would be needed from employer-sponsored plans.

Increase Social Security Contributions and Benefits

There are multiple ways to increase Social Security revenue in order
to finance higher retirement incomes. The most obvious would be to
increase the combined employer-employee FICA rate of 12.4 percent
of salary. The U.S. rate is low by international standards and could
bear incremental increases. The most just path, as argued in chapter 5,
would be to remove the cap on labor income taxed and begin taxing
investment returns, the main source of income of the wealthy. Still
another way would be to open up new revenue streams. Currently,
Social Security has three revenue streams: contributions, interest from
Treasury bond investments, and taxes on Social Security incomes.
Other possible revenue sources could be from general income taxes,
business taxes, and taxes on financial transactions.

Catch-up Contributions

As discussed in chapter 3, people with the same final earnings receive a wide range of Social Security benefits depending on how their work careers developed. People who had always been middle-income earners for their thirty-five highest-earning years receive Social Security benefits that replace 41 percent of their final incomes. But most people start their work careers at lower than their last earnings. Those that started at minimum-wage jobs and then worked their way up to final middle-income jobs replaced 31 rather than 41 percent of their final incomes. Because of the nature of the calculation of the Social Security benefit, lower-income years decrease the size of the retirement checks. This dilemma is the career pattern problem.

To fix the problem, we have to first recall, also from chapter 3, how Social Security calculates benefits. It first establishes an average indexed monthly earnings amount based on the thirty-five years of highest earnings. To that amount, it applies a progressive formula of different-sized multipliers. The result is the initial monthly benefit.

In almost all cases, the initial monthly pension amount would be higher if Social Security based it on the final or highest rather than average career income. Retirees could achieve this through a reform of Social Security that allowed them to purchase additional earnings credits to increase their average indexed monthly earnings. They would be paying back years of low contributions to Social Security to compensate for the significant negative effect of small earnings years on retirement benefits. They could do this by voluntarily rolling over part or all of their retirement savings accounts into Social Security in return for higher indexed pension incomes.

The right to purchase additional service credits is a parallel feature of many public and private sector defined benefit retirement plans. Social Security could adopt that right as well. A similar policy exists in several Central and Eastern European countries. They had mandatory personal retirement savings accounts carved out from public social security plans. When their governments realized that the savings accounts produced lower benefits than the public plans, they allowed account holders to reconvert part or all the funds back into the public plans.[3]

Here is an example of how a service credit purchase program could work. Consider a worker who starts with minimum wage jobs and then works his way up steadily so that at the end of his career, he is earning $51,795. That is the average for medium-income workers according to Social Security statistics (see chapter 3). Because his low earning years pull down his salary average, his annual retirement benefit would start at $16,034, which is less than the average for middle-income workers. Following Social Security's methodology for calculating benefit amounts, he could pay Social Security $65,533 out of retirement savings, if he has them. That would bring his average salary up to his final one. He then would get an extra $5,214 yearly benefit, bringing him up to a total annual benefit of $21,248, the amount for someone who had always earned his final salary. The payout rate for the indexed extra benefit would be 8 percent, much higher than anything available on the commercial annuity market. It would be money well spent.

Such a service credit purchase program would be an excellent deal for most, but not all, Social Security participants. The payout rate for the extra benefit purchased rises up until the higher part of the medium-income range. Then the payout rate begins to decline. This pattern is a reflection of the progressive nature of the benefit formula. The higher the income category in the formula, the lower the percentage of it that translates into a higher benefit. It is still a considerably better deal than commercial annuities for the great majority of workers who started their careers with low salaries and then worked their way up to high final ones. But by the time we get to those trying to obtain Social Security's maximum benefits, the payout is less than that of commercial annuities. There is, in statistical terms, a curvilinear relationship between the amount of benefit and the payout rate: it rises and then drops. But still, the vast majority of participants would be better off putting their savings in Social Security to bring up their career earnings averages, were this reform to exist, than by purchasing commercial annuities.

An alternative reform to accomplish the same goal would be if Social Security allowed people to make voluntary extra catch-up contributions as they approached retirement age to compensate for earlier low-contribution years. There is precedent for such a reform in that the tax code allows for extra catch-up contributions to 401(k) and other defined contribution plans beginning at age 50. Either way, through rollover of retirement savings or catch-up contributions, the opportunity to purchase higher Social Security checks should be available to workers.

Social Security Annuities

Close to half of workers approaching retirement have accumulated savings in 401(k)s, Individual Retirement Accounts, and other retirement savings vehicles. The sizes of their savings vary greatly between token and substantial. The median amount, as discussed in chapter 13, is approximately $109,000. Currently, there are no good ways for individuals to translate their savings into optimal retirement incomes. Commercial annuities are expensive, continued active management and withdrawal risky.

If workers were able to redeem their savings through the purchase of nonprofit Social Security annuities, which would be better deals than commercial ones, they could optimize their retirement incomes. There are several possible Social Security annuity programs that would advantage workers.

1. Short-term Annuities. If workers were allowed upon retirement to purchase short-term indexed annuities, that would enable them to delay beginning their Social Security benefits to later ages up to age 70. Every year of deferral would increase significantly both initial and lifetime Social Security retirement incomes.

Those who voluntarily or involuntarily begin taking retirement benefits at age 62 sacrifice considerable lifetime income compared to those who start taking it at Full Retirement Age or later. The age 62 early retirement benefit is 27.5 percent lower than the Full Retirement

Age benefit. Every year of delay of initiation of benefits after the full retirement age, currently 66, results in an 8 percent increase in the benefit. Put simply, if people take early retirement, they receive lower retirement checks. If they take deferred retirement, they receive higher checks. The decreases and increases are so that total lifetime benefits remain the same.

The idea of this proposal is that people could retire at age 62 and pay Social Security for an annuity that would provide them monthly income up until the age they wanted to initiate their regular benefit. Let's say that someone wanted or needed to retire at 62, the age of earliest retirement permitted by Social Security. Let's suppose, further, that she wanted to delay initiating her Social Security benefit to age 66 when it would be substantially higher. At the same time, however, she would still need income to cover her expenses between ages 62 and 66. Under this program, she would be able to purchase a four-year annuity from Social Security that would return to her a monthly payment that would equal what her payment would be at age 66. The only unknown would be the sizes of future cost-of-living adjustments. One way to handle that would be to purchase the annuity in two payments. The initial payment, at age 62, would be for the value of the pension checks up to age 66 without consideration of future cost of living adjustments since those would be unknown. Once she reached 66, the age to initiate her regular Social Security benefits, she would make a second payment to cover the costs of the COLA increases. Social Security could design the reform so she could pay for the COLA increases in total or through deductions from subsequent pension checks.

Those with sufficient retirement savings can, in theory, already defer taking their Social Security benefits to reap the higher later age benefits. Their savings can support them in the meantime. But that strategy incurs risks. If they invest the savings, the market might decline significantly. There is also what we can call "rationality risk." The holder of the savings might not be able to figure out exactly how much can be spent or resist using the savings for other purposes. Converting the savings into additional, known Social Security income at age 62 would be much simpler and predictable than continuing to manage and spend down the savings for living expenses. It would be possible to resolve some of that risk by purchasing a four-year certain commercial annuity. But then she would run into the problems of knowing about and knowing how to do this, choosing a company, the expensive nature of those annuities, etc. Far better and more certain would be to be able to lock in the extra retirement income by directly rolling the retirement savings into Social Security.

2. Life Annuities. This reform would benefit those who still had retirement savings after employing the first two policy proposals of catch-up payments and the purchase of short-term annuities. Or, in the case of the first two proposals not being enacted, it could be a stand-alone proposal of relevance to participants with all levels of retirement savings.

When 401(k) plans began to replace traditional defined benefit pensions in 1981, as we have seen, there was an implicit assumption that retirees would convert their accumulations into life income annuities to mimic pension incomes. This did not occur on a large scale due primarily to commercial annuities becoming increasingly expensive. Also, commercial annuities charge higher prices for women because they live on average longer than men.

Availability of government-issued (Social Security or Treasury) immediate indexed life annuities for purchase would enable retirees to obtain more income than otherwise available from commercial annuities or continued active management of their accumulated retirement savings. How much more income would depend on the nature of the Social Security investment model. Using the present Social Security investment model in Treasury bonds, its annuities could have an approximate 10 percent higher payout rate than commercial annuities. An additional benefit for women is that they would have the same payouts as men since Social Security uses gender-blended longevity assumptions. A still higher payout would be possible if Social Security began to invest some of its trust fund surplus in stock market equities.

It is important to note that the original Social Security draft legislation in 1934 contained a program that would have allowed participants to use savings to purchase annuities issued by the Department of the Treasury. It was thus clearly thought feasible by its proponents then. The proposal did not survive the final legislation due to opposition from private life insurance companies that had their own annuities to sell and did not welcome competition from a public option in that market.[4]

3. Deferred Annuities. With this reform, workers voluntarily would be able to purchase Social Security deferred annuities while still working. They would be able to redeem the annuities upon retirement for higher pension checks.

A Public Option Employer-Sponsored Plan

Social Security could also develop its own public option occupational retirement plan that employers could choose to switch to from their existing individual retirement savings plans. The Social Security Administration already has the infrastructure in place to develop such a plan. Employers and employees could make contributions as set percentages of salaries, as with any defined contribution plan. The difference is that there would be defined pension benefits. One possibility would be to base the plan on employer and employee purchases of deferred annuities, as in the previous reform. Because of the enormous national risk pool, employers would be immune from having to make up pension fund shortfalls. Like occupational pension plans, a Social Security optional pension plan could invest in higher-return equities as well as in its current Treasury bond investments. Other national social security systems, such as that of Canada, invest in stock equities.

Concluding Words

As discussed throughout this book, pensions and individual retirement savings accounts are the two poles of the American retirement system. Since 1981, the center of gravity of that system has shifted to the right toward personal accounts. Some would like to see pension provision become extinct. Privatizing Social Security and ending remaining employer-sponsored pension plans would be the final steps. While such actions would enormously benefit Wall Street interests and be cheered on by neoliberal ideologists, they would decrease further the retirement security of workers.

Other countries, such as France, Austria, and the Netherlands, maintain their national and most of their occupational retirement plans as pension plans. As a result, their workers enjoy much more secure and adequate retirement incomes than do Americans.

There is nothing inevitable about the rightward shift in retirement provision in the United States. The continuation of secure pension provision in other countries indicates that it is possible, and their populations fiercely support that continuation. Like much of public policy, including healthcare, it is a matter of choice and who has the power to make choices. Any improvement in retirement security in the United States will require reversing the trend and moving back toward pension provision. There are several ways to do that, with the goal being to ensure that all Americans receive at least 70 percent of their pre-retirement incomes.

Increasing Social Security retirement income is the most direct way to achieve more pension provision. We have described several reforms to expand Social Security by allowing people to voluntarily make more contributions to it, such as through purchasing annuities. More encompassing is to expand the basic system itself. That is, employers and employees should pay higher tax contributions to it in return for higher benefits. The OASI tax rate of 6.2 percent of salary from employers and employees is lower than rates for national pension plans in many other countries. Americans could pay more to Social Security and simultaneously reduce what they pay to employer-sponsored plans so that overall payroll reductions would remain the same. Despite the famous American aversion to paying taxes, most Americans make an exception for Social Security and Medicare taxes because of the popularity of those programs. They would most likely support paying more taxes to them as long as it was clear that in return they would receive more benefits.

Obtaining these reforms to realize Social Security's potential to resolve the retirement crisis will require putting popular pressure on Congress and an administration to do so. It is like universal healthcare, which we know is technically possible because many other countries have it. So too would be providing more retirement income from guaranteed secure lifetime pensions through the federal government's most popular program, Social Security.

Glossary

Anyone investigating retirement plans for the first time will encounter a large number of terms that present challenges for understanding. Some might be thoroughly unfamiliar, such as "adverse selection" or "bend points." Some, such as "freeze," will be familiar but used in ways different than their everyday meanings. To make matters even more potentially confusing, the meanings of some will differ according to who is employing them. The definition of what constitutes a pension is an example. Some writers describe 401(k)s as pension plans. I do not.

I have explained specialized terms for the most part within the book chapters, either with direct definitions or through descriptions. But not everyone, including myself, is always able to remember the definition of a term encountered on an early page when the word without definition pops up a hundred pages later. For that reason, I've constructed this glossary. I've also put it together so that readers can see how I've used the terms when other writers may use them differently, as in the case of what counts as pension plans.

The definitions may of necessity include other specialized terms. Readers may want, in such cases, to consult the definitions of those terms.

401(a): Internal Revenue Service Code section number for a type of defined-contribution tax-deferred retirement savings plan sponsored by governments, educational institutions, and nonprofit organizations. Employers, with or without employees, contribute to individual employee savings and investment accounts that are dedicated to accumulating funds during working years to provide income for retirement years.

401(k): Internal Revenue Service Code section number for a type of tax-deferred defined contribution retirement savings plan sponsored by for-profit private businesses. Employee Retirement Income Security Act (ERISA) provisions govern 401(k) plans. Employers or employees contribute to individual employee savings and investment accounts that are dedicated to accumulating funds during working years to provide income for retirement years.

403(b): Internal Revenue Service Code section number for a type of tax-deferred defined contribution retirement savings plan sponsored by governments and nonprofit organizations. Unlike with 401(a) plans, the Internal Revenue Service does not require employers to contribute to these plans. Employees, with or without employers, contribute to individual employee savings and investment accounts that are dedicated to accumulating funds during working years to provide income for retirement years. Some employers that sponsor 401(a) plans also sponsor 403(b) plans so employees can tax defer additional retirement savings. In these cases, the 403(b) functions as a supplemental defined contribution plan.

457(b): Internal Revenue Service Code section number for a type of tax-deferred defined contribution retirement savings plan sponsored by state and local governments for their employees. These are also called deferred compensation plans. Employees, with or without employer matches, contribute to individual employee savings and investment accounts that are dedicated to accumulating funds during working years to provide income for retirement years. This type of plan is similar to a 403(b) plan. Some organizations sponsor both types, which allows employees to increase tax-deferred contributions. Unlike 401(k), 401(a), and 403(b) plans, job changers can withdraw funds from the plan before age 59½ without paying a 10 percent tax penalty.

Accumulation: The amount of funds built up in a retirement account through contributions and returns on investments.

Accrual: In defined benefit pension plans, the yearly buildup of guaranteed retirement benefits. These may be in the form of percentages of final income in traditional final salary pension plans or cash values in cash balance plans. It is important to note that, unlike with defined contribution plans, already accrued cash balances cannot lose value because of stock market investment losses.

Actuarial Science: Applied mathematical field that estimates the probability that certain risks will occur to insured populations. For example, actuaries use probability statistics to determine how long people will live on average so that pension fund managers will know how much revenue (contributions and investment returns) is needed to cover lifetime pension payments to retired plan members.

Adequacy: The extent to which a retirement plan will provide enough income during retirement years. A rule of thumb is that retirees should receive from all sources, including Social Security, at least 70 percent of pre-retirement income. It follows that an employer-sponsored retirement plan should deliver the difference between the 70 percent replacement rate and what Social Security provides.

Adjustable Pension Plan: New type of defined benefit pension plan first offered in 2014. In it, the amount of accrued benefit varies yearly, like that of a cash balance plan, according to collective investment returns. Different from a cash balance plan, the benefit is expressed as a percentage of final salary or dollar value for each year of service.

Adverse Selection: Entrance of unusually risky individuals into insurance plans. Because they are more likely to file claims, insurance plans must compensate by charging more for the plans. This is an issue for retirement annuities when their purchase is voluntary. Retirees in good health who think they are likely to live a long time are more likely to purchase annuities that make payments for their remaining life than those who think they will live for just a few years more. And people who think they are going to live longer in general do live longer. That, in turn, drives up the cost of annuities. Social Security payments, by contrast, are immune from adverse selection because its participants make up nearly all of the labor force, and they cannot cash out their benefits as lump sums even if they think they will live for only a few more years.

Annual Required Contribution (ARC): The Employee Retirement Income Security Act (ERISA) mandates that employers with private pension plans make specified payments each year that vary according to the financial ability of the trust fund to meet pension and accrual obligations.

Annuity: Financial product sold, usually, by a life insurance company. In return for a specified price, the life insurance company pays the purchaser a specified amount through regular payments over a period of time that can vary according to the terms of the agreement. Retirement annuities are usually sold for the remaining years of the purchaser's life. They were important for original conceptions of retirement saving plans in which participants would transfer accumulations into annuities that were like pensions. (See **Immediate and Term Annuity.**)

Average-Salary Pension: A pension plan in which the pension amount is calculated according to the career average rather than final salary. The Social Security benefit formula is an example.

Bend Points: Thresholds within the Social Security benefit formula that determine initial pension amounts. The Social Security Administration establishes two bend points each year, which represent amounts of average monthly income. To determine the initial monthly pension payment for a new retiree, it starts with the worker's average indexed monthly income over the thirty-five years of highest earnings. It then multiplies income up to the first bend point by .90. Income, if any, that exceeds the first bend point up to a second bend point is multiplied by .32. Income, if any, that exceeds the second bend point is multiplied by .15. The product of the multiplications is the initial monthly pension amount. The bend point dollar amounts change each year.

Capitation Fees: Per person rates that Medicare pays private insurance companies that administer Medicare Advantage plans.

Cash Balance Plan: A defined benefit pension plan in which employers and employees share investment risks. Accrued past benefits are guaranteed. Future benefits can vary according to investment returns. Employers or employees contribute to a collective fund that is invested. The collective fund is organized so that each employee has an individual cash account balance. The final balance is used to finance retirement, either through an annuity, which must by law be offered, or a lump sum payment.

Commercial Insurance: Insurance offered through a private for-profit company.

Contingent Annuitant: Annuities may have a feature that should the holder die, a spouse or other named individual will continue to receive all or a portion of the annuity amount. The named individual is the contingent annuitant.

Cost-of-Living Adjustment (COLA): Feature of many, but not all, pension plans wherein payments increase along with inflation.

Decumulation Problem: Term used to describe a general problem with the spend-down phase of retirement savings plans, such as 401(k)s. Retirement savings plans go through the phases of accumulation of savings through contributions and investment returns and then decumulation or "spend-down" of those accumulations for living expenses in retirement. The problem is that either (1) the accumulations are not enough to provide for enough funds for decumulation; or (2) there are no good ways to transition between accumulation and decumulation.

Deferred Annuity: An annuity that begins payments at a specified point in the future, as opposed to an immediate annuity that begins payouts right away. Between the time of purchase and payout, the company issuing the annuity will invest the monies received from the purchaser. The payment amounts, after the term is up, will be calculated, taking into consideration investment returns.

Term annuities deliver more income to purchasers than immediate annuities because of the investment returns during the time before payouts are made.

Defined Benefit Plan: One of the two fundamental types of retirement plans, along with defined contribution plans. Employers or employees contribute to a collective fund, out of which guaranteed retirement pensions are paid. Defined benefit is a synonym for pension plans. There are several different types of defined benefit pension plans, including final salary and cash balance plans.

Defined Contribution Plan: One of the two fundamental types of retirement plans, along with defined benefit plans. Employees, with or without employer matches, contribute to individual personal savings and investment accounts that are dedicated to accumulating tax-deferred funds during working years to provide income for retirement years.

Dependent Benefits: Benefits that the dependent of a Social Security participant may be eligible to receive.

Disability Benefits: Benefits that a disabled Social Security participant may be eligible to receive through SSA's Disability Insurance program. Some employer-sponsored retirement plans also contain disability benefit features.

Discount Rate: In estimating future funding ratios of pension trust funds, actuaries subtract plan liabilities—pension payments owed to participants—from plan assets. The overall liability is "discounted" by an assumed rate of growth of plan assets from investment returns.

Dollars x Years Pension Plan: A type of defined benefit pension plan in which participants accrue set dollar amounts of regular retirement pension income according to the number of months or years worked.

Employee Retirement Income Security Act (ERISA): The 1974 legislative act that governs private-sector employer-sponsored retirement plans. Among other provisions, ERISA mandates that pension plans make progress toward full prefunding.

Employee Stock Ownership Plan (ESOP): Tax-deferred defined contribution retirement savings plans sponsored by private companies. Employers contribute cash to a trust that uses it to purchase stock shares in their companies. These stock shares are assigned to individual employee accounts. When employees retire, they sell their shares back to the company and use the proceeds to finance their retirement years. While ESOPs provide a type of employee ownership of companies, they can be very risky if the company declines in value or goes bankrupt.

Final Salary Averaging: A form of final salary pension reduction. Instead of basing pension amounts on the last year of work salary, they are based on the average of, say, the last five years. That usually results in a lower pension amount.

Final Salary Pension: A type of defined benefit pension plan that calculates pension amounts as fractions of final salaries multiplied by years of work.

Financialization: Recent term used to capture the rising power of financial institutions (banks, investment houses, insurance, and retirement plan companies) in the U.S. economy.

Freeze of Pension Plan: When an employer stops a pension plan. With a *soft freeze*, existing employees continue in the pension plan, but it is not available for new ones. With a *hard freeze*, existing employees no longer continue in the plan. This is a special hardship for veteran employees since their final career years are more valuable in terms of pension benefits than earlier ones. However, the plan sponsor must honor accrued benefit commitments.

Funding Ratio: The ratio between assets in a pension plan trust fund and accrued pension liabilities.

Hard Freeze of Pension Plan: See **Freeze of Pension Plan**.

Immediate Annuity: An annuity that begins payments right after its purchase.

Indexing: Adjustments made to Social Security benefit determinations and amounts to take inflation into account.

Individual Retirement Account (IRA): A defined contribution tax-deferred retirement savings plan to which individuals, as opposed to employers or employees, make contributions.

Investment Risk: The risk that the value of a retirement plan investment will lose value. Also referred to as market risk.

Longevity Risk: The risk that retirees will outlive their retirement incomes.

Lump Sum Payment: Retirement plan payment in terms of a one-time cash payment of accumulated value rather than as a series of regular pension payments, annuity payments, or withdrawals.

Multi-employer Pension Plan: A jointly funded pension plan created by two or more employers and a union. The plans are usually in the same industry, such as trucking, hospitality, and construction. Such plans allow workers in those industries to move from employer to employer and still build up pension rights.

Normal Cost: The amount of contributions necessary to keep a pension fund in actuarial balance when there has been full funding. Pension costs are divided between normal costs and costs of unfunded liabilities, which are extra costs usually resulting from past underfunding.

Pay-As-You-Go (PAYGO): A type of pension system in which employers make pension payments exclusively from current revenues. They do not build up trust fund reserves to cover the future accrued benefits of retired or current plan members. Prefunded pension systems, in contrast, have the goal of building up trust funds with enough assets to cover both present pension payments due and future accrued benefits of current and retired plan members. PAYGO systems require much less funding than prefunded systems. Social Security largely operates on a PAYGO basis, as did most public and private pension plans in the past.

Pension Plan: A form of retirement plan for which employers with or without workers make contributions to a collective fund out of which retirement benefits are made, usually in the form of remaining lifetime pension payments. (See also **Defined Benefit Plan.**)

Pension Benefit Guaranty Corporation (PBGC): Established under the Employment Retirement Income Security Act in 1974, the PBGC is a federal insurance company that insures the benefits of private pension plans. It is financed by contributions from plan sponsors. The PBGC guarantees that pension payments will continue, though not always at the same level, should a pension plan become insolvent.

Portability: A type of retirement plan that workers can continue participating in if they change employers. Social Security is the most portable retirement plan in the United States because employers covering approximately 94 percent of the labor force participate in it. Defined contribution employer plans are generally more portable than defined benefit pension plans.

Prefunding: See **Pay-As-You-Go (PAYGO)**.

Privatization: Transforming a publicly owned retirement plan, such as Social Security, to private ownership.

Replacement Rate: The amount of retirement income provided by a retirement plan expressed as a percentage of pre-retirement income. Replacement rates have been expressed in terms of final or average career salaries. But there is a great difference between the two. A 40 percent replacement rate for a final salary is usually much higher than one for a career average salary. Many retirement advisors recommend that workers strive to have enough combined retirement income from Social Security and their employer-sponsored plans to replace at least 70 percent of their final incomes.

Required Minimum Distribution: Internal Revenue Service regulations require holders of tax-deferred retirement savings accounts to begin making at least minimum withdrawals at age 70½. The amount of the minimum varies according to account balances and age. It generally starts at 3.6 percent and rises each year.

Retirement Incentive Program: Occurs when pension plan sponsors encourage employees to retire by offering them higher pension amounts as incentives. Retirement incentive programs are controversial. Though often beneficial to employees, they are unfunded, thereby increasing a plan's unfunded liabilities.

Retirement Savings Account: Type of retirement plan in which employees with or without employer matches save and invest money through individual accounts that will be used to finance their retirement years. (See also **Defined Contribution Plan**.)

Risk: The possibility that an adverse event will occur. Adverse events for retirement plans include outliving retirement income and loss of accumulated retirement savings due to investment value declines. With pension plans, all or most risks are borne by employer sponsors. With retirement savings plans, all risks are borne by the holders of the accounts.

Risk Sharing: See **Risk**.

Roth Plan: A retirement savings plan in which taxes are paid on the amount contributed at the time of contribution. Subsequent investment gains and withdrawals are not taxed.

Service Credits: For pension plans that calculate benefits in part on the length of employment, service credits are the time units, for example, months or years, of work. Many pension plans allow members to purchase extra service credits that will increase their pension amounts.

Single Employer Pension Plan: Pension plans that are sponsored by single, as opposed to multiple, employers. (See also **Multi-employer Pension Plan**.)

Social Insurance: Government-sponsored insurance, as opposed to private for-profit insurance. Social Security is an example of a government-sponsored insurance program. Social insurance could also be offered through a nonprofit entity.

Soft Freeze of Pension Plan: See **Freeze of Pension Plan**.

Spiking: The practice of final-salary pension plan participants driving up their final income, mainly through overtime work, to increase their final-salary pension amounts. Many frown on the practice of spiking because it delivers unearned extra pension amounts through gaming the system. The unearned pension amounts, in turn, increase unfunded liabilities that threaten plan solvency.

Summary Plan Description (SPD): The Employee Retirement Income Security Act of 1974 requires that each private employer who sponsors a retirement plan provide participants with access to a description of the plan. Many public employers, though not required to, voluntarily publish SPDs.

Supplemental Security Income: Program administered but not

funded by Social Security that provides income to low-income old
age or disabled adults.

Survivor Benefits: Social Security benefits that may be available to
spouses and children of deceased Social Security participants.

Tax-Deferred Plan: Type of pension or retirement savings plan for
which contributions and accumulated gains are untaxed until
withdrawn during retirement.

Timing Risk: The risk that an investment will begin to lose value
soon after being made.

Underfunding: Sponsors providing less contributions to a pension
plan than necessary to keep the plan in actuarial balance. This is
the major source of unfunded liabilities in pension plans.

Unfunded Liability: See **Normal Cost**.

Variable Pension Plan: See **Adjustable Pension Plan.**

Vesting: a legal term that indicates that a person is entitled to payment from a pension plan. For most pension plans, contributions
must be made on behalf of workers for a period of time, up to several years, before being vested. If workers leave employment before
vesting, they may be entitled, depending on the plan, to a lump
sum payment of some or all of the contributions.

Notes

Introduction

1. Social Security Administration, Trust Fund Data, 2017, https://www.ssa.gov/cgi-bin/ops_series.cgi.
2. Ted Benna, "The Introduction of 401(k)," in *401(k)—Forty Years Later* (Maitland, FL: Xeron Press, 2018).
3. See David Webber, *The Rise of the Working-Class Shareholder: Labor's Last Best Weapon* (Cambridge, MA: Harvard University Press, 2018).
4. "Step by Step," words from nineteenth-century miners' union song, modern music by Pete Seeger.
5. James W. Russell, *Social Insecurity: 401(k)s and the Retirement Crisis* (Boston: Beacon Press, 2013).

1. The Retirement System

1. Irina Dushi, Howard M. Iams, and Brad Trenkamp, "The Importance of Social Security Benefits to the Income of the Aged Population," *Social Security Bulletin* 77/2 (2017).

2. Social Security: The National Pension Plan

1. Elisa A. Walker, Virginia P. Reno, and Thomas N. Bethel, *Americans Make Hard Choices on Social Security* (Washington, DC: National Academy of Social Insurance, 2014), Table 1.
2. Quoted in Philip Bump, "Either Paul Ryan Doesn't Understand Insurance or You Don't Understand Paul Ryan," *Washington Post*, March 9, 2017.

3. Alfred C. Mierzejewski, *A History of the German Public Pension System* (Lanham, MD: Lexington Books, 2016), chap. 5.

4. Source: Lillian Liu, "Foreign Social Security Developments Prior to the Social Security Act," Special Study #8, Social Security Historian's Office, Social Security Administration, Washington, DC, December 2001.

5. Nancy J. Altman, *The Battle for Social Security* (Hoboken, NJ: Wiley, 2005), 15–37.

6. Ibid., 28.

7. Edwin Amenta, *When Movements Matter: The Townsend Plan and the Rise of Social Security* (Princeton, NJ: Princeton University Press, 2006), 59.

8. "Memorandum on Conference with FDR Concerning Social Security Taxation, Summer, 1941," Franklin Delano Roosevelt Presidential Library, Hyde Park, NY, https://www.ssa.gov/history/Gulick.html.

9. Joseph McAuley, "80 Years After the Birth of Social Security, Remembering Miss Ida May," *America: The Jesuit Review of Faith and Culture*, August 14, 2015.

10. Robert J. Myers, "Old-Age and Survivors Insurance: History of the Benefit Formula," *Social Security Bulletin* 18/5 (May 1955).

11. Certain groups, including public school K-12 teachers in states such as California, Connecticut, and Texas, remain uncovered. There is also a distinction between the coverage rate today and whether a particular employee approaching retirement has been in covered employment her whole career. If someone shifted back and forth between paid and self-employment, the latter would not have been in covered work unless she paid the requisite taxes, which many people don't. Many people concoct self-employment jobs after losing paid employment jobs as a way to maintain some income until able to obtain paid employment again, especially positions that come with benefits. There is also under-the-table paid work in an informal economy in which employers hire temporary workers off the books for whom they do not pay Social Security taxes. And periods when someone is collecting unemployment benefits and does not accrue Social Security credits. All of this is to say that any particular worker or employee may have significant periods during a working career for which they do not receive Social Security credit, and that will decrease the amount of their retirement benefit. Social Security bases its monthly retirement check on the thirty-five years of highest pay.

12. Social Security Administration, *Annual Statistical Supplement 2020*, Table 5.A1.

13. Federal Reserve Bank of Minneapolis, Consumer Price Index, 1913, https://www.minneapolisfed.org/community/financial-and-economic-

education/cpi-calculator-information/consumer-price-index-and-inflation-rates-1913.

14. Altman, *The Battle for Social Security*, 216.

15. Kathleen Romig, "Social Security Lifts More Americans Above Poverty Than Any Other Program," Center on Budget and Policy Priorities, July 19, 2019.

16. Irena Dushi, Howard M. Iams, and Brad Trenkamp, "The Importance of Social Security Benefits to the Income of the Aged Population," *Social Security Bulletin* 77/2, 2017, Table 1.

17. Office of the Chief Actuary, *2018 OASIDI Trustees Report* (Washington, DC: Social Security Administration, 2018). Table II.B1.

18. Congressional Budget Office, "Administrative Costs of Private Accounts in Social Security" (Washington, DC: Congressional Budget Office, 2004), 15.

19. Federal Data Center, Federal Employees Salaries, https://www.fedsdata center.com/federal-pay-rates/.

3. What to Expect at Retirement

1. Stephen Goss, Michael Clingman, Alice Wade, and Karen Glenn, "Replacement Rates for Retirees: What Makes Sense for Planning and Evaluation?," Actuarial Note 155, Social Security Administration, Office of the Chief Actuary, July 2014.

4. Not a Ponzi Scheme

1. For purposes of comparison, I have chosen the original fifteen-member countries of the European Union plus Norway and Switzerland. For more about the choice of this unit of comparison, see my *Double Standard: Social Policy in Europe and the United States* (Lanham, MD: Rowman and Littlefield, 4th ed., 2018).

2. For more on the differences between the U.S. and European welfare states, see ibid.

3. Nancy Altman, "Social Security Isn't in Crisis. It Just Needs a Tune-up," *Los Angeles Times*, August 14, 2019.

5. Privatizers and Means Testers

1. Milton Friedman, *Capitalism and Freedom* (Chicago: University of Chicago Press, 1962).

2. Cited in Eric Laursen, *The People's Pension: The Struggle to Defend Social Security Since Reagan* (Oakland, CA: AK Press, 2012), 54.

3. Cited in Nancy J. Altman, *The Battle for Social Security*, 232.

4. Laursen, *The People's Pension*, 60.

5. Peter J. Ferrara, *Social Security: Averting the Crisis* (Washington, DC: Cato Institute, 1982).
6. World Bank, *Averting the Old Age Crisis* (New York: Oxford University Press, 1994), 239ff.
7. Jackie Calmes, "Simpson Apologizes to Critic," *New York Times*, August 26, 2010.
8. National Commission on Fiscal Responsibility and Reform Report, *The Moment of Truth*, December 2010, 49, Fig. 11.
9. Congressional Budget Office, *The Distribution of Household Income, 2014, Supplemental Data*, Fig. 16 (Washington, DC: Congressional Budget Office, March 2018).
10. Calculated from Social Security Administration, *Annual Statistical Supplement, 2017*, Table 4.B2, https://www.ssa.gov/policy/docs/statcomps/supplement/2017/4b.html#table4.b2.
11. Calculated from Internal Revenue Service, *All Returns 1990–2016, Selected Income and Tax Items*, Table A (https://www.irs.gov/statistics/soi-tax-stats-individual-income-tax-returns-publication-1304-complete-report).
12. Calculated from Internal Revenue Service, *Statistics of Income, Basic Tables—All Returns Filed and Sources of Income, Tax Year 2016*, Table 1.4,https://www.irs.gov/statistics/soi-tax-stats-individual-income-tax-returns-publication-1304-complete-report#_pt1.
13. Social Security Administration, *Annual Statistical Supplement, 2017*, Table 4B4.

6. Reversing Privatization

1. Raul L. Madrid, "Ideas, Economic Pressures, and Pension Privatization," *Latin American Politics and Society* 47/2 (1 July 2005): 24 and 34.
2. Raúl L. Madrid, *Retiring the State: The Politics of Pension Privatization in Latin America and Beyond* (Stanford, CA: Stanford University Press, 2003), 73.
3. Doris Elter, *System de A.F.P. Chileno: Injusticia de un Modelo* (Santiago de Chile: Universidad Arcis, 1999). Her 1995 thesis was published posthumously after she died in an automobile accident.
4. CENDA, *Principales Problemas del Sistema Chileno de AFP y Algunas Propuestas de Solución* (Santiago de Chile: CENDA, 2001).
5. Isabel Ortiz, Fabio Dura-Valverde, Stefan Urban, and Veronika Wodsak, *Reversing Pension Privatizations* (Geneva: International Labour Organization, 2018), 15.
6. Amanda Taub, "'Chile Woke Up': Dictatorship's Legacy of Inequality Triggers Mass Protest," *New York Times*, November 3, 2019; Ministerio

de Desarrollo Social (Chile), "Valor de la Canasta Básica y Líneas de Pobreza," *Informe Mensual*, December 2018.

7. Elaine Fultz and Kenici Hirose, "Second-Pillar Pensions in Central and Eastern Europe: Payment Constraints and Exit Options," *International Social Security Review* 72/2 (2019): 5.

8. Liviu Ionescu and Edgar A. Robles, *Update of IOPS Work on Fees and Charges*, IOPS Working Papers on Effective Pensions Supervision, No. 20 (Paris: International Organization of Pension Supervisors, 2014), cited in Ortiz et al., *Reversing Pension Privatizations*, 22.

9. Ortiz et al., *Reversing Pension Privatizations*, 10.

10. Armando Vidal, "Diputados Convierte En Ley La Libre Opción Jubilatoria," *Clarin,* February 27, 2007.

11. Ismael Bermúdez, "Jubilaciones: El Traspaso Será Desde Abril a Fin De Diciembre," *Clarin,* March 3, 2007.

12. "Críticas a Las AFJP," *Clarin,* August 23, 2006.

7. Medicare

1. Nancy J. Altman, *The Truth About Social Security* (Washington, DC: Strong Arm Press, 2018), 232.

2. T. R. Reid, *The Healing of America* (London: Penguin Books, 2009), 127.

3. Centers for Medicare and Medicaid Services, *Office of the Actuary, National Health Statistics Group, Age and Gender Tables*, Table 7 (2014), https://www.cms.gov/Research-Statistics-Data-and-Systems/Statistics-Trends-and-Reports/NationalHealthExpendData/Age-and-Gender.html.

4. Edward R. Berchick, Emily Hood, and Jessica C. Barnett, *Health Insurance Coverage in the United States: 2017*, U.S. Census Bureau, Report Number P60-264 (September 12, 2018), Table 2.

5. Ellen Nolte and C. Martin McKee, "In Amenable Mortality—Deaths Avoidable Through Health Care—Progress in the U.S. Lags that of Three European Countries," *Health Affairs* 31/9 (September 2012).

6. Kaiser Family Foundation, "Primary Care Physicians Accepting Medicare," https://www.kff.org/medicare/issue-brief/primary-care-physicians-accepting-medicare-a-snapshot/.

7. Phillip Tseng, Robert S. Kaplan, and Barak D. Richman, "Administrative Costs Associated with Physician Billing and Insurance-Related Activities at an Academic Health Care System," *Journal of the American Medical System* 319/7 (February 20, 2018): 691–97.

8. Steffie Woolhandler and David U. Himmelstein, "Single-Payer Reform—'Medicare for All,' *Journal of the American Medical Association* 321/24 (June 25, 2019): 2399–2400.

9.   Medicare, "Estimated Out-of-Pocket Costs," https://www.medicare. gov/find-a-plan/staticpages/medigap-out-of-pocket-costs.aspx.

10. Calculated from U.S. Census Bureau, Personal Income, https://www. census.gov/data/tables/time-series/demo/income-poverty/cps-pinc/ pinc-02.html#par_textimage_10, Table PINC-02.

11. Kaiser Family Foundation, *2018 Employer Health Benefits Survey*, Figs. 11.1 and 11.2, https://www.kff.org/report-section/2018-employer-health-benefits-survey-section-11-retiree-health-benefits/.

12. Centers for Medicare and Medicaid Services, *2019 Annual Report of the Board of Trustees of the Federal Hospital Insurance and Federal Supplementary Medical Insurance Trust Funds*, Table V.DI, 197; Kaiser Family Foundation, *Issues Briefs*, "An Overview of Medicare" (February 13, 2019), Fig. 5. Spending averages are for 2016.

8. The Pension Gold Standard

1.   U.S. Department of Labor, Employee Benefits Security Administration, *Private Pension Plan Bulletin Historical Tables and Graphs 1975–2017*, Tables E1 and E4; U.S. Census, *Annual Survey of Public Pensions Summary Brief: 2016*.

2.   Marc E. Fitch, "As Connecticut Drowns in Pension Debt, One Retiree Won't Cost Taxpayers a Dime," *Yankee News*, Yankee Institute for Public Policy, July 18, 2018, http://www.yankeeinstitute.org/2018/07/ as-connecticut-drowns-in-pension-debt-one-retiree-wont-cost-taxpayers-a-dime/.

3.   Beth Almeida and William B. Fornia, *A Better Bang for the Buck: The Economic Efficiencies of Defined-Benefit Pension Plans* (Washington, DC: National Institute on Retirement Security, 2008). If you read nothing else from these references, you should read this book. I learned a great deal from it.

4.   Social Security Administration, "Benefits Planner-Life Expectancy," https://www.ssa.gov/planners/lifeexpectancy.html.

5.   National Academy of Social Insurance, "The Role of Benefits in Income and Poverty," https://www.nasi.org/learn/socialsecurity/benefits-role.

6.   Bureau of Labor Statistics, *National Compensation Survey (March 2018)*, Retirement Benefits, Table 2.

7.   Jeff Manning, "Investors Fear Their Savings Gone to Pot," *The Oregonian*, February 3, 2016.

8.   Federal Reserve Bank of Minneapolis, "Consumer Price Index, 1913– ," https://www.minneapolisfed.org/community/financial-and-economic -education/cpi-calculator-information/consumer-price-index-and-inflation-rates-1913.

9. Solvency

1. NASRA, *Issue Brief: Public Pension Plan Investment Return Assumptions*, February 2019, https://www.nasra.org/files/Issue%20Briefs/NASRA InvReturnAssumptBrief.pdf.
2. Mark Miller, "Looking to Washington for a Retirement Lifeline," *New York Times*, September 12, 2019.
3. Ellen E. Schultz, *Retirement Heist* (New York: Portfolio/Penguin, 2011), 13.

10. Cutbacks, Freezes, and Bankruptcies

1. Ellen E. Schultz, *Retirement Heist*, (New York: Portfolio/Penguin, 2011), chap. 1.
2. *Annuity Shopper Buyer's Guide*, January 2019.
3. Mary Williams Walsh and Karl Russell, "$129 Billion Puerto Rico Bankruptcy Plan Could Be Model for States," *New York Times*, June 1, 2020.
4. Katherine S. Newman, *Downhill from Here: Retirement Insecurity in the Age of Inequality* (New York: Metropolitan Books, 2019), 96ff.

11. The Pension Wars

1. Guild-Consumer Reports Adjustable Retirement Plan Summary Plan Description, November 2018, http://www.ieshaffer.com/guild884/ SPD-ARP_11-2018.pdf (accessed May 18, 2021).
2. Without comparable accrual figures, it was not possible to calculate exactly how much *New York Times* employees lost in the switch from the old to new pension plans. With their higher employer contribution rate, they did not lose as much as *Consumer Reports* employees. Assuming similar investment returns as those to the *Consumer Reports* plan, they would have had an accrual of approximately 1.2 percent of current salary, still undoubtedly significantly lower than what their original plan would have yielded.
3. The union involved was the Washington-Baltimore News Guild, Local 32035 of the Communication Workers of America, AFL-CIO. Slightly more than half of the workers covered by the agreement were actual union members. The *Post* is an open shop, meaning that union membership and dues payment are voluntary. The Guild's contract, however, covers all non-managerial employees, regardless of whether they are dues-paying members.
4. Phone interview with Fredrick Kunkle, September 12, 2019.
5. Vanguard, *Amazon.com 401(k) Plan Highlights,* https://amazon.ehr. com/ESS/Client/Documents/BenefitSummaries/Amazon.com%20 401(k)%20Plan%20Highlights.pdf; Fidelity, *Q1 2019 Retirement Savings Update/4.*

6. Phone interview with Marilyn Katz, August 17, 2019.

7. Michael Cooper, "Chicago Symphony Ends Its Longest Strike with Pension Change," *New York Times*, April 27, 2019.

8. Morgan Brennan, "The Investment Zen of Sam Zell: Inside the World of the Grave Dancer's $4 Billion Business Empire," *Forbes*, October 7, 2013.

9. "The 2018 Forbes 400," *Forbes*, https://www.forbes.com/forbes-400/#57 eeb48b7e2f.

10. Phone interview with Steve Lester, chief negotiator for Local 10-208 of the American Federation of Musicians, August 19, 2019.

11. Chicago Symphony Orchestra Association, *2018 Annual Report*.

12. Ibid.

13. Phone interview with Joy Lindsey, January 30, 2021.

14. Pension Benefit Guaranty Corporation, "Introduction to Multiemployer Plans," www.pbgc.gov.

15. Katherine S. Newman, *Downhill from Here: Retirement Insecurity in the Age of Inequality* (New York: Metropolitan Books, 2019), 25.

16. John S. Topoleski, Multiemployer Defined Benefit (DB) Pension Plans, Congressional Research Service, 2018.

17. U.S. Department of the Treasury, "Frequently Asked Questions About the Kline-Miller Multiemployer Pension Reform Act," question 12, www.home.treasury.gov.

18. Center for Pension Rights, "Pension Plans That Have Applied to Cut Benefits Under the Multiemployer Pension Reform Act," August 31, 2020, www.pensionrights.org.

19. Phone interview with Kelly Stillwell, January 14, 2021.

20. Phone interview with Adam Krauthamer, January 20, 2021.

21. American Federation of Musicians and Employers' Pension Fund Trustees, letter to participants, December 2016, reproduced at www.musciansforpensionsecurity.com.

22. Joseph N. DiStefano, "The Musicians' Pension Fund Lost Big on Risky Bets," *Philadelphia Inquirer*, March 20, 2020.

23. Newman, *Downhill from Here*, 42.

12. Origins of the 401(k)

1. Gretchen Morgenson, "The Finger-Pointing at the Finance Firm TIAA," *New York Times*, October 21, 2017.

2. Ibid.

3. TIAA, *Compensation Disclosures* (TIAA: May 2019).

4. Ibid., 1.

5. Joint Committee on Taxation, House Committee on Ways and Means and Senate Committee on Finance, United States Congress, *Estimate of Federal Tax Expenditures for Fiscal Years 2018-2012*, Table 1.

6. Sarah Max, "The Inventor of the 401(k) Thinks It Has Gone Awry," *Barron's*, November 16, 2018.

13. Saving Up to Spend Down

1. Dutch Association of Industry-Wide Pension Funds, *The Dutch Pension System,* http://www.pensiondevelopment.org/documenten/ The%20Dutch%20Pension%20System.pdf.
2. Calculated from figures in Annuity Shopper Buyer's Guide, 1986 and 2019.
3. U.S. Bureau of Labor Statistics, "Usual Weekly Earnings Summary," Economic News Release, January 17, 2020, Table 3.
4. U.S. Government Accountability Office, *Retirement Security* (May 2015).
5. All Dow Jones Industrial Index dates and values from Samuel H. Williamson, "Daily Closing Values of the DJA in the United States, 1885 to Present," *Measuring Worth* (2020), http://www.measuringworth. com/DJA/.
6. David Blanchett, Morningstar, cited in Megan Leonhardt, *CNBC Nightly Business Report*, July 22, 2019.
7. George S. Mellman and Geoffrey T. Sanzenbacher, "401(k) Lawsuits: What Are the Causes and Consequences?," Center for Retirement Research at Boston College Brief number 18.8 (May 2018), 5.
8. Brian Croce, "Companies Start Suspending 401(k) Contributions Due to Economic Slowdown," *Pensions & Investments*, April 3, 2020.
9. William P. Bengen, "Determining Withdrawal Rates Using Historical Data," *Journal of Financial Planning*, October 1994.
10. Bill Bengen, "How Much Is Enough?" *Financial Advisor*, May 1, 2012.
11. Calculated from Internal Revenue Service, Publication 590-B, Table 3, Uniform Lifetime Table.

14. The Lone Ranger of the 401(k)s

1. Gretchen Morgenson, "A Lone Ranger of the 401(k)s," *New York Times*, March 29, 2014.
2. Phone interview with Jerome Schlichter, December 16, 2019.
3. ABB, *ABB Pension Plan*, https://new.abb.com/docs/librariesprovider27/ ch-karriere/vorsorge-publikationen/def_abb_pk_reglement-2018_e_ 20180110.pdf?sfvrsn=7d7cb013_2.
4. United Electrical Workers, "UE Local 1009 Members Negotiate First Contract with New Employer," *UE News*, August 1, 2019.
5. Schlichter, Bogard & Denton press release, March 28, 2019.
6. Supreme Court of the United States, *Tibble et al. v. Edison International et al.*, October term, 2014.
7. Quoted in Robert Steyer, "403(b) Litigation Driving Fiduciary-Role Awareness," *Pensions & Investments*, August 5, 2019.

15. Autopsy of a Retirement Plan

1. Major parts of this chapter are based on James W. Russell, "Autopsy of a Retirement Plan," *Academe* (American Association of University Professors), May–June 2018.
2. TIAA online advertisement, September 20, 2016, https://www.tiaa. org/public/land/results?tc_mcid=bn_10239603_2512007_1372156 15_73769488&tgtid=wallet2&rlsa=RLSAPARTR.

16. Reversing 401(k)ization

1. Tyler Bond and Dan Doonan, *Enduring Challenges: Examining the Experiences of State that Closed Pension Plans* (Washington, DC: National Institute for Retirement Security, August 2019).
2. Jennifer Levitz, "When 401(k) Investing Goes Bad," *Wall Street Journal*, August 4, 2008.
3. Bond and Doonan, *Enduring Challenges*, 13.
4. Phone interview with Jim Kaplan, March 22, 2020.
5. Kravitz, *2018 National Cash Balance Research Report*, https://www. cashbalancedesign.com/wp-content/uploads/2018/08/NationalCash BalanceResearchReport2018.pdf.

18. Retirement Security For All

1. For more information, see Christoffer Green-Pedersen, "Denmark: A 'World Bank' Pension System," in *The Handbook of West European Pension Politics*, ed. Ellen M. Immergut, Karen M. Anderson, and Isabell Schultze (Oxford: Oxford University Press, 2006). Despite the chapter title, Green-Pedersen concluded that "the explanation for the emergence of this multi-pillar system is not to be found in the World Bank recommendation itself. The Danish pension system has never been deliberately desgined and certainly not according to World Bank recommendations" (455). For other reasons, what emerged in the 1980s and 1990s approximated World Bank recommendations.
2. Organization for Economic Cooperation and Development, "Collective Bargaining Coverage," https://stats.oecd.org/Index.aspx?DataSetCode =CBC.
3. Elaine Fultz and Kenichi Hirose, "Second-Pillar Pensions in Central and Eastern Europe: Payment Constraints and Exit Options," *International Social Security Review* 72 (February 2019).
4. See Nancy J. Altman, *The Battle for Social Security* (Hoboken, NJ: Wiley, 2005), 69; and Altman, *The Truth About Social Security* (Washington, DC: Strong Arm Press, 2018), 211–12.

Index